CULTURE AND PLANNING

Culture and Planning

SIMONE ABRAM

ASHGATE

Published by
Ashgate Publishing Limited
Wey Court East
Union Road
Farnham
Surrey, GU9 7PT
England

Ashgate Publishing Company
Suite 420
101 Cherry Street
Burlington
VT 05401-4405
USA

www.ashgate.com

British Library Cataloguing in Publication Data
Abram, Simone.
Culture and Planning.
1. City planning – Social aspects. 2. Regional planning – Social aspects.
3. Culture. I. Title
307.1'2'01–dc22

Library of Congress Cataloging-in-Publication Data
Abram, Simone.
Culture and Planning / by Simone Abram.
p. cm.
Includes bibliographical references and index.
1. Culture – Case studies. 2. Social planning – Case studies. I. Title.
HM621.A29 2011
307.1--dc23 2011016246

ISBN 9780754677222 (hbk)
ISBN 9781409435068 (ebk)

MIX
Paper from responsible sources
FSC® C018575
FSC
www.fsc.org

Printed and bound in Great Britain by the MPG Books Group, UK

Contents

List of Figures *vii*
Acknowledgements *ix*
Foreword *xi*

1 The Idea of Culture in Planning 1

2 The Magic of Planning 19

3 The Body in Planning 49

4 Owning: House Society and Policy 69

5 Citizens and the Public 91

6 The Public and Time 111

7 Bringing it Together – Renewing Planning 133

References *139*
Index *151*

List of Figures

2.1	Model of the future housing estate from *Ten years of Housing* (1962)	24
2.2	Excerpt from the Housing Defects Survey of 1985	25
2.3	Excerpt from the 'Masterplan' – draft supplementary planning guidance	28
2.4	Images of houses/streets from the masterplan proposals	30
4.1	Excerpt from *Sustainable Communities: Homes for All,* Chapter 6	80
5.1	Extracts from Recommendation Rec(2001)19 of the Committee of Ministers to member states on the participation of citizens in local public life.	92

Acknowledgements

This book has taken some time to write, and builds on work that I have done over many years. To name everyone who has helped through that time would be an impossible task, but the contributions of many people have been much appreciated, while the responsibility for any faults and weaknesses in this book must remain mine. There are a few individuals who have given me particular help with this book, however, and I should like to thank them. Several people have read parts or chapters of the book and given helpful constructive comments. Eeva Berglund, Tim Rippon and Catherine Alexander have been supportive readers. Huw Thomas has been an inspirational advisor throughout the project and has heroically read almost everything with enormous patience. I thank him in particular for his support and friendship. I should also like to thank participants in seminars at the universities of Manchester and Aberdeen, Oslo and Tromsø, whose comments and questions have helped me to reformulate my ideas and avoid misunderstandings. I am also very grateful to Valerie Rose at Ashgate, who immediately understood my purpose and has been both generous and patient. I should also like to thank Gary for his wonderful cover illustration.

No book can be written without a degree of indulgence from academic employers, and I must give particular thanks to Mike Robinson for being endlessly supportive and considerate while this book has been in progress. Much of the research was originally funded by the Economic and Social Research Council and the University of Sheffield, to whom I offer my gratitude.

Most of all, I would like to thank the people who contributed to the empirical material in this book. Joan Hubbard, Colin Nuttall and their colleagues at the Norfolk Park Community Forum, members of the Regeneration Team, and residents in Norfolk Park who also participated in the documentary film Living Through Regeneration, especially Hermine, Jean and the late Peggy Seaton.

I would also like to thank three people whose involvement has been less direct but equally important. Firstly, Halvard Vike, for the many discussions we have had over the years that motivated me to propose the book in the first place. Secondly, I would like to mark my gratitude for the inspiration that I gained from working with the late Jonathan Murdoch. He is sorely missed. Thirdly, I must thank Luke Carver Goss, for putting up with me while writing, and for serenading me when not writing. There is more to life than planning, anthropology or academia, and I consider myself lucky to be regularly reminded of that.

Finally, I hope that my mother, D, will enjoy the fact that the book is written. Her support and encouragement have been invaluable.

Simone Abram
November 2010

Foreword

> '**Culture** is one of the two or three most complicated words in the English language.'[1]

What are planners doing when they talk about culture? If we ask this question, rather than asking what culture means, we discover rather more about planning than about culture itself. For too long, it seems to me, 'culture' has stood in planning theory as the extraneous non-rational human elements which create flaws in the workings of planning's central rationalities. Culture is a kind of black-box explanation for everything we cannot properly understand, everything that is not thought to be rational. The rationalities of planning were the focus of the book that Jonathan Murdoch and I published in 2001 called *Rationalities of Planning*.[2] In it, we showed how arguments about land-use planning (specifically planning for housing) became locked into a certain governmental logic. We traced this logic from central government through regional planning and through into local planning, and showed how a set of policy proposals that were supposed to be open to debate at each phase of their development were, instead, carried along on a 'cascade of numbers', becoming increasingly immune to challenge as they proceeded down a governmental hierarchy. Instead of being open to debate, housing numbers ended up locked in a contest between the competing rationalities of the economy and the environment. This seems to be the central conflict to all planning in capitalist democracies. How do we balance the need for economic growth that consumes resources with the need for citizens to live a peaceful and healthy life without suffering from resource exploitation? In other words, that book revealed the rationalities that are in play in planning contexts, and showed how they fall into patterns that are not necessarily either constructive or satisfying, but that effectively exclude many vital aspects of the quality of our lives.

In this book, I look outside those rationalities, complementing our understanding of 'rationalities of planning' by looking at all the issues that are excluded when planning's opposed rationalities clash. This book takes culture not as the stuff other people do, nor the inexplicable or irrational, nor even the way we do things. Instead, it thinks about culture as a concept in its own right, one with a social history and a world of analysis at its service. My aim is to reveal culture as one of the concepts we think with, and to show where our lack of thought leads us into dilemmas and dead-ends. With a little more thought about culture, we can employ it and other concepts beyond it to open up the tight limits of planning thought.

1 Williams 1976: 76.

2 Abram and Murdoch 2002.

Once we properly acknowledge the concept of culture, we have available a world of analysis, new ways to understand old problems and new ways to imagine solutions.

The aim of this book is to open up new ways for planners to think. It will not tell you how to plan, or how to solve planning problems, but it should help to explain why planning problems arise, and offer new ways to understand them. Using culture as an all-purpose category for things we can't deal with has not been a very satisfactory position for planners to hold. We have used the concept of 'power' in a similar way, to gloss the play of key actors and institutions searching for success in whatever terms that may be desired, whether economic, political, social, or in terms of status. Approaches like Latour's (based on Mauss) that see power not as the ability to influence others, or a capacity that certain people have ('I have power, you are powerless'), but as the illusion people get when they are obeyed,[3] change the nature of the problem rather than giving a new answer. At the same time, they challenge us to think in unfamiliar ways.

Many people shy away from this kind of mental work precisely because it is hard work to assimilate new ideas rather than coasting along with the ones we already have. So, it is little surprise that the work of Bourdieu[4] has become so popular in planning theory and practice, as it makes it possible to sort the messy arenas of human life into 'cultural capital', 'social capital', and so on. Translating the complexities of social relations into the metaphor of economy is a way to maintain the adherence to developmental versus environmental rationalities, since thinking in terms of 'economy' already provides the principal rationality used in governmental thinking. The language of capital is already present in much of the policy that planners work with on a daily basis. In other words, planners and planning theorists are used to thinking in terms of the economic, of quantifiable exchanges, and calculable actions. Economy provides a 'total model' into which all other processes and relations can be submerged. Re-casting the social into this totalising model has been largely a comfortable process.

It is not my intention to find a new way to squeeze an explanation for irrationality out of 'economy' as a total model. On the contrary, I aim to take seriously all those other ways of thinking, being and finding meaning or significance which do not fit and which are consistently excluded. I have no ambition to cause a global revolution in the manner of making government, but hope to offer a grain of thought which may inspire others to re-think the narrow and all-pervading economic rationalities which repressively dominate our political and social worlds.

The first task in this journey is to examine the idea of culture itself. In the first chapter, I take this bull by its fearsome horns, not in a head-on assault which asks what culture is (and already presupposes its scope as a 'something'). Rather than treating culture as some kind of conceptual container whose contents one can dissect, at the same time defining what is and what is not culture, the chapter

3 Latour 1986: 173.

4 Hillier and Rooksby 2002, Howe and Langdon 2002.

instead traces an intellectual history of the culture concept. It treats 'culture' as a specific historical concept whose meaning has changed and whose use has varied, in order to observe it from a distance. In this light, the concept of culture takes on a rather different tone. No longer a receptacle for all that is not rational, we see it as a frame for changing understandings of other large and ever present categories, such as nationalism, racism, elitism, and so forth.

With this rather more situated understanding of culture, we are ready to embark on an unusual journey through the vagaries of planning, delving here and there into local government practices, neighbourhood campaigning, management practices and organisational change. Detouring through ideas about magic, belief, emotions, calculability, the use of the body and the idea of the public, the book traces a new route through the idea of planning and opens a quite new field in planning studies – the study of the irrationalities of planning.

This irrationality has been approached before occasionally, though ideas such as government by 'muddling through',[5] in which Lindblom outlined how, in practice, policy-making was less rational than it might be assumed, or in the concept of 'ad hoc' organisational processes, which similarly acknowledge that all is not rigorous or impersonal in the running of organisations. These glimpses of non-rationality show us that people in official positions sometimes behave in unpredictable ways, and hint that this may be because they are following an alternative rationality which is less apparent to the observer, but in doing so they have often been interpreted in terms of other grand narratives of planning theories, such as 'power' which, for some, explains everything. Somehow, planning theories have remained trapped in their own hermeneutical web, explaining themselves through their own premise, that either a hygienic rationality or 'power' governs planning processes. As an explanatory concept, power is most amenable. It can be used to conceptualise all meetings between persons, and it can also explain their outcomes. For such an all-encompassing concept, it ends up explaining nothing at all, but merely reproduces what we know of human encounters, that they are only partially understood and are subject to prior events. In anthropological terms, we might say that persons always pre-exist in relations, both social and environmental. Such a statement opens up the circumstances in which political debates are subject to broader enquiry, because it does not reduce the meetings between persons to the weighing of amounts of power, and nor does it reduce the person to a singular identity. A person acts in relation to others and in relation to themselves in different times and under various constraints, and is therefore relational despite the emphasis in Western philosophies on individuality. We need not, in other words, be limited to the notion that individuals have identities that carry quantities of power, whether that be in terms of cultural or social capital, status, or any other basket of goods. Instead, we can let go of the popular assumptions that we use to categorise people and things and allow ourselves to reconceptualise what we are doing when we think about people, places or processes.

5 Lindblom 1959.

Let me give a brief example of how this might work. In *Rationalities of Planning*, we used theories of governmentality to show how complex issues fell into competing planning rationalities. By sticking to planning arguments and governmental theories, we were less able to show why this conflict is so persistent in planning debates, or how it continually took over interesting and relevant arguments about other things, such as community solidarity or qualities of space. To do that, we need to look to experiences and theories from studies of culture, to find explanations of how conflicts, feuds and contests persist. Gregory Bateson wrote about the conflicts that arise from what he called culture-contact, which he showed varied between different societies. Had we used Bateson's concept of 'schismogenesis'[6] (as Boholm does in relation to infrastructure controversies[7]) we might have shown how, at each stage, challenges to the governmental policy logic were increasingly locked into an oppositional mode, so that the argument developed 'sides' that adhered to increasingly exaggerated oppositional positions and logics. Bateson's theory of 'schismogenesis' describes situations where opposing groups become trapped in increasingly polarised positions, in which each gives out signals which are interpreted by the others, either 'symmetrically' (where each responds in a similar way, such as in an arms race) or 'complementarily', where responses are mutually reinforcing (such as in a dominant-submissive relationship). In the planning debates we researched, both these mechanisms were apparent, as competing ways of thinking became polarised through their supporters' use of similar tactics. What we saw was that the economic and developmental rationality of planning policy was represented in the policy process as a hyper-calculability, while challenges to it became locked into an environmental discourse which, although employing its own form of calculability, was increasingly characterised as emotional, unrealistic or idealistic. Even though the developers probably went home and fed the birds in their gardens, and the environmentalists built themselves a new shed, in their arguments they became more and more opposed, rather than moving towards any kind of mutual understanding or compromise. The two opposing rationalities, environment and development, we argued, persisted despite potentially radical policy changes even before New Labour took over from the Conservative government in the 1990s. They remain the shape of planning discourses and one might easily perceive that now, as some predict the total collapse of planning in England under an economistic regime,[8] it is even more apparent that these two rationalities dominate. One could argue that in a schismogenic way, each side has escalated its arguments into a caricature of itself.

When then-Chancellor of the Exchequer Gordon Brown commissioned economist Kate Barker to review the supply of housing, he implicitly promoted the logic of economy to the principles of land use planning. The aim of the report, in the brief that the Treasury supplied, was to explore how 'planning policy and

6 Bateson 1973.

7 Binde and Boholm. 2004.

8 Lovering 2009.

procedures can better deliver economic growth and prosperity alongside other sustainable development goals.'[9] Even the brief highlighted the schismogenic opposition with environmental arguments, and forced the two logics even further apart, pressing the resolution of the conflict between them further towards the use of force. If this sounds a little histrionic, we need only to refer to the history of British conflicts over road and runway construction throughout the early 1990s to see how environmental protest against financially-driven development did end in the application of physical force by the state (or the state-sanctioned private security forces acting on the instruction of development companies) against the physical 'force' of non-violent protesters occupying land and trees.[10]

In the increasing escalation of conflict between these dominant competing rationalities, alternative rationalities, or other ways of thinking about and acting towards planning, were eclipsed, and other ways of understanding what planning is and does have been overlooked. It can hardly be a surprise to us that economic and environmental logics are transformed into competing categories where the economic is seen as reason and the environmental as emotion, with the government sitting pretty squarely on the side of reason against everything from small village associations to national campaigning groups. I have written[11] about how the latter are continuously defined as 'out of context' in the governmental process. That is, they are always and continuously stripped of legitimacy and authority by the positioning of governmental agents and developers in the camp of economic-benefit-as-a-public-good. There is a long tradition of commentary on Western discourses of opposition between emotion and reason, from Descartes onwards (and no doubt before). On the other hand, Kay Milton[12] has written in depth on the relation of emotion to environment by addressing the gap between studies of culture in anthropology and studies of emotions in psychology. This sort of meeting between disciplinary approaches can offer new insight into familiar arguments. But current anthropological theory tends to do this in a rather subversive way. Rather than offering an alternative to known dichotomies (or oppositions), the trick is rather to offer an alternative to thinking via such rationalities at all. So, for example, in trying to find a way round thinking about structure versus agency, the anthropologist Bruno Latour suggests that rather than resolving the struggle or adding in other elements, we should rather think in terms of networks and drop the perspectival riddle that structure and agency lock us into. Contrast this with the ideas of the sociologist Giddens, for example, whose approach was to say that structure and agency beget each other, and we see how a lateral approach can get us beyond merely resolving a problem, towards opening up a new way of thinking altogether.

9 Barker 2006: 3

10 See, for example, North 1998.

11 Sheffield paper? Published?

12 Milton 2002.

A rather good case in point, which we will come back to, is a recent turn in long-standing debates about nature and culture. Early social anthropologists were first inspired by questions of whether human attributes were derived from nature or nurture, a question still lively in certain scientific fields. More recently, however, with the rise in interest in environmental questions, authors such as Marilyn Strathern have brought in a rather different perspective by showing us that among some social groups, the opposition itself is meaningless. Strathern is particularly good at spiking such binary oppositions and has used her fieldwork among the people of Mount Hagen in Papua New Guinea to recast many of our familiar ways of thinking. Alfred Gell described her use of Melanesia as less a geographical space than 'a manner of speaking', '...the site of certain problems of expression and understanding, peculiar to the cultural project of anthropology' in contrast to an equally non-geographical 'Euro-America', which he describes succinctly, as 'the setting for a sustained thought experiment'.[13] In this experiment, Strathern has rethought the oppositions between individual and society, between the individual as singular and society as plural, between people and the environment, and so on. For some readers (myself included), this is a superbly mind-liberating experience where the shackles of accepted knowledge fall away and allow the mind to examine how it travels the rails of its familiar structures. It is also immensely challenging and not always popular outside the sometimes heady realms of anthropological debate.

It may be becoming clear that my intention is not to pursue the description of the production of opposition between the economy and the environment, along the lines of the earlier monograph mentioned above. In contrast, this volume goes to the heart of these competing rationalities, not by seeking out the logic of those rationalities themselves, but by examining the areas not included in their reach. In planning theories and other studies, these alternative modes of thought have often been relegated to a kind of remainder area that attracts the label 'culture'. This category includes areas that scholars of planning have not been able to explain within the frame of the rationalities of development or environmentalism which are so dominant, as our earlier book showed.

I hope that this will be an enjoyable but challenging journey that will provide much food for thought, and many glimpses of new vistas for all those interested in planning. If it does not provide the answer to what 'culture' is as some readers might have been expecting, I hope that it will leave the reader thinking about the kind of questions they ask about culture, and the kind of questions that we are allowed to ask about planning, planners and policy.

13 Gell 1999: 34.

Chapter 1

The Idea of Culture in Planning

This chapter introduces culture as a concept. It outlines a brief history of the concept of culture and its study. It shows how it interacts with other concepts such as ethnicity and nationalism, and how it can be distorted through stereotyping. This chapter sets up an approach to culture that is developed through the following chapters.

There are three key areas where the term culture is used in planning literature. One is to refer to civic activity, the Arts and social events. Culture as music, visual arts, media and sports is a category of public activity that attracts its own bureaucracy, what we might call the *planning of culture*. I should make it clear straight away that Arts management is not the subject of this book. A second area where culture is used is to identify that different institutions have different ways of doing planning, or that there are *cultures of planning,*[1] and a third is concerned with questions of ethnicity, or social exclusion, what we might call *cultures in planning*.

The second area needs to be addressed straight away, as it is here that most planning attention has been focused, whereas this book goes in a different direction. There is now broad awareness that planning systems are not universally standardised, but vary between countries[2] and can therefore be compared. This approach has two main implications. Firstly, it suggests that planning cannot be universally rational but has particular histories in different locations. This recognition that planning is a practice with a history, that it is not, as Friedman puts it, 'a profession devoid of social, political, or cultural content except for its own specific professionalism',[3] is part of the concern of this book. The second implication is that much of the energy that could have gone into thinking about culture has been diverted into thinking about planning cultures. This is a well worn path trod by various industries over the 20th century. Keir Martin tells us how the Ford motor company began to realise in the 1970s that its traditional focus on numbers and systems was part of its problem rather than a solution, and that its focus shifted to the way social relations were organised in the company

1 Sanyal 2005 is an example.

2 For example, see Booth 2009, 1993; Clavel 1983, Cullingworth 1993.

3 Friedman 2005: 184.

itself.[4] The culture concept was ready and waiting, popularised by a generation of anthropologists as an 'all-encompassing determining system into which individuals are socialized… [that] Americans could use to make sense of social issues.'[5]

Something similar has happened in planning in recent decades. In the UK, interest in culture and planning has been stimulated by a UK government action to change the 'culture of planning', which started in the early years of the 21st century as a move towards spatial planning and increased governmental focus on efficiency. For neo-liberal governments, the identification of local government as a problem is based on an idea that there are rigid bureaucrats who do not participate with sufficient enthusiasm in new adventures.[6] With this definition in place, the answer to problems with the ways in which business or bureaucracy are done is to change the 'culture', or, in other words, change how practitioners think about what they are doing so that they do it differently. The idea of workplace cultures is well established, and draws on some of the earliest definitions of culture, as the customs and habits of social beings,[7] a set of observable characteristics attached to a particular group of people or among those in a particular place. This idea of culture acknowledges the tensions between shared and secret information, that cultures vary and can change, and that customs and habits can be learned, but it is still a rather old-fashioned model, one that Martin describes as an 'old, bounded, deterministic model of culture that many anthropologists from the 1980s onwards viewed with some disdain'.[8] It is an idea we are now very familiar with, though, so much so that the idea of organisational culture has become a normative tool[9] in the management consultant's box of answers to procedural problems, one that appeals to politicians and practitioners who look to organisational cultures to change how things are to how they would like them to be. Despite the lack of evidence that 'culture change' is an effective business tool, the idea of organisational cultures has become extremely popular, and planners have joined the party in adopting these ideas.

Andreas Faludi defines planning culture as 'the collective ethos and dominant attitudes of planners regarding the appropriate role of the state, market forces, and civil society in influencing social outcomes', focusing clearly on the planners themselves.[10] John Friedman, stretches things a little further, but keeps the focus tight in defining planning culture as 'the ways, both formal and informal, that

4 Martin 2010.

5 Martin 2010: 17.

6 Minister Tony McNulty defined culture change as 'making effective, creative use of these [policy] changes, not always looking to live in the comfort zone of a rigid, inflexible planning system (2003).

7 Tylor 1873.

8 Martin 2010: 18.

9 Wright 1994.

10 Faludi 2005: 442.

spatial planning in a given multi-national region, country or city is conceived, institutionalized, and enacted'.[11] He acknowledges a rather different definition of culture by Mary Douglas, renowned anthropologist and important contributor to organisational theory, but where Douglas thinks about culture as the production of meaning in a community, Friedman slides the idea of a community across into being a 'community of planners',[12] bringing us back into a field of organisational management: planners have their ways of doing things, and it varies from office to office. This is an ideal start to a project of comparing planning systems around the world, to show how the basis on which planning is done is different, and how those differences are also played out in different regulations, practices and languages. This, in itself, is a very important aspect of planning research,[13] alongside the study of planning history. Not only does planning history teach us about the plans of our predecessors and their relative successes and failures, it gives a sense of time and proportion to current problems.[14] It should also teach us that 'Planning Cultures' are not really cultures (in the anthropological sense) but managerial strategies. When we hear talk of Changing the Culture of Planning we should recognise that it alludes to changing the management of planning by putting new premises in place for bureaucratic practices.

The third area of culture focuses on the idea of thinking about people from different social, ethnic or national contexts as groups. This kind of work has been most effectively done in the planning field by Huw Thomas and his various colleagues, and is extremely important to try to ensure that planning is not inadvertently exclusive or racist.[15] Vanessa Watson has also pointed out how planning theorists' belief in the value of consensual politics relies on an essentialist and superficial understanding of cultural difference.[16]

I do not intend to repeat that approach here, though. Instead, this book challenges the very idea of distinct cultures and tries to put the concept of culture into perspective. Socially conscious planners strive to draw minorities into debates about development, to bring together people with conflicting cultural values as well as interests, to create debate and foster communication. There has been a heavy emphasis in planning theory on the potential for planning to build bridges, to open communication or even for planners to be cultural 'therapists', as though cultural differences were equivalent to psychoses that could be talked out through couple counselling. Rarely, though, do planning theorists stop to think about where the concept of 'culture' comes from. Where it is discussed, it is treated without the historical perspective and the theoretical critique that it requires to be properly

11 Friedman 2005: 184.

12 Friedman 2005: Footnote 1.

13 This is one that Sanyal's 2005 book does admirably.

14 See Fischler 2006.

15 See Thomas 2000, for example.

16 Watson 2003.

considered.[17] Ask yourself first: 'what is your culture?' What are the categories you seize on to describe it, and what are symbols you refer to, to distinguish it from others?

Culture and nationalism

My opening gambit on a course for postgraduate students in planning on 'understanding cultural difference' was to ask them to tell me five things about 'their culture'. Perhaps not a very innovative opening gambit, but a useful one none the less, because the answers were very revealing. Many of them described their culture in terms of their nation, in terms like 'I'm Welsh, and we Welsh like to do x and y', trying to describe the culture of the nation in terms of common practices. They also tried to describe other cultures in a similar way, 'ah, she's Scottish, and they are like this…' In fact, it seemed difficult for some students to sort out the culture from the nationalism, and indeed, the nationalism from the stereotypes. 'English people are always drinking tea' or 'British undergraduates drink a lot and don't take their studies seriously'. It is always striking how national stereotypes persist, and where only a trace of common practices needs to remain to keep the stereotype going. But more important are the mechanisms by which particular actions or habits – what used to be called 'customs' – are transformed from simple actions into symbolic emblems that are used to designate a whole group of people.

It should not be surprising that these otherwise well-educated students engaged in this debate, since it is regularly exploited by politicians and media to conjure up enthusiasm about the nation. What makes us British, or what makes us English (or any other nationalism), are common elements of slow news-day media discussion, or a helpfully distracting debate by beleaguered politicians. It is also encouraged by authors such as Kate Fox, whose entertaining book, *Watching the English* argues that English people share attributes and customs, behave in prescribed ways in the pub and generally display shared etiquette. There is nothing wrong with Fox's observations, but there is something highly dubious about the way that she projects her observations of pub behaviour and etiquette (mostly in the South of England) to generalisations about the meaning of being English.[18] She does this work of translating habits into the emblems of nationalism by generalising particular practices into characterisations of a population. This is a kind of hidden category-shift, a linguistic trick, which scales up observed characteristics to the larger category of nation that includes very many individuals who may not indulge in any of the actions described, and at the same time includes others, perhaps not nationals, who might participate in the same activities. Take a simple statement

17 Young (2008b) seems to think that Raymond Williams invented the concept of culture as everyday life in the 1950s. This will not do.

18 Mills 2006.

about English people taking tea at 4pm. This is a classic national stereotype in that 'everyone knows' that English people drink tea in the afternoon, yet we know that many English people never drink tea at all, and that lots of non-English people might drink tea in the afternoon. Yet it is enough that *some* English people drink tea in the afternoon, that cafés offer afternoon tea (especially in popular tourist destinations), and that English people are represented having tea (in films, books or other media) for the stereotype to persist. It is precisely the kind of nationalism that Benedict Anderson analysed as being based on an imagined community among people who have never, and are never likely to, meet each other. Casual readers of Anderson (or those who repeat second-hand versions of his thesis) have leapt to the conclusion that all communities are imagined, yet this is not at all his argument. The object of his study is the nation, a fictional unity that gains traction through the belief that there is a large number of people with whom we believe we have something in common, even though we have never met. That is, he notices how we transpose our experience of being part of a community to a larger cohort or population. We may still ask, how it is possible for such imaginary wholes as 'nations' to persist over such long periods of time? One way is surely through our acceptance of images and stereotypes that suggest commonalities among larger abstracted populations.

Stereotypes are very convenient ways to think, to simplify the world, and yet we know that stereotypes applied to ourselves are rarely accurate, sometimes not even recognisable. I was puzzled by French stereotypes of English people eating jam with dinner, for example, until I realised that the reference might be to cranberry sauce with Christmas turkey, or apple sauce with pork. It hardly needs pointing out that it doesn't apply to every meal or every English person. On the other hand, it is not strictly untrue that some English dishes include both meat and fruit. Stereotypes are effective because they take a fact that might be found to be true in some circumstances, and generalise broadly. Stereotypes play with what we know to be true and how we generalise ideas about difference, making what Maryon McDonald calls 'categorical mismatches'.[19] As she points out, how we identify ourselves depends very much on the social and political maps of the day, that is, 'the categories available for the marking of self/other or us/them boundaries'.[20] McDonald notes that 'difference does not exist simply and solely between supposedly homogeneous wholes called "cultures" coincident with these categories'[21] and that the lack of fit between the categories we use and those we observe is often transformed into a confirmation of our existing prejudices about our own rationality and the irrationality of others. A long history of Western nation-building has left us with systematised sets of oppositions into which we can fit our category mismatches: reason/emotion, logic/intuition, facts/values, intellect/passion, and so on. McDonald's broader point is that when we

19 McDonald 1993.

20 Ibid: 228..

21 Ibid.

identify cultural difference, we often attribute such differences according to our own understandings, and do not recognise that we are actually meeting different classification systems.

We do not only do this in relation to nations, of course. We use stereotypes equally eagerly about internal classifications, characterising men and women, for example.[22] We attribute a person's actions to the features found in our stereotypes, reinforcing the difference we observe and classifying the person exhibiting that difference as a representative of a cultural group, who will then be expected to share the other attributes we include in that stereotype. That we do this so often on the basis of national categories is a product of our socio-historical context which also produces the idea that nations are a natural category, one that we have internalised so deeply that, like the students I mentioned above, we find it difficult to think about culture without thinking about nations. Marianne Gullestad has shown eloquently how these discourses allow prejudices to appear 'plausible', by being grounded in everyday life experience,[23] where ideas of nation and culture are mixed and blurred.

If we tend to blend the categories of culture and nation, then transposing them into multiculturalism and multinationalism, makes the distinct and contrasting realms of the terms unavoidable, and highlights the slippage between actual nationalism and the popular idea of the nation. Although it is often thought that culture is intrinsic to the nation (and vice versa), it is rarely argued that multiculturalism is intrinsic to multinationals.[24] In fact, current debates about multiculturalism reveal more about nationalism than culture, and seem almost completely divorced from thoughts about the existence of multinationals. A number of critics have argued that the politics of multiculturalism have failed to produce a tolerant society. The Bishop of Rochester, for example, publicly argued that multiculturalism had led to the government endorsing extremist teachings in the mistaken belief that they were being tolerant of difference (Nazir-Ali, 2006). In response, Anthony Giddens claimed that these attacks misunderstand what multiculturalism means. Rather than encouraging tolerance for extremism, multiculturalism proposes the generation of understanding and dialogue across cultural boundaries. Despite his evident good intentions, Giddens continues to treat culture as a set of bounded categories, and in responding to criticism of multiculturalism in its own terms, does little to move the debate on. This simplistic idea of multiculturalism has been

22 Kerfoot and Knights, and Cullen (1994) give excellent accounts of how women get trapped in certain bureaucratic positions while men are promoted, when similar actions are interpreted as the demonstration of different kinds of abilities and women are associated with certain kinds of skills.

23 Gullestad 2006: 34.

24 Indeed, multinationals often foster their own explicitly stated unifying 'culture' to encourage employees (and clients) to identify themselves with the company over and above whatever national or cultural affiliations they may have – see Wright 1994 for an explanation of the culture-concept in commercial organisations.

taken up by some planning theorists whose ambition it is to bring about dialogue between ethnic groups and across cultural boundaries. Leonie Sandercock, in particular, has argued that planners should become cultural therapists, negotiating between conflicting parties in land disputes (2000). In her haste to be inclusive, though, Sandercock (2006) falls into the very trap that Giddens warns of, for example, in taking reports on ethnic riots in northern England at face value.[25] Imagining herself to be cosmopolitan, instead she remains trapped in a vision of cultures as separable categories, across which understanding might be sought. Her vision of a 'mongrel city' is also posed in opposition to the dystopian vision of a city of purified culture – the Australian 'white' city always just out of sight in the relatively recent past is a relevant model here – yet ignores the rich history of 'impure' cities of the past, the Istanbul of the 19th century, cosmopolitan Cairo, the many mixed cities of the southern Mediterranean, and so forth. We need a longer historical perspective to notice the purifying work of imperial powers, and we also need to see how our stereotypes and representations of our societies as national differs and has always differed from the actual mix of people to be found in them.

These sorts of notions about culture owe more to nationalism than might be imagined. The notion of a holistic shared identity, common to people from one place, is the central theme of Western ideas about the nation. It is the idea that Anderson highlighted in the 1980s, and which anthropologists criticised heavily in the 1990s.[26] The realisation that the connections between community and place were far from universal, but actually a product of colonial ideologies has been discussed for at least 15 years, yet it seems barely to have registered in planning studies.

Culture and ethnicity

One of the weaknesses of planning approaches to culture has been the tendency to assume that culture is a descriptive term. Culture is imagined as a set of practices, a way of thinking, or a bounded set of beliefs, traditions and ideologies. Culture describes what holds groups of people together, enforced by socialisation and reproduced through the generations. There are various texts which help to reinforce this impression. I will not attempt a complete review of the developments in the concept of culture but will instead highlight a few key areas.

25 Sandercock takes a government report on the riots and interprets it as though it were ethnographic research. She notes that Amin's *Ethnicity and the Multicultural City* (2002) is a 'think piece', yet she generalises wildly from stereotypes of 'types of neighbourhood' where racism is activated. A report written for a government department makes politically informed proposals which should not be confused with refereed academic research.

26 see Gupta and Ferguson 1992, 1997, and Olwig and Hastrup 1997.

Early anthropological texts established the idea of culture as the elements of embodied and received knowledge learned during socialisation. E. B. Tylor's definition of culture[27] (1878) included knowledge, belief, art, morals, law, custom and other capabilities and habits. This definition has been extremely long lived, the idea of culture as a kind of school of living particular to certain social groups. It has become so widespread that it has become a way of conceptualising the world itself, which makes it a cultural object in its own right. We can ask how this concept of culture has spread, who shares it, how it has changed, and what kind of thought and action it encourages and enables. The significance of this definition of culture was its incorporation of social organisation and social institutions into a general concept of culture.[28] In Britain this was developed into a social anthropology focused on the institutions and organisations of historically particular cultural unities that was very concerned for some years with the idea of social structures. In America, in contrast, a theory of cultural patterns became the central theme of a cultural anthropology focused more on ideas, symbols and artefacts. Throughout the years of structural functionalism and structuralism, culture was thought of as shared by co-located social groups, socialised from birth into certain ways of being and believing. Imaginary maps were constructed that located social groups (be they tribes, clans, societies) onto territories, often ranged into scales of remoteness, civilisation or contact with 'Western' civilisation.

Into this serene and timeless vision of clearly bounded socialised cultures, Modernism was seen to intrude as a corrupting process, incompatible with social cohesion. Much of this early research was based on the presumption that it was people out there, far away in the colonies or in traditional rural settings, who had 'culture', whereas civilised colonial masters had education, science and knowledge.[29] Critical reflection on the concept of culture helped to change this perspective, not least the study of language systems and elite societies, and to convince us that we are all culturally shaped. However, the idea that there were distinct cultures located in particular places has persisted. Modern urban culture was thought to obliterate local differences, much as we still think that globalisation will make us all 'the same', and much effort was put into documenting what were often thought of as the last remnants of timeless pristine cultures under threat of extinction from modern man. By the 1960s, interdisciplinary teams were conducting 'urgent ethnography' in Europe too, combining studies of folklore, agriculture, economics and politics into attempted holistic accounts of complete societies.[30] In Britain, not uncoincidentally, an extremely successful series of television documentaries about indigenous people was called 'disappearing

27 Tylor 1878.

28 Jenks 2005: 33.

29 However, as Williams points out, Herder was already criticising this as early as the late 18th century (Williams 1976: 79).

30 A large multi-disciplinary study of the Aubrac plateau by CNRS researchers is a good example of this: CNRS 1970–79, 1974.

world'. Whether or not there were people whose way of life was under threat from capitalist exploitation of resources (such as the destruction of the Amazon rainforest) is not the point here. The point is that all these approaches were based on an idea that people had holistic and distinct cultures that could be documented, and that were under threat from being polluted by the intrusion of other cultures, such as 'contact' by imperial or colonial powers.

It was, however, after a wave of village-studies, such as Frankenburg's study of a Welsh borders village published in 1957, that criticism coalesced around the idea that cultures could be imagined as whole, static and isolated. Even so, some of the work criticised was not as isolationist as criticism imagined it: Frankenburg's book was a study of change through the lens of football.[31] In any case, the idea that village life was conducted in a timeless bubble of tradition regardless of wider socio-economic and political processes was roundly rejected, and it became impossible to imagine that even so-called 'isolated' Amazonian tribes were not actually deeply affected by the existence of states, by development policy and changes in international capitalism.

Fredrik Barth, writing in 1969, observed that cultures were not really noticeable in everyday life except in the encounter with difference.[32] His approach shifted the focus from what was included within a culture, ie, what were cultural ways of doing things, to how cultures became defined through their boundaries. How do we differentiate ourselves from others? How do we define a common 'us' in the face of different 'others'? Barth argued that ethnicity, as an expression of cultural cohesion, was only apparent in the face of competing ethnicities, and that it was at the boundaries between groups that cultures became noticeable. These boundaries are not fixed, but appear in relation to whichever 'other' is encountered. While we might see ourselves as different from our neighbours, we might feel we are more like our neighbours than some stranger that happens into our village. Sometimes our enemy's enemies are our friends, that is, people from whom we distinguish ourselves normally, might become part of 'our' group if we are under threat from further afield. Evans-Pritchard described African societies that were organised into clans defined in opposition to each other, where the divisions could also be understood as hierarchical, since local disputes between close clans were put aside and local clan divisions overruled if conflict arose at higher levels.[33]His observations highlighted the contextual nature of loyalty and identity, showing how persons identified with different corporate units according to how their enemies were defined. Liverpool and United fans, for example, might all support England in the World Cup, even if at home they are vehemently competitive. In this model of boundaries of difference, the idea of constant and coherent cultures starts to be destabilised and reimagined as contingent, fluctuating and differentiated. That is,

31 Frankenburg 1957.

32 Barth 1969.

33 Evans-Pritchard 1949.

what we consider to be the boundary of our culture or our community changes according to the context.[34]

One of the most widely popular theorists of culture is Clifford Geertz. In creating his own definition of culture, Geertz famously adopted Weber's image of a web of significances tying people together, creating spaces of meaning and barriers of misunderstanding.[35] Geertz shifted the ground from culture as a set of practices to culture as shared meanings. He appeared to offer instruction into how one might describe these webs of meaning by bringing literary criticism to bear on culture. Inspired by the philosopher Gilbert Ryle, Geertz argued for descriptions of culture that went beyond a kind of distant factual observation (or 'thin description'). Instead, the description of culture (or 'ethnography' – writing about ethnos) should include knowledge that a fieldworker had gained through detailed and in-depth engagement with the people described. This he called 'thick description'.[36] In doing so, he wanted to highlight the difference between describing events and elaborating on their meanings and significances, and the method for doing this was to use literary critical techniques to analyse culture. This has been called imagining culture as if it were a text, and analysing it as so. Geertz's proposals inspired a generation of literary experiments, culminating in the recognition that writing about culture was as much about the writing as it was about the culture, and that the notion of culture was itself another meta-category generated by talk about culture itself.

By this stage, culture as a linguistic category had taken on a life of its own. Clifford and Marcus's landmark volume, *Writing Culture*,[37] argued, in particular, that the texts which represented culture were themselves written from particular positions. They attacked early anthropological or ethnographic texts as the documents of colonialism, and showed anthropologists that their writing about culture used the same styles and narrative strategies as colonial travel documents. Even though many anthropologists were explicitly subversive of colonial ambitions, Clifford and Marcus, and, in particular, Mary Louise Pratt argued that anthropological texts were still often implicated in colonial concepts of self and other. The resultant focus on writing and authors was perhaps a long overdue period of reflection for anthropological writers and others. It was an essential process of revelation – literally an uncovering of the socio-political and economic conditions under which ethnographic studies had been taking place. It allowed anthropologists to face up to the myths of contact and to address the ethical implications of comparative research in colonial and post-colonial situations. In terms of writing styles, it made anthropologists much more self-conscious about writing in a realist-style, because writing in the present-tense about a study which may have taken some years to write up inevitably downplayed the longer term changes happening even in remote

34 As Antony Cohen (1986, 1989) has also pointed out in relation to 'community'.

35 Geertz 1975.

36 From Ryle 1949.

37 Clifford and Marcus 1986.

islands or states. The force of the criticism was that there were anthropologists who still used the kinds of exoticising descriptions that Jonathan Swift satirised in *Gulliver's Travels,*[38] and these styles of writing were political and not at all neutral. These criticisms also began a process of interrogation into the role of nationalism in writing about culture, alongside critical reflection on realism as a literary style.

On the other hand, since these early anthropological writings, at least one or two generations of anthropologists had devoted their careers to fighting colonialism, and to righting the wrongs of developmental dependency, for example. Because anthropology is a comparative enterprise, it offers the opportunity to challenge even our most taken-for-granted assumptions and beliefs about the world. With the rise in anthropological studies across the world and the increasing accessibility of international texts, the voices of dominated people (sometimes called subaltern voices) have contributed to the debates about culture. They have helped to make visible some of the central paradigms in Western thinking and challenged the traces of colonial thought which persist in different forms.

One of these central 'tropes' (or dominant ways of thinking) has been the idea that rural villages house societies whose social relations are somehow more timeless and authentic than those found in urban societies. Such an idea goes right to the heart of sociological studies based on Tönnies' 1887 distinction between 'gemeinschaft' and 'gesellschaft'.[39] Tönnies wished to distinguish what he saw as two basic types of thought associated with two kinds of social group, an essential will expressed in small-scale, face-to-face communities (family, neighbourhood), and arbitrary will enacted in wider societies (city, state). It was in the city that Modernity was supposed to be located, in the tumult of dispossessed contractual relations. This linking of small communities with the somehow more authentically emotionally human in contrast to a modern, rational and impersonal city has flowed through the history of social sciences in an astonishingly thorough way and can be spotted popping up all over the place. It struck chords with the assumption that out of the way villages were 'backwards', in contrast with increasingly 'modern' cities, in other words, that we conceptualise them in different temporal schemes – that is, we think of villages as being in the past, while skyscraper cities are in the future. This placing of societies and places at points on linear timescales was intrinsic to the discourses of Western colonialism and was absorbed into common sense thinking in many academic disciplines, as both Fabian and Wolf have pointed out.[40] For the argument here, though, the significant point is that one of the very large assumptions we often take for granted is that 'real' communities either live together and know each other face-to-face, or that they once did, and, in contrast, business people and cosmopolitans who live in cities don't really live in proper communities. That is, we keep the idea of the village as the icon of an

38 Swift 1726.

39 Tönnies 1955 (there are several translations available).

40 Fabian 2002; Wolf 1982.

authentic society,[41] both as the place where real society is found and as the sign of an intrinsic link between geographical location and cultural identity. Even when describing social circles in cities, we use the metaphor of the urban 'village' to emphasise personal knowledge, repeated face-to-face encounter and tightly-drawn relations.

The notion that place and culture are intrinsically linked has been central to Western thinking for some time. European folklore traditions of the late 19th century were influential in formalising an association between authentic customs and culture and particular places, as I noted above. Culture and place were thought to define the identities of rural people immersed in traditional culture, defined in opposition to urban 'moderns' who were cultured or cultivated yet non-specifically cultural. But to define themselves as mobile and cosmopolitan, urban moderns needed to be able to point to traditional ruralists to demonstrate the difference. Such ideas are remarkably persistent, and the intimate connection between place and identity underlies many Western ways of thinking and of governing. The exception to this overwhelming model has always been the nomad whose 'authentic culture' lies in their nomadism. Yet nomads are simultaneously romanticised and feared – gypsy camps are regularly attacked, even while we enjoy stories about Gypsy Rose Lee and sing about life on the open road. British imperial authorities consistently attempted to settle nomads, and settlement policy remains central to many states' approach to nomads, from Bedouin in Egypt to Travellers in England. One reason nomads have so long been considered a 'problem' is precisely because they do not conform to the normative link between place and culture that defines our notion of geography and society. Nomads remain mystical, romanticised and often frightening figures in the Western imagination. And of course, it is harder to tax people if you do not know where they live.

So central was the place-culture nexus to Western sociological thinking, that Gupta and Ferguson argue that the anthropological method of going to the field was itself implicated in the over-determination of fieldwork sites, where cultural difference was naturalised into geographic locales (1997). Bronislaw Malinowski was hugely persuasive in founding a tradition of anthropology at the LSE (London School of Economics) which required individual ethnographers to spend long periods studying 'native' society. Despite the activities of many ethnographers working in teams and doing local studies, many still believe that this was the only way to access culture, and that authentic culture is to be found in out of the way places with isolated people. But critique of the idea of a 'field' of work suggested that a new anthropology had to accept that culture and geographic locale were not coterminous. The field was not out there waiting to be discovered by the researcher, but the researcher themselves defined a field of research and then discussed it as if it were somehow natural, pre-existing the researcher's interest in it.

This is not to suggest that anthropologists had only studied so-called exotic others: urban anthropology is nearly a century old and ethnography of migration

41 See also Abram 2003.

is no longer new. Yet the observation that anthropological fields were the product of concepts of culture that shared a model with the concept of nations ushered in a new way of thinking and writing about the idea of culture and nation alike.

This icon of the authentic community then reappears in quite different debates, sometimes in disguise, sometimes explicitly. It informs the model for our ideas about how politics works too. In much political discourse, and recently in the discussions of urban renewal and the new urbanism, an ideal society should be community-like with social relations so intense and comprehensive that it should be possible to communicate its views through a singular representative. In debates about including minorities in policy processes, government officers most often identify minority communities and treat them as though they approximated to simple face-to-face communities whose viewpoints can be communicated by a spokesperson.

Iris Young calls this approach one of cultural imperialism. Cultural imperialists take their own values and perspectives as normal and universal. In contrast, they identify other people as part of groups, such as ethnic minorities, 'marked out, frozen into a being marked as Other, deviant in relation to the dominant norm'.[42] Whereas members of a dominant cultural group need not notice their own group at all, seeing themselves as neutral or mainstream, Young argues that it is the 'victims of cultural imperialism' who are never allowed to forget that they have a group identity, being constantly reminded of it. They are addressed as though their group-specific interests override any others, and are rendered invisible as subjects. Young calls this a kind of violence, and considers the ways in which prejudices can result in physical violence to the body, as well as symbolic violence to the self. It is enough, for our purposes here, to appreciate that seeing some people as groups, separate from the main population, is problematic, sometimes to the point of violence. However, we should not allow ourselves to think that this is an isolated problem with the way we identify 'others' in groups. We can see that it is the same logic that we use to identify citizens as members of a nation. If we can imagine that a nation can be represented by individual people who carry the traits of the nation and understand its history, traditions and customs, then the idea that a culture can be represented by a spokesperson is an obvious parallel.

Nationalism, multinationals

What does it mean to say that culture is a similar notion to nation? Historians such as Antony Smith,[43] Benedict Anderson[44] and Eric Hobsbawm[45] make clear that an idea of nations emerged in an historically specific process and show how the idea

42 Young 1990: 123.

43 Smith 1998, 2001.

44 Anderson 1983.

45 Hobsbawm 1990, and Hobsbawm & Ranger 1983.

spread among populations hitherto highly differentiated. A nation, by definition, implies a people with common language, history and traditions. By including some, a nation clearly excludes others, so nationalism can be seen as a kind of purifying ideology, defining a collectivity, tying it to a territory, and excluding others. The idea of a shared culture has been central to nationalist projects, despite its fragility and tendency to dissolve under scrutiny. The amazing feature of nationalism has been people's ability to make a conceptual leap from shared experience at a personal and local level to the idea of a shared experience at the broader level of a population. The link to territory has been implicit; explicit examination of territory always shows it to be contested, difficult to define around the fringes and usually inhabited by significant numbers of people peripheral to ideals of the imagined nation, such as Celts in Britain, Sami in Scandinavia, Bretons and Basques in France, and so forth. Nationalism has been closely associated with race-thinking since the early colonial period, and it is, paradoxically perhaps, in attempts to discredit racism that nationalism has sometimes been strengthened. The term nationalism is used here not to denote national supremacy but rather thinking through the nation – using the nation as an unreflected category of thought. It is this unreflecting categorising that makes the stereotypes raised above serve to confirm prejudices.

Marianne Gullestad shows us how these prejudices can seem terribly plausible. She was one of a number of Norwegian authors who highlighted race-thinking in European multiculturalism, and her analysis of a public debate between two anthropologists in Norway offers insightful and counter-intuitive analysis of the co-implication of culture, nation and race as currently circulating modes of thought (Gullestad 2006). The example is interesting since both authors have published widely on questions of racism in Norway in both academic and public media. First, she takes Inger Lise Lien's argument that acts such as staring at non-whites is not a form of racism but a racialisation of difference. Defining racism as 'acts with negative intentions based on feelings of hate' (Gullestad 2006: 233) allows Lien to conclude that there is little actual racism in Norway. However, Gullestad argues that this ties in too neatly with a self-image of Norway as a non-racist society. On the contrary, Gullestad suggests that 'the idea that Norway is a homogeneous society and that racialisation is a response to a new phenomenon in a new situation' hides an unconscious racism embedded in what Rex calls the linguistic categories of advanced industrial societies (Gullestad 2006: 234). It is not the white Norwegian's encounter with persons of colour which is significant, but the meaning of this encounter in a much broader and enduring history that extends the geographical reach into colonialism, and the anti-Semitism and eugenics movements between the two World Wars.

In contrast, Gullestad considers the work of Unni Wikan, a well known anthropologist and commentator on the Middle East, who has written extensively about racism and integration in Norway. Wikan has argued apparently in the interests of immigrant women that the Norwegian government has been too tolerant of moral differences. In particular, she has suggested that the Norwegian government ought to make stronger demands on immigrants to adopt Norwegian moral codes and behaviours, to become more Norwegian. Wikan argues that culture is a new term for race, since it allows people to be understood as products of their culture, and applies different criteria of human-ness to different groups. Wikan argues that if we say it is acceptable for some women to be circumcised, for example, because it is 'their culture', although genital mutilation is forbidden under Norwegian law, then we are suggesting that people with 'other culture' are less fully citizens, and subject to different moral standards.

For Gullestad, these statements change the scope of the term 'culture' in Norwegian. Culture (or '*kultur*') relates to the arts, to ways of life and to patterns of social action, and is contrasted with nature, as in English, but the term is ambiguous in terms of value. Whereas at one time, culture would have been something attributed to foreigners (just as whites in Britain were not considered to have ethnicity), recent debates have normalised the idea of a Norwegian culture, so Norwegians' own culture is contrasted to the strangeness of other, foreign cultures. The Norwegian government has tried to imply that intrinsic to Norwegian culture is respect for the culture of others, yet at the same time, it emphasises the value of Norwegian culture as being of value simply by being 'ours', inherited from generations before. Gullestad argues that this constitutes a hegemonic frame where national belonging is conceptualised through descent and idealised notions of 'basic Norwegian values'. These basic values are often at play in governmental contexts and are often counterfactual. One such example is the centrality of integration services for immigrants arriving in Norway. The framing of integration is already problematic and sets up a set of dilemmas over the extent to which immigrants might learn to behave like Norwegians in order to integrate into Norwegian society. Integrating into a society that defines itself as tolerant and open is somewhat paradoxical. Wikan's arguments are typical in that the national identity that is threatened is precisely this tolerance. Should the Norwegian state tolerate domestic violence, should it tolerate female circumcision in the name of tolerance of other cultures?

Norway is also a missionary society. and yet missionary work presumes a moral superiority implicit in the religious frame, one at odds with the notion of tolerance and equality. Yet as a relatively new nation, only a century old, there is a great deal of debate about what the national identity might be and what those basic national values are. In trying to define such values, a definition of what they are not is also produced, and since, as Barth has indicated, ethnicity is defined in relation to others, defining the basic Norwegian creates a potential ethnic boundary with immigrants. This is additionally complex in Norway given the presence of an aboriginal population of Sami who were increasingly colonised by Norwegians over the 19th and 20th centuries. Norway was also much occupied by Danes and Swedes as well as Finns, over the centuries. This has led to persistent efforts to define Norwegians as distinct from other Scandinavians, efforts to purify the definition of Norwegians whilst simultaneously trying to incorporate ethnic others into the nation-state. At the same time, Norway is home to two of the world's larger multinational companies (Hydro and Statoil), who contribute to a cosmopolitan circulation of service and labour through the country and globally. This kind of circulation, however, is never discussed in terms of ethnicity, integration or nationalism or, even, in terms of multiculturalism. It is an invisible multinationalism that reminds us of how partial national debates about culture actually are.

Metaphor

Running through all these discussions about culture, how to define it and how to describe it, it has been taken for granted that culture is there to be defined. We know, somehow, that we do things differently from others, yet the same as some, and that the patterns of this similarity and difference are not smooth. The barrier to our conceptual understanding, though, is the failure to recognise that culture is a metaphor and not a descriptor. All our models and discourses attempt to establish new metaphors even as we think of them as better conceptualising what culture really is. Furthermore, in planning studies, attempts to understand culture almost always incur a normative desire to resolve cultural differences, to disempower them, to take away the sting in the differential tail. Planners' desires have been directed towards resolving conflict, and often this desire over-rides the need to understand the meaning of conflict itself. I've attended many community planning events, for example, where the pressure to reach consensus has become evident when someone has dissented. Sometimes people who criticise proposals are accused of 'being negative', for example, whether or not they have good reasons for seeing flaws in policies. But most crudely, policy forums often invite a single person to represent 'the black community', for example, neatly subsuming any areas of difference that might exist between people so designated. At a meeting of a local authority in southern Norway in the early 2000s, three councillors of Pakistani origin (first and second generation immigrants) explained their relief that they could stand up as representatives of different political groupings rather than being seen as a representative for all immigrants, as though all immigrants shared the same political views. Although my example is from Norway, it could as well have been from Britain or from many other countries. The point is that we use cultural groupings as a convenience, whereas it is often anything but convenient for the people grouped into them.

Where Barth imagined ethnic and cultural boundaries as the place where different kinds of substance meet, we might try a different metaphor, one of electric currents, to challenge our imaginative constructs. Electricity is created between differences in voltage, known as 'potential difference'. It is when a connection is made between two conductors that a current is generated. The potential difference cannot be seen in one conductor at a particular voltage, since it has nothing to be different from. It is only in relation to another that the potential difference is found. Where there is a potential difference, currents may flow, and will continue to flow until the difference disappears. Imagining cultural difference in this way reflects the sense that culture is not noticed if we are simply going about our daily lives – rather like the swallow on the electricity line. Only when we connect different elements does the potential become apparent and a current of communication can be created. Of course, this is a very simple metaphor, yet applying a new metaphor is a way to jolt us into new ways of thinking. The comparison between multiculturalism and multinationals similarly confronts us with the different ways in which culture and nature are constructed and forces us to think through analytically what nation and culture signify. However, neither metaphor does justice to the complex historical routes of our addiction to 'culture'.

Culture is not a substance out there which can merely be described. The concept of culture is an invention into which we load meaning. It then circulates and accumulates layers of significance in different contexts. The efforts of ethnographers like Geertz to be descriptive have given a false impression of innocence to the descriptive act. Once recast as an authorial act, it is harder to deny the linguistic categorisations which allow us to think with culture. The problem with culture, though, is that without this nuance of understanding, like national identities, they make for poor anthropological analysis but effective politics.[46] The politics of culture and multiculture have led to an impasse between liberal laissez-faire and nationalist exclusion. If we are to move beyond the dichotomies of us/them, our/their culture, tolerance/integration, we will need new ways to think about culture. And we will need ways to think about our social worlds that do not fence off 'culture' as all those things that we find difficult to think about. This book, then, tries to open up some of those areas that we routinely exclude from planning to show how a shift in our understanding of what 'culture' means might help us to become more open not only to the possibilities of planning, but also to its limits.

The chapters ask you to play some thought-games, to think about things you might usually expect to ignore, and to ask what they tell you about conventional approaches to thinking about planning. The next chapter confronts convention head on by asking what the role of magic is in planning, certainly an area that is hard to find in most planning studies. The book goes on to consider bodies and relations, and to think about houses as persons. These unusual approaches to conventional subjects define the thread that runs through this book. They might not lead to a new definition of culture itself, but they use ideas from the studies of cultural difference to rethink what the realm of planning is, and to jolt the theories of planning into new fields.

---

46 As Kaneff and King suggest, 2004.

Chapter 2
The Magic of Planning

'Concern with an inherently capricious future makes all kinds of planning seem "mystical" at times.'[1]

> This chapter takes a fresh look at how planning works and introduces empirical material from a regeneration project in Sheffield. Using ideas and examples from anthropology, the chapter considers the consequences of practices that are usually dismissed as not-planning, or the parts of planning that we consistently choose not to see.

How does planning actually work?

Planning is usually represented as a very rational activity, despite what are now long-standing criticisms of rational theories. Classic textbooks suggest the policy-maker identifies a problem, examines the evidence and recommends a solution based on sound evidence, then later evaluates the outcomes of the policy, identifies a problem and so forth. This sounds very convincing and professional, and makes policy seem benign and sensible, but once you actually start to look at how policy is made, it becomes much more difficult to see how this model relates to what actually happens. There have been various challenges to this version of policy-making, often stemming from Lindblom's argument that, in practice, policy is made by muddling through complicated circumstances rather than proceeding in an orderly manner.[2] If you look closely at plans and try to match them to what has happened in particular places, there are usually significant differences that raise questions about how you would ever know if a plan had done what it set out to do.

The main puzzle that struck me when I first started to study planning was exactly that, how you might know if a plan had worked. Thinking about forward-plans or policies, rather than project-plans or blueprints, I wondered how people could be convinced that it was worth writing a long-term plan, say for 20 years hence. Looking back at plans of even ten years ago, the most consistent feature was how few of the goals identified had ever been achieved or even remained unchanged. Yet all sorts of people were busy working on new plans, expending great energies in fighting for particular policies, or striving to achieve one form of wording over another.

---

1 Robertson 1984: 191.

2 Lindblom 1959.

Evaluation seemed to be something of a mirage, given that a long-term plan is never evaluated at its end but in the middle. If we set out a plan to reduce car transport in 20 years, but after 3 years we revise the measures and change the goal, how can we know whether our plan was effective? Our plan might be based on a forecast that the population will increase by 4 per cent over ten years, and household size will diminish by 1 person, requiring an increase in the housing stock of 2 per cent, but after four years, we might decide that the population has decreased but the number of single-person dwellings has doubled. Is that because the plan allowed developers to sell studio flats, because more people decided to invest in small properties or because there was a whole generation of single people just waiting to move into their own flats? And how could we ever know for sure? These are simple examples, but they all point to the fact that we cannot really tell what social changes are the effects of plans and which are independent of them.[3] Why is a plan worth such trouble, I wondered, when its effects are hard to discern?

But this is not the end of the puzzle. Once the planning office has done its research and recommended a plan, politicians start to debate it, demand changes and generally pull and tweak the plan, not only according to their assessment of the evidence, but in line with electoral pressures, their party ideology (if they have one), or the deals they have made with other politicians. Hopefully, it does not depend on deals they have done with private investors, as this is called corruption, but politicians – and planners – are regularly lobbied by developers to persuade them that development is a good idea. In any case, political pressures shape plans just as much as technical assessments of evidence, and this is not necessarily a bad thing. It does make plans less predictable, the 'evidence base' rather more diffuse, and more difficult to understand without following the process of debate in detail. This adds another layer of complexity to the idea that we can retrospectively evaluate long-term planning strategies, since they are not always consistent, even within themselves. And then, of course, we know that just because a policy is in place does not mean that its implementation is automatic. In planning, policies are interpreted by practitioners, lawyers, applicants and others, and policies are challenged, decisions appealed, exceptions made and illegal developments either prosecuted or not. Enforcement is an important but often under-funded aspect of planning activity.

This brief summary, even without considering the more fringe or specialist activities of planning, suggests that planning is hardly a straightforward activity with direct relations between cause and effect that are easy to identify. Eric Reade pointed out as much more than two decades ago, suggesting that planning had little claim to be either scientific or technical.[4] On the contrary, he thought planners' approach to social science was 'naïve'.[5] It might be more helpful to think of planning instead as a set of models or ideas, that we use to think with,

3 A problem common to most policy evaluation.

4 Reade 1987.

5 Ibid: 101.

and that we also use to help us to accept the messiness of actual development in practice. Planning offers us a set of relatively simple images and rules that suggest to us that there is, or will be, some kind of order, irrespective of what order we do or do not see on the ground. Since none of us can really tell what the future holds, our lives are beset by uncertainty, but we have our ways of holding that uncertainty at bay. We create routines for daily or regular activities, notably divided up by mealtimes and drinks (morning coffee, dinner time[6]) we have rituals and ceremonies to manage big upheavals such as birth, marriage, death,[7] and through these we create different forms of time.[8] We have linear life-times, the circular repetitive time of daily and weekly routines, and annual cycles of seasonal events and activities.[9] Beyond this, the universal time of physics or religious eternity can feel terrifyingly large. In contrast, for more practical and political activities we tend to choose limited timescales that seem to be more or less within our grasp, timescales in which we think we can anticipate how society will be. In planning, this commonly translates into forward plans of about 5 or even up to 20 years, although occasionally audacious plans for 50 years are not entirely unknown.[10]

In choosing these periods for ordering the world, planning configures a future that holds out hope that things might be better.[11] This has always suggested to me that planning is rather like a belief-system.[12] We persuade ourselves to believe that there is a system, based on a set of written rules and statements, with a benign (or not) ruler at the top (the Secretary of State), and a higher purpose – the public good. What makes it seem even more like a belief-system is not that there are non-believers but that people who make objections are often within the system. If you don't believe that the system had any effect, you wouldn't bother to participate in it at all. I clearly remember being driven around the most picturesque villages of Buckinghamshire by a belligerent developer who vehemently pointed out that all the areas recognised by plans as particularly lovely and worthy of protection were built prior – often centuries prior – to the introduction of planning law in England. And yet the reason I had even met this developer was because he had lodged an objection to the regional Structure Plan. Despite his scepticism to the way planning worked, he clearly did believe that it achieved something, even if it

6 Douglas 1987.

7 Van Gennep 1960.

8 See Zonabend 1984.

9 See Eriksen 2001 on how modern time has increasingly speeded up.

10 The longer the time, the less convincing the plan though – policies for managing climate change have been very far-reaching, but are then largely considered less realistic as the level of uncertainty goes up.

11 A hope that we have elsewhere characterised as an 'elusive promise': Abram and Wezkalnys forthcoming.

12 A conclusion also considered by Robertson 1984 and Reade 1987.

was a something that he did not like.[13] This sounds a little like Michael Herzfeld's argument, that even the critics of nation-state rational bureaucracy believe it is the ideal system, but that the human actors in it are flawed.[14] It has all the hallmarks, he suggests, of a religious doctrine, and so he takes up a religious question posed by Weber, of what he calls a 'secular theodicy'. That is, how do we continue to believe in a system (or a God) when its weaknesses or flaws continually confront us? Grumbling against the system is a kind of idiom in which we manage this contradiction, and Herzfeld thinks that complaining about particular bureaucrats (in our case, planners), is a way that we resolve this mismatch between what we expect from an ideal planning system and the system we actually experience.

In all of the planning controversies I have followed, often it is actually the objectors or protesters who have the strongest belief in the ideal planning system that should produce the best of all possible worlds. For them, the reason that we do not have the best of all possible worlds is not because planning is not the way to achieve it, but because planning is not being done properly, or the proposed plan is not the right one, or is not being interpreted correctly. Systems of belief are deeply embedded in ways of thinking and acting, exclude arguments or evidence against them, and the sufferers of its consequences may believe just as much in the system as those who seem to benefit from it. Yet people believe in all sorts of weird and wonderful systems as having effects, so belief in the system is hardly proof that they work, nor an explanation of why they work, or why people participate in them.

So, there are two problems here. One is the puzzle of why planning continues, why people believe in it, and the other is how to recognise the boundaries of what planning considers as relevant evidence to make decisions on, and what is ruled irrelevant. How do we define what is a problem, and how do we decide that a particular policy might be the answer to that problem? How does something become a matter for planning policy, and what kinds of evidence are to be considered in relation to it? Thinking about planning as rational and tied to evidence keeps it on the plane of the real, in what we might call a realist approach to the concept of planning. But in this chapter, I also want to look a little at what is thought to be the opposite of planning, and use it to reflect on where the limits of the 'material' lie.

If we focus on an actual plan it will help us to elaborate these ideas in practice. Rather than take a long-range general forward plan (like a district plan or a community plan), or a blueprint design (like an architect's instructions), the rest of the chapter looks at something in-between, often known as a 'masterplan', one that appears to offer a vision for the future of a fairly well defined area, a particular landscape, a plan decorated with welcoming drawings and maps, full of facts and figures and statements about the past, present and future. Masterplans are a device to navigate the temporal transition to an ideal future in an ongoing and tenuously

13 Planning's achievements include preventing certain kinds of building being built as well as enabling others.

14 Herzfeld 1992.

consolidated present. They offer an insight into imaginations of temporality as well as spatiality and also stand as physical objects, or the concrete manifestations, of culture which themselves circulate (or don't) in routes which can trace social relations of planning, as I will show.

Where is the plan?

First, as in all good diagnoses, we need to find a plan to examine and begin by taking a brief case history. The case here concerns a large urban council-owned housing estate built in the 1960s in the glory days of slum-clearance. The estate was built on open land only a mile or so from the city centre of Sheffield in the north of England. It was an area that had seen some mining and small-holding, and consequently had only a few buildings on it, and various disused mineshafts. It lay adjacent to the Duke of Norfolk's deer park, which was given to the city council to become Norfolk Park, more recently renovated and renamed Norfolk Heritage Park. In the 1950s, a grand vision was put forward for the renewal of the whole city, the latest in a series of post-war grand visions by the city council. In this plan, Norfolk Park was presented as a modernist vision of clean living in parkland landscapes. Between 1963 and 1966, nearly 3,000 dwellings were built in system built houses, maisonettes and 15 double tower blocks. This large council-owned estate was visited by international architects and sociologists, and was included in a book about the city's post-war housing estates published in 1962 in English, French and Russian (Figure 2.1).[15]

The Estate was built under direct contract from the city council within the space of 3 years, and was managed for the next 30 years by the city council's housing office. It is not the original masterplan for this estate which I will examine here, but the plans for its regeneration in the 1990s and 2000s. Although this estate did not suffer the worst conditions of the decline of council housing under the Conservative government, by the 1990s flats were hard to let, many of the concrete buildings suffered from structural faults (such as spalling, where steel reinforcing rods inside the concrete rust), damp from the single glazed metal window frames not having been insulated from the walls, and a small number of dispersed properties had been sold to private owners. The Housing Survey listed a catalogue of structural problems in the flats that contributed to them being perceived as 'depressing' (see Figure 2.2). Norfolk Park became a focus for urban regeneration, and after several attempts the city council gained Single Regeneration Budget (SRB) status for the estate as well as funding from the Estates Renewal Challenge Fund. This meant that a pot of money was made available for complete regeneration managed by the city council in partnership with commercial and charitable organisations.

---

15 Sheffield City Architect 1962.

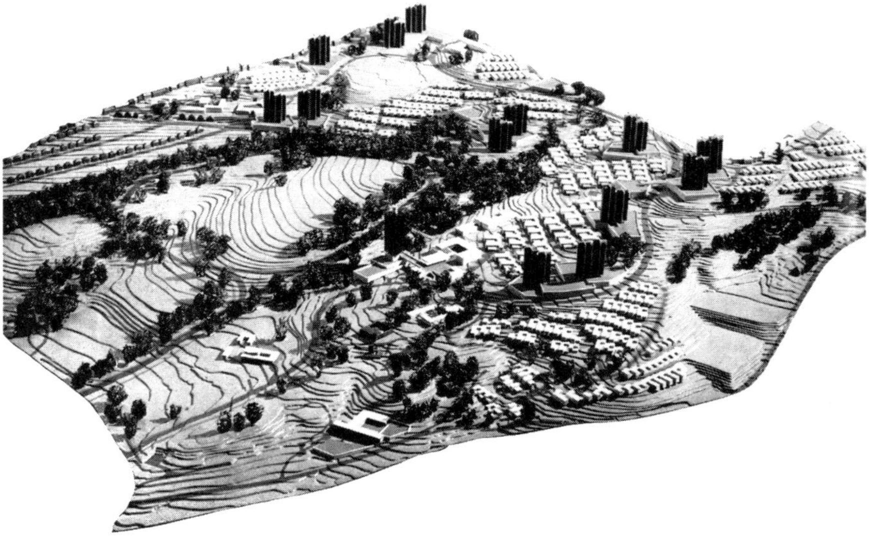

Figure 2.1 Model of the future housing estate from *Ten years of Housing* (1962)

Source: Sheffield City Architects *Ten Years of Housing* (1962)

All government housing policy since the mid 1990s has emphasised the general shortage of housing and an urgent need for an increased housing stock.[16] The policy response has been to favour increasing the density of housing to accommodate a greater number of smaller households in urban areas. In Sheffield, the market has also been favourable for the production of private sector high-rise city centre flats, which have been built in large numbers, in a similar way to nearby cities such as Leeds and Manchester, although Sheffield saw this building spurt a little later than other cities. Paradoxically, then, with a high-density urban housing estate on the edge of the city centre, plans for Norfolk Park aimed to reduce the housing density on the site, to demolish the tower blocks and maisonettes and to build just over a thousand low-rise dwellings to replace them. Sheffield as a city has been through a kind of morphological change, from a low-rise dense industrial city packed around the central hill, which retained many of its Victorian little factories, to high-rise dwellings built in the 1960s around the fringes of the city, only to be replaced then in the 1990s and 2000s by high-rise densely packed dwellings in the centre with low-rise suburbs all around.

16 As we outline in Murdoch and Abram 2002.

<u>Sheffield Housing Defects Survey 1985</u>

The 15 'twin towers' are 16 storeys in height and each contains 126 dwellings.

The typical floors (1st to 15th) consist of 8 flats, 6 number 2 bedrooms 3 person and 2 number 1 bedroom 2 person. The ground level consists of 2 entrance halls, a caretaker's room and 6 number 2 bedroom 3 person flats.

The basement consists of service rooms and small tenants' stores. Circulation is via a central stair unit and 2 lifts. They were designed by Sheffield City Architects Dept. Five towers were built by Gleeson and ten were built by P.W.D. The towers were completed between 1965 and 1968.

External – small areas of spalling concrete. Only means of escape is central stairs. Fire doors and screens not up to standard. Some screens have asbestos panels.

Metal windows on timber subframes... rot in subframes... window posts worn... no draught seals or ventilators... wind pressure can suck windows open and break glass... extreme condensation... runs down the glass and saturates the sill and wall leading to mould...poor security... depressing atmosphere.

Figure 2.2 Excerpt from the Housing Defects Survey of 1985

Source: Sheffield Housing Defects Survey 1985

As with any major building project, the first stage of the redevelopment of the Norfolk Park estate was to draw up plans. The development was managed by a small team of city council planning officers, called a Regeneration Team, working in a part of the council known as the 'neighbourhoods division'. This means that they were separated from the general planning offices, which themselves were divided between forward planning, development control, highways, and so on, and also separate from the city's housing office. Government funding for the demolition and rebuilding of council estates through public-private partnerships was supplied on condition that residents were represented in the process, and eventually the council succeeded in securing funding in partnership with a new local organisation called a Community Forum that represented the residents. The regeneration team faced the challenge of reconstructing the estate in partnership with private investors, using commercial construction companies, and also satisfying Housing Associations, while using only a limited public budget. In other words, the expectations for their work were rather ambitious. The large budget allocated from public funds, nominally £20 million, was intended to cover the costs of making the whole site attractive to investors. The money was to be used to demolish existing buildings and cover the difference in cost between building on 'green field' and 'brown field' sites. As budget holders for this process, demolition was more or less the one function over which the team had something like control.

At the start of the project, flats and houses were defined as 'hard to let'. This meant that at the lowest point, housing officers were handing over bunches of keys to prospective tenants and letting them visit flats until they found one they wanted to live in. For housing officers, therefore, Norfolk Park represented housing failure, with high crime rates, fairly open drug dealing and many derelict flats, as the housing defects survey shows. That there was also a strong core community of families who had lived in the estate since the 1960s did not counteract a general view that this was a 'failing estate'. The structural and social problems in the flats became a surrogate for the whole estate, so that the peaceful and long-term population who were mainly very happily living in the terraced housing were not recognised until they put up a huge fight to prevent their houses being demolished later in the process. Instead, the whole estate was labelled as a failure. The reasons for this failure were associated with the catastrophic unemployment suffered in Sheffield estates with the collapse of jobs in the steel, engineering and coal industries, and with the social fallout of poverty and the lack of investment in estate maintenance. Years of starvation of public funding under the Conservative government had left many similar estates chronically under-maintained. Housing policy was addressed from the top down, by selling off public housing to housing associations or private owners, or through the transformation of local authority housing management into 'arms length management organisations'. The energies of regeneration teams then began to focus on changing the buildings and landscapes of public housing areas.

Late in the 1990s, the team invited developers to enter a competition for the right to be the principal developers of Norfolk Park. At this stage, there were documents relating to the redevelopment, of course, but no masterplan. The masterplan would emerge as a result of the competition and a range of associated activities. The winner of the competition appointed an architectural consultancy and a planning consultancy to develop site-specific plans. The architects met with local residents on a fortnightly basis over several months to fully develop their plans, before putting forward a masterplan. This masterplan was a large paper document, presented in landscape format as architects often prefer, with colour illustrations, maps and figures.

I heard about the masterplan long before I actually saw a copy. For some time, a short summary was downloadable from the architects' website, but a polite request for a copy of the full document went unanswered. I was also told that there was a copy in the offices of the local Community Forum. But it didn't actually appear in physical form for several years and then only by chance. I was also told that the original models built to show the plans for the 1960s estate had found their way into the Community Forum offices at one time, indeed, they had been stored in the back of the toilets, but had eventually been disposed of (not down the toilet, I was assured), to the regret of the Forum staff. I made enquiries at the city council's planning office, but again no response was forthcoming. Over several years, I directed a student research project about the estate, and several students went to the council's enquiries office and asked to see the masterplan. All returned with the same response, that no one at the reception desk or in the council planning offices believed in the existence of a masterplan for Norfolk Park. The students' response has always been rather indignant, that the city council does not seem to archive their plans properly, followed by doubt that there ever was a masterplan for Norfolk Park. And yet they have by that time heard so much about it that they did believe that a plan existed.

One day, when I called into the Community Forum's offices, the deputy chief-executive, Colin, happened to have a copy of the draft plan open and began to talk to me about it, pointing out that it specified clearly that community regeneration should be the core of the regeneration of the estate. Some time later a manager in the Regeneration Team handed me an electronic copy of the formal plan. Even with a copy of this lodged in the university library, students requesting plans for Norfolk Park from the City Council planning office are still told it does not exist. And indeed, although widely referred to as 'the masterplan', this is not its formal name (Figure 2.3).

Revised plans put forward by the architects were adopted by the city council's planning committee as what is called supplementary planning guidance, that is, policies that apply only to the specific site, in addition to normal planning policy. It is this supplementary planning guidance that is the formal plan from the council's perspective, rather than anything called 'a masterplan'. It was and is widely held among *non-planners* that these plans formed a blueprint for the regeneration of the estate. That is, it seemed to be commonly understood among residents on the estate that the drawings that were discussed in detail in the preparatory stage of the regeneration were representations of what would be built. This is not too difficult to sympathise with, since if the plan was not a guide to what would be built, then what was it for, and why had they spent so many Tuesday evenings discussing the shape and size of the 'cyber-centre' that would form the hub of the regenerated estate? (Figure 2.4) The planners and regeneration officers, and politicians, also regularly complained of local residents seeing the plan as a blueprint, expecting it to be followed to the letter as if it were a contract.

These residents were formally represented by two organisations, the community forum (NPCF) mentioned above which was formed in 1993 to be the community development partner in regeneration, and the tenants and residents' association (TARA), a longstanding organisation founded in the 1960s by the tenants in the new estate. Primary formal communication between planners and residents took the form of regular public meetings of the regeneration team and the Forum, at which other organisations were also represented, including local churches and businesses. I interviewed a number of older residents and attended several meetings, and it is indeed clear that most held early expectations that the images presented in the plans would somehow become replicated in real buildings. They did not naively believe that the world would look like the architects' drawings, but they did expect that the commitments made in the plans would be honoured, that the fact that they had been officially corroborated would give them some authority and that appeals to the plan would ensure that development would be predictable. Some of these residents had lived in the estate from its construction, which had largely taken the form envisaged in architects' drawings and plans circulated at the time, a few design details notwithstanding. A few of the residents had raised money and campaigned to have facilities built, such as a community centre with

Proposals

The Developer's proposals should make full use of the opportunity to provide outstanding views from dwellings and use purpose designed buildings to achieve this and provide appropriate architectural scale and presence in this prominent location which is a landmark site. As the site is surrounded by open space and or lower ground on three sides, buildings should be outward facing on the site's perimeter and designs should create a visually interesting skyline. Topography and other factors require that road access be only from Kenninghall Road which gives the oppotunity to create gateway buildings at the junctions. The eastern end of the site, prominent from Park Grange Road and near to the Beldon tram stops and proposed non-residential facilities, would be a suitable location for a taller multi-faceted flat development. The Developer should maintain and enhance all existing pedestrian routes through and around the site and respond to the existing footbridge by proposing built form and landscaping which could link communities on either side of Park Grange Road.

Density - this site is identified in section 2.3 as being appropriate for higher density at over 70 dwellings per hectare and the Developer should use purpose designed buildings where required to achieve the recommended density.

Extract from Masterplan drawing (not to scale)

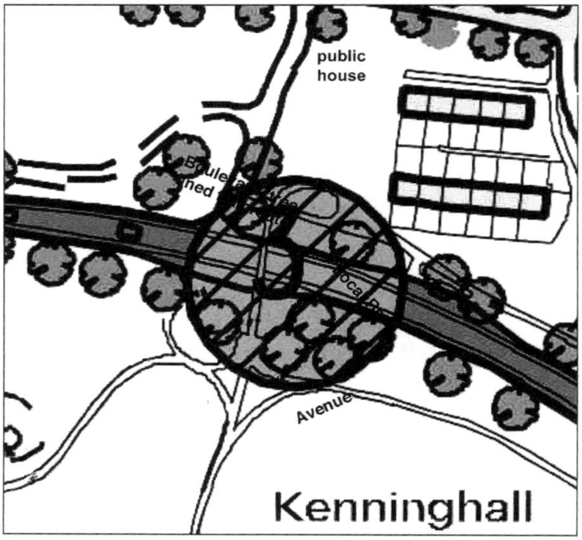

Figure 2.3 Excerpt from the 'Masterplan' – draft supplementary planning guidance

Source: HTA Architects

SITE FEASIBILITY & DESIGN PRINCIPLES STUDIES | 6.0

6.10 Design Principles Study: Site 9, Kenninghall Mount

Schedule of Accommodation

Site 9, Kenninghall Mount:

Total	**80 no. dwellings**	**Land parcel area:**	**1.65 hectares**	**4.07 acres**
		Developable area (assumed 75%):	**1.23 hectares**	**3.06 acres**
		Area for density calculation:	**1.39 hectares**	**3.44 acres**
		Density	**57 dwellings per hectare**	

A subjective developable area has been assumed for the purpose of establishing realistic unit numbers for this study. This area takes into account restrictions of extreme slopes and tram power supply furniture zones.

Indicative Layout (not to scale)

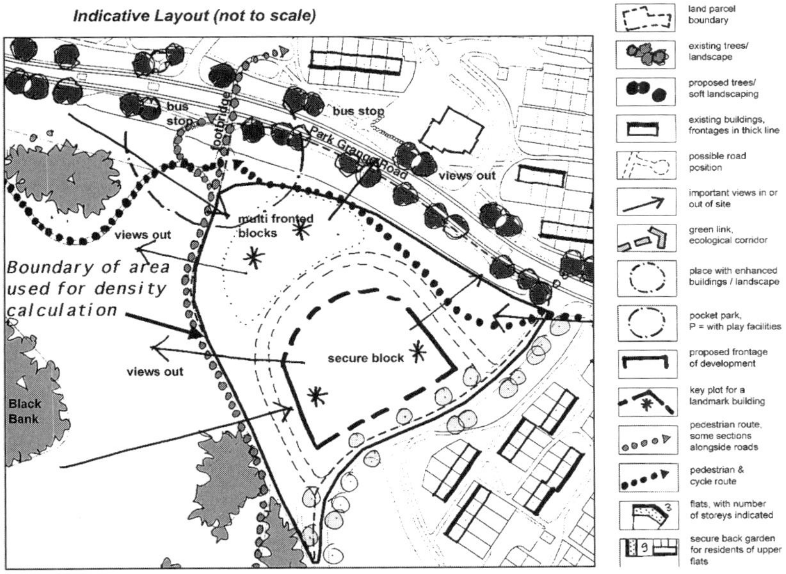

NORFOLK PARK
REGENERATION PLAN

HTA ARCHITECTS LTD
for THE MILLER GROUP LTD / M J GLEESON plc

ballroom, stage and café, and for years they had held frequent events and annual review-shows.[17] In those days, they met directly with the head of city housing and the chair of the housing committee, and although promises were hard to extract, once they were made, they could be used to produce results. Promises, either verbal or on paper, offered a solidity that could be referred to at a later date.

17 These events were also captured on film by the TARA. Some excerpts from these films are included in the documentary *Living Through Regeneration* (Abram and Allam 2005).

Figure 2.4 Images of houses/streets from the masterplan proposals

Source: HTA architects

On the other hand, among the planners, politicians and developers, it is a self-consciously apparent truth, owned by those experienced with regeneration (or planning more generally) that plans are not pictures of how the future will be manifested. Plans are not like architectural drawings which serve as codified instructions between designer and builder. You need to have a plan to show the government (or EU agencies) that you know what you are doing; you need to have a plan to 'draw down' money. In other words, the plan becomes a symbolic object used to cement different kinds of relationships.[18] Between plans being drawn – especially when they are drawn as images by architects – and large scale regeneration becoming concrete, there are many unpredictable events and relations to be secured. Relations are perhaps the most significant variable and the most magical, being fragile, vulnerable and difficult to describe.

In practice, a key use of the masterplan, highlighted by local councillors, for example, was as evidence presented to state funding agencies as proof of competence, as part of the documentation required to demonstrate the legitimacy of the request for finance. Beyond this function, any actual proposals within the plan were seen as 'flexible' and dependent on circumstances, including capture of private investment. In the context of urban regeneration, thinking about divination as a way of invoking fully social futures is potentially useful. Planning is seen to

18 As Alexander (2001) argues for contracts.

change not only the place but the people in it. So one might say that writing plans is a form of magic through which residents will be transformed into fully human beings in properly socialised neighbourhoods, engaging in clean and lawful activities. The plan will not achieve this alone, but it is a powerful tool in attracting various positive forces that may first help to diagnose and then to counteract the negative forces identified (perhaps with the help of a 'culture change'). And such positive forces were clearly very significant in the eyes of planners and developers. For them, the estate was beset by negative forces. As shown above, the estates from the 1960s were not only seen as physically dilapidated, but as sites of social degradation. Dereliction, drug-dealing, theft, the burning of stolen cars and so forth, were the signs of people not fully human, or at least not fully social – hence the term 'anti-social behaviour' takes on a powerful resonance in relation to 'problem estates'. In response, the magic of planning can be applied to create a civilised well-behaved (middle-class) residential area.

Human-non-human planning

If we look again at the connection between the buildings and the humans, we can see that the original plans aimed to perform some kind of healing magic to make both healthy again. There are, of course, alternative readings of the development process, and it is worth trying these out if we are to find new understandings of complex projects like regeneration. How are human, material and other aims put together, and why do unexpected things keep happening? And how do the magical transformations we hope for actually come into being (if they do)? If we focus for a while on the knowledge that connects people to things, we can start to reveal the less rationalist effects that are hidden in the unrecorded things that people and things actually do. First, we need to think about how information works, and try to understand the difference between explicit and implicit or shared and partial knowledge, so we can isolate the more mystical aspects of planning and regeneration.

In the Norfolk Park case, community development, economic development, job training and so on, were written into the original aims of the regeneration programme, joining material change to social change to build a 'better future'. Rather than seeing planning as a success or failure, Latour's metaphor of a fragile network of relations and of materials, human and non-human, offers an alternative perspective that helps us to see a broader range of non-human elements as significant in planning activities. By not categorising everything into either social or material, we can start to see how the social and material are tied together. In Norfolk Park, the non-human intrudes into the planned future not only in the form of planning documents, but most notably in the form of what are known as 'abnormals'. Abnormals in Norfolk Park were primarily holes in the ground, and they seem to have arrived in this project like surprising new knowledge at almost every stage. The estate was built on clay and limestone that had previously contained mineworks, shafts, potholes and faults. In the 1960s, the 15 storey tower blocks were built on concrete rafts, and older residents remember that one of the blocks was built on two rafts, after the first raft began to slip. It came as a surprise to them that rows of two or three storey houses could not be supported on land that had until recently supported high-rise tower-blocks. Similarly, when a new primary school was built, the development was held up when large potholes were discovered and had to be filled with substantial volumes of concrete, substantial in both scale and expense. A scheme to build green-homes on another of the sites was held up for nearly two years after it was discovered on site (ie not in geological records beforehand) that expensive gas-cooled electrical cables ran under the site.

James C. Scott points out that working only with formalised externalised knowledge is like 'working to rule', which is always less efficient than working with social cooperation, compromise and goodwill.[19] On the contrary, we rely on practical or experiential knowledge (that he refers to with the Greek term *metis*) to achieve anything from everyday to specialist tasks. This is knowledge that is often not made abstract or externalised, and Scott points out that grand plans often fail where they do not accommodate practical and local knowledge, although he also reminds us that grand schemes often succeed where space has been left for unofficial or illegal activities to supplement the formal planned development. Scott is making legitimate space for what is often called 'local knowledge' – such as the memory of Norfolk Park residents about where the holes in the ground could be expected. On the other hand, Alberto Corsin-Jimenez has an original way to show us just how social knowledge is and why it might be ignored, by suggesting that information has varying degrees of morality that might be located in different places.[20] Knowledge that circulates freely outside morality he describes as public information. Fully accessible information in Western societies might be such things as clock-time, so easily accessible that anyone can find it with the basic ability to read numbers, or uni-dimensional facts stripped of additional context, such as land altitudes. He argues that information is conflated with knowledge, but that truly transparent information is like a truly free gift, that is, without a social life. A really free gift doesn't put you under any obligation to offer something in return, whether that is money, a counter-gift, or an obligation to be grateful. Which is why we usually understand that there is no such thing as a really free gift (or a lunch, for that matter), since giving a gift by definition draws us into some kind of social relationship between the giver and the recipient.[21] We can see how deep this obligation flows if we only consider the exchange of words: you ask me what the time is, I tell you: so far we have merely exchanged information in one direction. But you are obliged then at least to say to me 'thank you', which is a courtesy that you offer in exchange for the information I have given to you, and already

19 Scott 1998, Chapter 9.

20 Corsin-Jimenez 2005.

21 Summaries of the large literature on the gift, starting with Mauss's seminal essay 1925/2002, can be found in Sykes 2005, Davis 1992, and Parry and Bloch 1989.

we have entered a basic social relationship (of courtesy and civility), which might easily be extended by a further exchange. In other words, gifts draw people into relationships with one another, just as we need relationships with other people to gain knowledge and experience. Some forms of information, such as gossip or opinion, are more explicitly moralistic, since we know that gossip is passed on in order to pass judgement on people's behaviour, to maintain principles of moral behaviour, and there the trust is in the person who tells us the information as a reliable source. But ideally, technical information should be free-standing and immune to social relations, making it reliable in any context. Whereas we normally trust information because we have it from a reliable source, we can feel trust in this kind of unattached information because it appears not to be entangled in personal relationships.

Planning documents lie somewhere between these two, as they contain knowledge which is specific, as well as information which is general. Their effectiveness is limited since existing plans are drawn into complex negotiations, rather than simply over-ruling other sources of knowledge. They also go far beyond merely technical procedure as they are also always inherently political. Any document which espouses a particular general future over others is political, and even the most technical land-use plan inherently favours the interests of some people over others. In the case of Norfolk Park, the interests of investors who sought to gain profit from the redevelopment of the estate were intrinsic to the success of the plan, even while the original planning guidance emphasised the needs of residents and the centrality of community development. If we are to trust the knowledge included in plans, then we must either have plans that contain only known externally verifiable facts (with the drawback that such knowledge is extremely limited, as Scott explains), or we must trust the people who write, legitimate and use plans, through personal experience (with the drawback that such trust is hard to create or maintain). As trust in public authority diminishes, perhaps we should not be surprised that there is pressure to make plans more 'technical'. If they are less well socialised, then they must gain their authority elsewhere.

Planning as a belief system

So at this point, we might recast the image of planning that we started with. Strategic planning by state actors is an activity with many rationalist alibis, yet at its core it is a set of practices engaged in to invite prosperity and other forms of good, and to ward off unwelcome changes. Plans can be aspirational, idealistic, and may attempt to co-opt unknowing actors over whom the planners have no particular authority or control ('the public', 'communities' or imagined benign commercial 'partners' spring to mind). Planning systems have expert practitioners with protected, even secret, realms of knowledge: planners, who are sometimes perceived by others as casting 'blight' (evil), with material consequences that can lead to suffering, ill-health and even death. Their motivations may be questioned, and often attributed to personality traits or secret intentions (corruption). Expert practitioners also do their best to form their clientele according to their own preferred worldview, that is, to try to coerce a public into activities and actions which meet the requirements of the art of planning. As noted, planning is premised on the prediction of future worlds, events, conditions and so forth. These futures are conjured in ways that few outside are in a position to either understand or criticise. That is not to say that others do not have the technical competence to challenge future scenarios, but that challenges seldom reach into the self-fulfilling procedures of planning practice. Critics' voices can be defined as inappropriate, as illegitimate, or as untrustworthy. They might be called 'NIMBY', or told that complaints about street lighting are not relevant to strategic planning, or they may be told that their arguments are not as important as the technical strategies of the planning office. That is to say, critics are seldom in an appropriate position to make challenges effectively. Planning also relies on descriptions of the present, and the partiality of these descriptions is seldom acknowledged.[22] Again, in practice, alternative descriptions are often inadmissible to planning procedures.

As I suggested above, there is no coherent theoretical or empirical model which demonstrates how the theory of planning reaches the outcomes which people experience. Textual plans never exactly correspond to actual material changes on the ground, and they can never robustly be tested for effectiveness. Effectiveness in planning – in common with many bureaucratic procedures – is only measured (in the UK) in terms of bureaucratic handling, speed of decision-making, that is, process efficiency rather than outcome evaluation. Descriptions of the present in relation to past plans are always contingent: plans are always under revision which helps to muddy the relation between plans and presents, as well as futures. It is also extremely difficult to show how planning effects its outcomes, if it can be said to do that, and explanations of planning can soon become rather mysterious themselves. What explanations and models that do exist tend to be normative accounts of what should happen, which remain steadfastly theoretical to the extent that implementation of plans becomes an art form in its own right, reliant on judgements and hunches of planners and politicians as much as on skills and experience. So it may be useful to see plans as the symbolic objects of divination, smoothing our path over the troubled waters between a difficult present and a better future. Plans appear to make the future fixable, to tell us how the future will be, to guide us into the future as we desire it, and not into something which resembles the past. Where there are conflicts between the many parties to contemporary planning processes, they are often over different expectations and understandings of the function and symbolic values of plans.

22 As Forester 1996 has shown.

Explaining non-rationality and the intangible

There is much we can learn from ethnographic studies of witchcraft that might cast new light on planning. From the earliest days of anthropology, and particularly among the British anthropologists primarily at Oxford University in the years between the two World Wars, there was a great interest in the practice of witchcraft in Africa. Colonial governors and missionaries generally saw continued belief in witchcraft as a sign that Africans were superstitious and somehow living in the Dark Ages (ie in a period of history that predated the sophisticated West)[23]. E. E. Evans-Pritchard, though, studied witchcraft to show how, understood in its own terms, it was as rational an explanation of the world as any Western explanatory system and was complementary to science, rather than contradictory to it. Witchcraft operates in the explanation of why things happen, whereas science tells us how things happen, and these are quite different fields of explanation.

As Laura Bohannan's novel of African life shows,[24] a tree might fall because it is rotten and has been eaten by termites, but if it falls on a man and kills him, then chance and coincidence are not satisfactory explanations – why that man, at that time, and that tree? Or a youth may stumble on an exposed root, but he may do this a hundred times, so why does it get infected one time in particular, and why does the infection not heal? Whereas we talk of bad luck, fate, or divine retribution, the people that Bohannan and Evans-Pritchard describe, talk about witchcraft. The reason for illness, bad hunting or injury is related to witchcraft, even if the details of the kind of witchcraft and how it works may vary, with some witches consciously acting on grudges,[25] and in other contexts unwittingly carrying witchcraft substance.[26] Witchcraft is an unavoidable fact of life in parts of sub-Saharan Africa and continues to inspire many fine studies, such as Smith's analysis of its role in contemporary neo-liberal development in Kenya.[27] But witchcraft is more than simply an idiom for the discussion of inexplicable illnesses or accidents. It is what is called a total social fact, a deep-seated truth and explanatory framework that helps us to make sense of the unpredictability of life. Planners, too, believe in invisible substances that can cause things to happen and which some people use to harm others for their own benefit. They call it 'power' and refer to it to explain many twists and turns in urban development. Yet who has ever actually seen something called power? It is as shady and flimsy as witchcraft substance, and equally effective as a total explanation of why things happen just here and just now. Power, too, is not just an idiom, a game of language that we know, but runs as a current through the way we think about the world, politics,

23 See Wolf 1982, Fabian 1983.

24 Bowen 1954.

25 Favret Saada 1980.

26 Evans-Pritchard 1937.

27 Smith 2008.

planning and everyday life. If we stop to interrogate it, it requires just as much explanation as witchcraft.

Most commentators who take this approach tend not to refer to witchcraft, as it sounds rather too exotic, but focus instead on magic and ritual as similar to policy. Robertson points out how it is possible to understand development planning as a symbolic system, identifying the use of key phrases and jargon as a parallel to the performance of magic.[28] Practitioners of magic, for example, use words that evoke the desired state – whether that is a state of health for health healers, or prosperity for economic healers. This is key to the effectiveness of the magic. Although the explanation for how this magic works might vary, it isn't too difficult to see the parallel with the language of political slogans, and Robertson lists everything from the Tennessee Valley Authority's 'grass roots theory' to Malaysian five year plans – from 'Success' to 'Self-Reliance' and on to 'Renewal' – as examples of the use of slogans to encourage progress. The website of the British Government Ministry with responsibility for planning shows how central such slogans remain: 'community, opportunity, prosperity', and 'strengthening local democracy' loom large,[29] and the planning pages are headlined with the phrase 'our planning and building regulation involvement ensures that we get the right development, in the right place, at the right time'.[30]

These are just slogans, you might say, they are just ritual. Indeed they are, but we should not underestimate the value of ritual in keeping a symbolic system on its feet, for helping us to believe that things are in order, that the state exists, or that planning 'delivers development' at the 'right place and time'. What if planning itself was an elaborate form of political ritual? It can hardly have escaped most planners' attention that they are sometimes accused of rubber stamping, and perhaps it is not so difficult for planners to admit that they, themselves, sometimes feel that they are going through the motions, rather than really planning in the way they thought they would when they decided a career in planning was for them. Ritual should not be too easily dismissed. Ritual can be a way of countering the anxiety that comes from the difference between the way things actually are and how we like to think about them.[31] How many of us really believe that planning actually always delivers development at the right time and in the right place? In the right time and place for whom? I have yet to meet a planner who does not regret at least one development for being untimely or inappropriate. And as Reade points out, there is no 'right' time or 'right' place, only 'a pattern of physical development which will suit *some* interests, and a pattern which will suit *others*'.[32] Planning and planners are not infallible, and nor are they completely responsible for the outcomes of development. Even so, going through the ritual of preparing plans is

28 Described by Malinowski, cited in Robertson 1984: 107.

29 http://www.communities.gov.uk/corporate/ 26.08.09.

30 http://www.communities.gov.uk/planningandbuilding/ 26.08.09.

31 Leach, in Mosse 2006: 940.

32 Reade 1987: 103.

important to legitimise both the principles of planning and the power of the state to regulate. In everyday use, 'ritual' is often associated with the idea of 'empty formality' or 'pure rhetoric', and, in the field of planning, ritual is not understood as an intrinsic and essential element but as the opposite, as the decoration on top of the cake, so to speak. Ritual is associated with the Lord Mayor and her[33] robes and chains, but not with the leader of the council and her management of political debates. Discussion of ritual in relation to planning is liable to be side-tracked into a discussion of the relation between speech acts and action, or between decisions and implementation, rather than head directly into an analysis of what difference speech and text make. Yet rituals do not necessarily have to be 'empty'. They are closely linked to routines that ensure the reproduction of organisations like bureaucracies and make them appear independent of the people who carry out the routines and rituals that are the bureaucracy.

Indeed, rituals are neither irrational nor a distraction. At the very least, they present concrete evidence of social life, of shared meaning and continuity. The concrete elements of rituals are probably easiest to recognise and appreciate in planning and politics. Rituals of the state such as the opening of parliament or commemorative events are familiar, and their pomp and formality, and, in particular, the costumes that participants sometimes have to wear (like 'Black Rod' in the British Parliament) quite explicitly prioritise roles over persons. Where it all goes a bit wobbly for planning is when we introduce the idea of magic. Or, even worse, witchcraft. Witchcraft and magic are, after all, often taken to be the direct opposite of modern, civilised life.[34] And in even mentioning magic, or in going on to discuss the significance of witchcraft discourses in Africa, there is a danger of simply confirming prejudices that the language of witchcraft has promoted – that believing in witchcraft is somehow 'backward'.[35] This sort of prejudice leads Margaret Weiner to argue that Modernity needs magic and witchcraft as opposites by which to define itself as rational and scientific.[36] Magic was a term applied by Europeans to colonial societies to demonstrate the superiority of the Europeans and their science, and to convince themselves that colonial societies needed to become civilised. In the longer run, these arguments – that colonial peoples needed to be civilised by whatever means necessary – were used to legitimise an often violent European presence. But the feelings of Europeans about civilisation and magic were not quite so clear cut in practice. Weiner describes an ambivalence towards magic among European colonial populations on the airy verandas of colonial Java. Here 'Europeans shared tales about ghosts, sorcery and inexplicable incidents or played at table turning and telling fortunes'.[37] In other words, the Europeans were telling stories about native magic as fake and as a danger to public order, but at

33 In the mid-2000s, Sheffield had a female Lord Mayor and a female council leader.

34 See Geschiere 2003.

35 See Pels 2003: 6.

36 Weiner 2003.

37 Op Cit: 150.

the same time, they themselves were playing games of the uncanny and the occult. And at home, too, upper-class Europeans also played games of the occult. So, if magic exists for Modernity as its opposite, it also exists within modern states. While strenuous efforts are often made to distinguish magic and religion,[38] the latter certainly takes the occult seriously. Many European states have established churches, which suggests that modern states are happy to accept certain kinds of mysterious and spiritual worlds, even if these are tamed into relatively narrow roles in political or policy processes. Bishops may bless politicians without rationality collapsing about their ears, but they also regularly make pleas for the spiritual, the integrity of nature, or the value of community that can be nicely translated into political concerns, if not planning ones.

But whereas I have characterised British – and generally Modernist – planning as realist planning, what about other planes of existence? Why is the evil eye not a valid planning consideration? Why is geomancy or *feng shui* not the principal logic of urban design? Of course, in some countries these are aspects of urban planning,[39] but a fully qualified British planner is trained into scepticism, to see such things as outside their field of competence or interest. Our well-trained British planner might start, instead, to talk about the material considerations that planning committees or inspectors can take into account to make decisions, but this does not answer the question of why some things are material considerations and others are not. Do our planners never question whether non-material considerations might be worth taking seriously? If we can acknowledge that there are lots of less than rational or technical elements to planning practice, perhaps we should examine other unexplained effects.

I noted above that the language of policy often uses jargon to invoke desired futures, and Michael Taussig takes a similar view of material objects like statues and commemorative objects. In his book on the magic of the state – itself quite a mystical work – Taussig brings to life the statues of colonial heroes and 'great' statesmen, and asks us to see them not merely as statues and memories, but as spirits of the dead that are worshipped and honoured as though they could still do things.[40] He calls to mind political protests that gather around statues of political figures, and reminds us how public events are held in historically significant places, as if to imbue them with the spirit of events past. When politicians invoke the name of great leaders of the past, pioneers or heroes, they seek to infuse their own plans with reflected greatness, but by what means is this achieved, other than through some magical infection that is created by the invocation of special words or names? Taussig blurs the distinction between actual practices of spirit possession and metaphorical attempts to use the spirit of dead political leaders to give substance to the nation-state. Spirit possession is certainly a kind of magic,

38 See Tambiah 1990.

39 See Kalland 1996, or for more journalistic evidence, see Lyall 2005 or Gruber 2007.

40 Taussig 1997.

and it sounds terribly exotic, but if we start to think of how often we try to capture a disembodied spirit of the past, we can see that the past – and the dead – are still with us in some kind of spirit, be it material or mental. So perhaps the spirit world is not quite so exotic as we might have thought, if we re-jig the language that we use to think about it.

Spirit possession rituals are not a common cultural practice in the urban regeneration I will refer to in Sheffield. Yet the spirit of the past is often invoked, especially among residents, and the spirit of the future is repeatedly called on, particularly by planners and developers. A common contemporary explanation for plans not fulfilled, promises broken and processes incomplete is referral to the market. In this kind of sweeping 'explanation', 'the market' becomes a kind of black box, a shorthand term for a myriad of separate processes that together appear to have some kind of causality. Planning, too, can seem to be a black box that from the outside appears to be either magical or mysterious, depending on one's point of view. It is this kind of 'magic' that is worth thinking about here. There are many ways of managing temporal transitions, and there are many responses to the lack of fit between the world as it is and the world as we wish to talk about it. Between them lie the unexplained and what cannot be understood, and magic and mystery can serve as residual categories to resolve these confusions. According to Evans-Pritchard, magical causes are often invoked when material causes meet their limits, since magic, by definition, operates beyond the knowable.[41]

Learning to be rational

Referring to magic and ritual shows us how plans are more than inert objects. They draw people into relationships with each other and with things, like buildings, land or vehicles. But plans are also socialised knowledge in another sense, through the socialisation of planners themselves. How do we know things, and what does it mean to say that planning knowledge is 'embodied'?

Planning knowledge gives an impression of being externalised into objects or documents, codified into graphs, trends or policy statements which planners imagine that anyone could read. In other words, planning knowledge is disinvested from the planner's body, in what we might call un-embodied knowledge. Yet this very imagination of disembodiment and accessibility is a product of the planner's initiation, through several years of training, of an easing into professional life, through periods of 'experience', where aspiring planners learn how to behave in a planning office, how to talk to non-planners, how to relate to politicians and to people defined as 'members of the public', as well as how to dress, behave in committee meetings and how to guard their silence. Through their training, which in Britain is closely codified by their professional institution, planners are taught to read the signs, one might say, to appreciate a particular way of being in the

41 Evans-Pritchard 1937.

world and certain forms of order. They are taught to understand their environment as legible landscapes, and construe communities through indices of deprivation and income, and some come to understand that there may be some people who will neither understand nor sympathise with them. This is common to most forms of the bureaucratic life, in that we need to use statistical categories to make the complex and diverse world somehow more manageable.[42] Planners are also taught, however, that they have a morally righteous goal in life, and that it is their duty to seek social harmony, economic growth and environmental sustainability. One might argue that they also experience a kind of seclusion from the world – as far as any other student is removed both from a domestic and a wider social world – in order then to be reintroduced as 'professionals' through a long period of training in junior positions in a classic 'rite of passage'.[43] What emerges is a professionalised body. Even if planning knowledge is still imagined as disembodied, the body of the planner is carefully disciplined, and the knowledge planners have is not free.

So, on the one hand, we tend to think of planning knowledge as information, knowledge that is disconnected from the person of the knower, but, on the other hand, the planner's body is disciplined and the planner takes control of the knowledge that they have privileged access to. There are many ways in which knowledge can be embodied, and a brief foray into comparison might help to highlight the Western case. Let us go back to magic and divination to think about where the power of knowledge is to be found. African witchcraft is a discourse that is used to explain much about the world. Rather like religion, it does not seek to explain the physical causes of things like illness or what we call bad luck, as much as to consider the metaphysical causes of why misfortune happens to particular people at particular times. Skilled diviners go into a special kind of trance to diagnose the supernatural causes of the afflictions of their patients, and they need to have very special qualities as well as intense training to do this. De Boeck and Devisch describe how Luundu diviners in southern Zaire gain the high level of ritual knowledge and expertise that divination requires. They spend a long period of training under the guidance of a senior diviner, and undergo complex rituals themselves. Luundu diviners use chickens as a tool to help them with their divination, and as part of the initiation into their profession, they are implicated physically into the relation with chicken-oracles.[44] A rooster is killed and a special meal is shared, but parts of the heart of the animal are retained. The diviner later swallows the reserved parts, which enter 'into his heart',[45] giving him an intensification of the feeling in his chest and heart, which enable the diviner to be possessed by the medium and to become attuned to the gift of clairvoyance.[46] Knowledge alone is not enough to become a skilled diviner; the diviner's body

42 As both Scott 1998 and Herzfeld 1992 have explained, following Weber.

43 van Gennep 1960/1909.

44 De Boeck and Devisch 1994.

45 Ibid: 114.

46 Ibid: 116.

must be attuned through long and complex rituals, so that the knowledge becomes effective. This knowledge is then embodied – it is part of the diviner's body – and it is also highly socialised, even if secret, as part of the tradition that diviners share. The diviner's clients know that the diviner possesses extraordinary skills, confirmed through ritual process and the tests that this demands of the diviner, and legitimised by the completion of an apprenticeship with a well known and skilled senior diviner.

One might safely say that the initiation of planners is rather different, but the knowledge planners have is not quite as free-standing as it is often imagined. Even truly transparent and freely available information may accrue a social life, when it is taken up and circulated partially. Information about the geological conditions of the land of Norfolk Park, for example, was derived from expert analysis in the 1960s, yet it appears to have become folk knowledge, rather than the restricted expert knowledge it might have been expected to have been. It was not secret, but planners appeared not to be party to it, even when residents tried to convince planners that their knowledge was valuable and relevant. But since planners and developers appeared unable to believe that residents might have trustworthy technical knowledge, and also appeared incapable of securing technical knowledge themselves, they suffered the financial penalties of not-knowing. By ignoring local knowledge, the developers faced significant technical and financial setbacks, problems that came back to haunt the planning team who then had to seek gap-funding to keep the regeneration going. So far, so familiar. This can also be interpreted as un-shared knowledge, an ignorance of local memory often observed in classic development studies. Residents interpreted this lack of knowledge as a form of immorality ('how could they…'[be so stupid as to not hear us]), yet for the council officers and developers it was put down to bad fortune. 'Abnormals', for the latter, were obstacles thrown up by the ground itself, not a result of oversight on their part of otherwise known information. Abnormals appeared 'as if by magic' to disrupt a realist project. 'Abnormals' themselves became an expected part of the process, with their own name. The abnormal became routinised as part of the development process.

Members of the Community Forum also experienced how the form in which information and/or knowledge was conveyed played a role in the extent to which it was incorporated into the process. As we know from studies of the way government works in practice, and of the 'mentalities' of governing that Foucault called 'governmentality', there are modes of communication which serve powerful interests, and modes which can be excluded by them.[47] Language is not separate from power, but, rather, can be an instrument that is used to influence, coerce or even control. This much has been recognised and written about widely in planning theory. The 'communicative turn' in planning theory suggested that the range of evidence that might be considered has been limited by the kind of language or presentation used to represent it, and authors like Healey, Innes, Sandercock and

47 Foucault 1978, Scott 1998.

others have argued that changing the way we communicate can expand the range of issues to be considered as significant in planning debates.[48] For example, they have suggested the importance of stories for organising knowledge, as part of the critique of the rationalist approach to planning. Yet the weakness in these studies is a desire to believe that inequalities can be set aside and talk made meaningful through earnest exchange. This desire has been inspired from the work of the philosopher Jürgen Habermas who aimed to describe the ideal speech situation. In doing this, he acknowledged all the conditions that would need to be in place for such perfect communication to be possible. Habermas concentrated on the qualities of speech needed to achieve rational argument between a pair of speakers and listeners, making this approach very unlike the actual situation of public politics that we know from experience. As various theorists have attempted to apply the idea of ideal speech into public contexts,[49] they have tended to see the ideal speech situation as an actually achievable goal, rather than a philosophical construct that illustrates how complex communication really is.

A more useful approach can be found in work that analyses speech acts as performance, and asks, what does speaking do?[50] How do certain terms in a debate become established as natural, obvious, objective?[51] And how do certain statements, spoken or written, carry authority while others do not? Sometimes this can be a subtle process of not hearing the voices from certain quarters, but unwanted commentary can also be despatched in quite concrete ways. The Norfolk Park Community Forum attempted to tap into powerful discourses to challenge the organisation of the regeneration process. The deputy-chief executive of the forum had, himself, studied planning and therefore had access to some of the processes, at least in theory. In the early days of the regeneration, the Forum's committee were included in many consultative meetings. Yet after a few years, they realised that the difficult questions they were raising about community development were not being addressed. Three years into the regeneration programme, after the demolition of nearly 2,000 dwellings, only 33 new houses had been built on the estate. At this point, one of the Forum's key volunteers, a founder member of the original tenants' association, asked the council's area panel officer for advice in getting funding for external advice. Their aims were to highlight the lack of progress in the regeneration, to see if their own concerns were legitimate and to find a way to resolve the problems they were encountering by securing an independent academic report. With this funding, the forum commissioned Michael Carley, a planning academic at Heriot-Watt University, to assess the regeneration programme and to report on it. The resulting report criticised the lack of commitment to community development, and examined the delays and failures in organisation, proposing new

48 Forester 1969, Healey 1997, Mandelbaum et al 1996, Sandercock 2000, Innes Hillier 1999.

49 See Renn, Webler and Wiedemann (1995) for an introduction.

50 Or in Austin's terms, what is it that words do? (Austin 1978).

51 Gal and Woolard 2001: 4.

forms of organisation to remedy these problems.[52] Rather than respond formally to the report, I was told that the senior regeneration officer began a grievance procedure against the area panel officer for assisting the Forum in gaining funding to produce negative reporting. Rather than prompt the regeneration into action, the report generated bad feeling. It is worth noting here, also, that this episode was not spoken about by any of those directly involved. Discussing (or not discussing) past failures in this process absolutely fitted the model described by Mosse of a long-term development project in India,[53] where project reviews always focus on future challenges and past successes, and where discussion or evaluation of past failures is at best a failure of tact and at worst an attempt to undermine a project's future.[54]

Bad feeling is the negative kind of magic found in policy-making and development planning, a dangerous emotional power that can endanger material developments. It bears relation to 'negativity', a sentiment embodied in critical documents or spoken words.[55] Critical words might endanger the 'goodwill' (ie, the magic) that planners strive to build with private commercial operators and government agencies, in order to cajole them into investing in risky projects. The risk is thus not purely financial, but may latch onto reputations too. 'Negativity' and 'criticism' might drive away flighty and risk-averse investors, and are to be avoided at all costs. That this commitment to the power of positive speech was widespread within the council was also clear at a public meeting on the future of the city of Sheffield, which was organised by a firm of architects as a panel debate in the city's art-house cinema in the autumn of 2005. The four panel members who were each invited to give a 15 minute presentation about the future of the city included a member of the city council's cabinet, a Labour politician and the cabinet member for planning, economic regeneration and culture, and, incidentally, also councillor for the Norfolk Park ward. The politician used nearer half an hour to extol the wonderful work of regeneration already going on in the city. He referred to the regeneration of various housing estates in glowing terms. During the debate following the panel speeches, audience responses varied. Some were very careful to praise the achievements so far achieved while asking about future plans, but others challenged the interpretation of success attached to the widespread changes in the city. Some were very critical of the architectural and design standards of city centre redevelopment, and one audience member interpreted regeneration efforts as gentrification, and asked how they benefited those who were moved out to further flung estates. After a fairly long and heated debate, the councillor started to complain about the criticism, saying he couldn't stand 'all this negativity'. Reiterating the achievement of huge changes in the city in recent years, he finally

52 Carley 2002.

53 Mosse 2005.

54 Mosse's own critical book met an emotionalised hostility in which he was seen to have betrayed the project team, apparently producing real hurt and bad feeling among his former colleagues: Mosse 2006.

55 c.f. Salaman 2000a,b.

exclaimed that people who didn't like what the council was achieving could go elsewhere.[56] Paradoxically, when he shortly afterwards lost his cabinet position, he explained to me that he thought it was because he himself had been too critical, questioning senior party officials and members and challenging council policies.

The mysticism of negativity bears uncanny resemblance to the words, death and spells that Favret-Saada describes in the Bocage in her study of the power of words within and about witchcraft[1].[57] Taking an interest in witchcraft in this part of France, she discovered that to talk about witchcraft is a dangerous thing to do. Either you are accusing someone of witchcraft, which could cause them to afflict you, or you are suggesting that you have an ability to protect from witchcraft, but either way, you are implicating yourself in a dangerous world and acknowledging it as real. In Favret Saada's work it is the power of words which creates the effect of witchcraft, where words out of place may be seen as the cause of both illness and misfortune, and where the accusation of witchcraft itself causes a material change in the health of the social body. Although witches' activities may not be observed, it is talk to them or about them which changes the relations between persons. Quite irrespective of material exchanges or movements, the circulation of words can in itself cause disease and lead to unfortunate consequences. The parallel in Norfolk Park is the idea that saying something negative or critical about the regeneration might cause bad things to happen. Perhaps that most magical of qualities, 'confidence', may be lost, the market will collapse, or the investors might pull out, or progress may be stalled. This can be rationalised as projecting an impression of competence, yet it goes far beyond avoiding misrepresentation, resembling the more spiritualised positive consciousness of the organisation that Salamon describes in relation to New Age businesses in Denmark.[58] As none of the participants really experiences control of the process, none can fully account for its success or failure, and hence, although I have yet to hear anyone refer specifically to witchcraft, there is ominous talk of negativity, of difficulties, of secrets and lies and hidden agendas. The reference is not to the supernatural, but to the emotional. The morality is, in Corsin-Jimenez's terms, attributed to persons and to organisations, sometimes interchangeably, and is described in terms of what Stapely has called the 'personality' of the organisation.[59] In other words, although we know that an organisation might just be an assemblage of people and things in a building, we still think about it as if it had volition, a personality, and character traits. Councils might be accused of being brutal, uncaring, thoughtless, or forward-looking, caring, efficient, or perhaps described as muddled, uncoordinated, the right hand not knowing what the left hand is doing: all qualities that are those of a single person, as if a great bureaucracy of a thousand people might somehow coalesce into one entity with an identifiable personality. This person is, indeed,

56 I paraphrase the stronger language used at the time.

57 Favret Saada 1980, 1985.

58 Salamon 2005.

59 Stapely 1996.

moody, mysterious, often unpredictable and full of internal contradictions, sometimes flighty, but generally gets on with the job of keeping the city turning on a day-to-day basis.[60]

The image of the organisation as one body is clearest when it is held responsible for the worst consequences of change. In the face of increased fragmentation of government activities, the council no longer provides or directly contracts its building activities. On the contrary, it has become just one partner in a complex and fragile network of actors, reliant on persuading reluctant investors to align their interests. At the same time, services which have been devolved to community-sector organisations are gradually being reclaimed as the legitimate activities of local government. Funding for training and environmental services are being withdrawn from charitable organisations and drawn back into the remit of the council. Yet the council is still 'seen' as a body which governs, even in the knowledge that it is fragmented. The director of a neighbouring development trust said a colleague had described the council to him as a dinosaur: a massive beast with a very small brain. If it happens to sit down or swish its tail near you, you get squashed or knocked over. The council, he said, is a massive organisation, with just a very few powerful people directing its activities. While these people may be intelligent, a slight change of direction can crush other organisations in its wake. These metaphors which describe the council add to the impression that it is a unitary whole, even while they acknowledge that seen as a whole it is irrational and unpredictable.

In Norfolk Park, as plans changed, a decision to retain one high rise tower block for elderly residents was reversed, and the block was demolished after all. Some of the residents were frail, some in their 90s, and had been told that they would never need to move again. Moving even into a well run comfortable new care home was a huge upheaval for many of them, and the care home manager pointed out that since moving house was known to be one of the most stressful things to experience in life, some of the residents had needed much more care when they arrived than when they had been assessed prior to the move. Some had even not survived the move after all. Certainly the transition had not been completely smooth, and with several different agencies and private organisations involved, the feat of organisation was not simple. For some of the residents, though, 'the council' was a callous beast that if it had not caused, had hastened the death of their friends. Seeing the move as a failure in the plans, from the residents' perspective, planning does, then, have potentially fatal effects, even if the cause is hard to pin down.

Conclusions

Using the concept of magic and witchcraft as metaphorical tools to investigate planning opens up the possibility of seeing governmental procedures as mirages,

60 Alexander 2002, Herzfeld 1992.

fragile networks of people, objects and ideas, as social and material relations which together give the impression of state presence or absence. Where governmentality approaches may offer an insight into the structuring of relations of power, a magical analysis brings forward the affective in those relations: the importance of feelings such as confidence, and the centrality of the relations themselves and shows that the state is not always an actor with rational repressive intent, but often a collection of persons thrust together with different intents and abilities.

Although I have pointed mostly to magic, there might also be much to be learned from a closer examination of scholarship on divination which, according to de Boeck and Devisch, 'does not so much offer a mimetic model of a social context, but rather *makes* a world'.[61] That is, rather than seeing plans as models of the world, we might also see the plans and those engaged in the tactical dance around them as performing the making of a world, in which the plans, as such, are part of a symbolic-socio-technical constellation rather than any simple means to an end. I raise this point to indicate that there is much more to be learned from these studies than the points that have been made in this chapter. Using the metaphor of magic here has offered an opportunity to view planning as it is rather than how we would like it to be. We can see it as a set of practices of compromises, mistakes and misunderstandings, held together by post-hoc rationalisation, coincidences, collective memory-loss and fragile confidences. In contrast to the majority of planning theories which see it as a power struggle between competing actors, classes or interests, or as a banal if contested political process, seeing the magic in planning shows us how amazing it is that we continue to believe in planning as a way into the future, and how far it creates its own barriers.

It is important not to push the metaphor too far. There is no suggestion that UK planning processes engage with spiritual or other worlds, although they may do so elsewhere.[62] However, appeals to higher authority certainly do exist, even if these are human authorities, and as I have pointed out, the use of documents to substantiate arguments in ways that, to most participants, are purely symbolic is certainly a similarity worth noting. Even within a most secular context, semi-articulated indications that outcomes are the result of decisions and powers 'higher up' have often been made to me.[63] Experienced activists often follow a pattern of experience by which they gradually try to influence processes higher up the governmental hierarchy, yet often never feel that they actually meet the higher powers behind planning frameworks flowing through those hierarchies.[64] It is in those gaps, where it is so difficult to explain why one's actions are not being effective, despite following all the right rules and tips, that we find often

61 de Boeck and Devisch 1994: 98, emphasis in original.

62 Smith 2008.

63 And indeed to other anthropologists, as demonstrated in my version of Halvard Vike's film, which I entitled *Much Ado about Norway*, in which a communist alliance politician invokes 'higher powers' to explain local disputes.

64 Murdoch and Abram 2002, and see also Damer and Hague 1971.

increasingly exotic conspiracy theories or alternative accusations of corruption, modern forms of witchcraft accusation that cover the gap between how we believe the world should work, and how we actually experience it.

Chapter 3
The Body in Planning

> After a voyage through the realm of magic, this chapter focuses on something much more material, the body. It asks what happened to bodies in planning. The chapter outlines links between our understanding of bodies and our concepts of culture, showing how the production of opposites such as mind and body, culture and nature, reason and emotion are constantly reproduced, with serious consequences for plans and planning. It also reminds us that planners have bodies too, and that we learn to discipline our bodies into certain kinds of behaviours that serve to distinguish planners from others.

A resident said [...], 'Have you taken into consideration the wind on the estate?' It was like they were patting her on the head and saying, 'There, there, old lady. We all have wind.' They wouldn't believe her that the wind on the Park can be extremely fierce. This went on for a few months, and all of a sudden we did have a huge gale on the estate. It was so bad that vehicles were blown over, and one of these cars belonged to someone on the design team. So all of a sudden a week later we had a wind specialist. So they were only half listening to people. It didn't seem what people were saying was going to be valued.[1]

How is it that such obvious and everyday things like the wind can be ignored in planning and building? Sometimes it seems to people living in areas under reconstruction that the most obvious mistakes are always made, and no amount of reminding or warning on their behalf leads to problems being avoided. Somehow, the residents of Norfolk Park who repeatedly asked for handrails on steep paths were just ignored time after time. Yet in the days of consumer-participation, how can it be that common knowledge is not shared by professional planners and builders?

Professionals are trained to be aware of statements that fall within their knowledge-field, and to prioritise the factors that they have the skills to manage. Indeed, this is part of what our training aims to achieve, the ability to sift out significant information. The trouble is that these skills are not failsafe but can often lead to us missing crucial information which lies on the fringes beyond or between professional fields. This means that when people talk to us about issues that are not within our professional field, their comments can seem to pass unnoticed. From the perspective of residents concerned about local conditions, it can often seem that there is no legitimate arena to discuss important issues, if they lie just between

1 Interview CN-SA 2006.

departments of the state, or are not the direct responsibility of one particular public servant or private contractor. But it can also be more than just kinds of talk that are unheard.

In planning, it is often talking about bodies that seems to meet a bit of a blank. Abstracted into populations we can treat them with statistics, and collectivised into 'communities' we can accept that there may be differences in group culture – ethnicity, identity, or whatever other grouping is in favour. Finding space for a particular number of houses on a hillside plot is a challenge that architects are well equipped to achieve and planners to approve, but accommodating the bodies of elderly ladies who are liable to be swept away by strong winds can easily end up being no-one's responsibility in particular. Our plans often have details about transport, routes, access, and, these days, more attention is beginning to be paid to wheelchairs and prams and bicycles. But bodies barely get a look-in. It is as if, in our efforts to remain impersonal in planning questions, we cannot face the variety, physicality and particularity of bodies themselves. Bodies pose a problem that resembles the one we will find in Chapter 5 about citizens, since actual bodies are always particular and therefore personal. So, in this chapter I ask what cultural concepts of bodies can tell us about planning, and what a focus on bodies tells us about culture.

In Chapter 1 I discussed the significance of categorising, as one of the most important ways in which humans order the world around them to make sense of it. Any system of ordering needs its remainder category, and as we saw in Chapter 2, magic is a classic category for things that are hard to explain. The British planning system has its own useful remainder category used in considering planning policies or decisions, which is the notion of 'material considerations'. Basically, things that we ought to take into account but are not obsessive (or far-sighted) enough to list comprehensively come under the category of 'material considerations'. But it is not an entirely open category. On the contrary, the category is not simply 'considerations', but 'material considerations'. In principle, the definition of material considerations is relatively flexible, trimmed by case law, but described as 'related to the development and use of land in the public interest'. Material considerations must also fairly and reasonably relate to the application concerned'.[2] Government statements are identified as material considerations, as are access to sites, landscaping, impacts on the neighbourhood and availability of infrastructure. Although it might sound fairly comprehensive, this leaves large areas of the physical, economic and social environment outside the realm of planning and effectively irrelevant to planning concerns, and tends to mean that other issues that are extremely important to many people in practice are subverted, or translated into problems with access or infrastructure.

Inordinate amounts of planning time are spent battling over issues such as the density of housing and the number of parking spaces available per dwelling, when what these issues often conceal can be anything from a sense of neighbourliness

2 ODPM 2005 Paragraph 11.

to concerns about the environmental effect of increasing car use, the aesthetics of streets lined with vehicles or the tendency for people to prefer parking spaces right outside their own house rather than just around the corner. One of the things that is difficult to press through as a material consideration is precisely the effect of gusts of winds on the bodies of frail elderly women, such as the one who was blown down the steep hill that Norfolk Park is built on, before calls for handrails on paths were heeded. To turn an anecdote about Mrs Taylor being blown over into a formal material consideration, you would need a systematic survey of wind speeds at crucial points around a site. This presumes access to an anemometer and the knowledge of how to make recordings from them, and since strong gusts occur only occasionally they are very difficult to record. So, the likelihood of local knowledge becoming a material consideration is low unless bodily experience is legitimised as sufficient evidence for materiality.

People who lived in Norfolk Park knew that there were often high winds there. They did not know it because they had pored over bar charts or meteorological data or invested in anemometers and recording equipment, but because they had battled along the paths on windy days, had seen debris blown about or had heard the wind ripping through the trees in bad weather. Their problem was in translating this kind of knowledge into the kind of knowledge that those involved in the planning system – planners, developers, politicians and so on – could recognise as valuable. This problem of communication can be understood as a kind of muting, where some people are rendered mute because their voice is not heard. This phenomenon is discussed later in the chapter. But before going back to the familiar realm of speech and hearing, we can focus, instead, on the place of bodies in planning process and policy. In particular, the idea that knowledge can be found in our bodies as well as in our brains is one that has the potential to transform planning process. In this chapter, the ways in which bodies are used in planning will be explored, to show how the ordering of bodies is a kind of cultural phenomenon that requires exploration and explanation. Thinking about bodies as mindful and social will tell us something about how far concepts of culture go, and offer different ways to think about nature and the environment too. The way we use our bodies is not necessarily a 'natural order of things' that must simply be adhered to, but a set of ideas and processes that produce order themselves.

Mind the mindful body

If thinking about bodies is going to help us, we will need to look a little more carefully at what we think bodies are and see that our approach to bodies falls within a general emphasis on the individuality of the person. Talking about bodies feels a little odd, since we usually talk about people, yet our way of thinking about bodies, in particular, is core to the way we think about people in general, and deserves closer attention. On the one hand, we recognise that we have bodies, and we consider our body as something we own, which suggests that our selves are not identical with our bodies. Yet the idea of the body is a potent metaphor for both individual and social effects. As the eminent anthropologist Mary Douglas pointed out,[3] we use the body as a symbol to think with, and not just human bodies. Annoying things are a pain in the neck, we have a West wing, or a 'publishing arm', we digest news and we ruminate on complicated thoughts. Nancy Scheper-Hughes and Margaret Lock[4] go further and identify three kinds of body: the individual body-self that recognises itself as separate from other bodies and that all people share some understanding of; the social body that uses the body as a natural symbol to think about nature; and the body politic that refers to the control and surveillance of bodies. It is the first body, the body-self, that feels most natural, but one of the key lessons of comparative anthropology is that the parts of the body, that is, the mind, psyche, soul, organs and limbs, are not consistently separated or identified in human thought. Even within Western thought, we are familiar with the conflicting concepts of Christian soul, and the psychoanalytical psyche that share the Cartesian division between body and mind. Scheper-Hughes and Lock refer to Buddhist traditions that do not perceive a 'self that stands outside the body and apart from nature', but perceive interiority as 'connected to, indeed identical with, the entire essential being of the cosmos'.[5] Among Melanesian people, it is known that the concept of the 'person' is not current at all.[6] Marilyn Strathern explains that the people of Mount Hagen in Papua New Guinea are, instead, more dividual than they are individual. People are as multiple within themselves as between themselves. There is no conflict between society and the person, as society is a person and a person is society.

Papuans are not the only people in the world who do not think of individuals as we do. Turner confirms that 'socially patterned, willed bodily usages' are used by the Kayapo people of the Brazilian rainforest, to emphasise the reproduction of social forms. In this case, these forms emphasise the combinations of internal and external relations rather than the singleness of bodies. It is actions, not things that are thought to define the natural world and its effects on the flesh of Kayapo, flesh that in many situations is thought of as continuous across social relations, whether they be parent-child or age-set relations.[7] The Kayapo mark such relationships on their bodies through certain kinds of painted decoration and through cutting their hair at particular times of their life, so that Kayapo flesh, jewellery and hairstyle become emblems of their relations to each other rather than demonstrations of their individuality. Turner describes this to argue that focusing on the body does not necessarily imply that we have to focus only on the individual as a product of changing social relations. On the contrary, analysing bodies 'points toward the integration of body and social relations as parts of a single continuum of material

3 Specifically, Douglas 2003/1970.
4 Scheper-Hughes and Lock 1987.
5 Ibid.: 13, citing from Robert Paul 1976
6 Ibid.: 16, Read 1955.
7 Turner 1995

activity'.[8] We do not have to assume 'Cartesian' subjects, pre-existing as single units, but can see bodies as inherently social and cultural.

It can be difficult for us to understand the idea of non-individual persons given that the very language we use is characterised by separating the singular and the social, whereas Strathern argues that for Hageners, such differences are irrelevant and meaningless. For us, not thinking about the individual constitutes an absence, but for Hageners, there is nothing missing, just as we do not feel the lack of a concept of the dividual (until we encounter it, at which point we might find it attractive). Nor should we think of these examples as exotic and remote – they are merely conveniently available in the ethnographic record for us to think with. Suffice it to say for our purposes that a wide range of ethnographic studies show that the individualism of the individual is not a universal human concept, but a socially and historically situated idea.

What Scheper-Hughes and Lock show is that once we accept this point, we can also see that Western thought is also not exclusively divided between mind and body. The social body, that is, the body as a useful symbol to think about the natural is a good example. We use body metaphors almost unthinkingly, with the healthy body as an image of organic wholeness or of mechanical sophistication, and the idea of illness describing social disharmony, conflict or disintegration. How often do we refer to the death of communities, for example, or to ailing housing estates riddled with drugs, etc.? We talk of the heart of a community, or dismiss certain areas as 'shit-holes'. The latter sometimes need 'intensive care' or life-saving intervention, the closure of a major employer might be described as a 'fatal blow'. The body politic also adopts biological and social metaphor, but on a more social scale, which is where witchcraft and magic come back into play as symptoms of sickness in a social group, where social order is threatened, as Douglas might put it. Sandy Robertson tells us that 'before the Renaissance and the invention of 'modern mercantile morality, bodies were profoundly implicated in the interpretation of behaviour'.[9] Nowadays, corporations use metaphors of life and growth to the point of cliché while they have lost touch with real bodies outside. Nonetheless, bodies are always important – and he reminds us how obsessed employees can be with executive toilets or dining rooms.[10]

Scheper-Hughes and Lock note that social groups, or bodies politic, also contrive to produce certain kinds of physical bodies that they need, such as warriors, and define particular kinds of bodies as 'healthy'. They also point out that the use of torture to produce political gains is a very physical demonstration of the potential power of the political body. They argue further that political unrest is nowadays channelled into feelings of bodily illness, for which people visit the doctor rather than blaming the politician[11] – we suffer from stress from overwork,

8 Ibid.: 168.

9 Robertson 2006: 10.

10 Ibid. See also Pringle 1994, Ouroussoff 2001.

11 Op.Cit.: 27.

or feel depression when unemployed, for which we seek medication.[12] Emotions, in and of the body, are expressed in terms of the body politic and vice versa. As they say, 'Emotions affect the way in which the body, illness, and pain are experienced and are projected in images of the well or poorly functioning social body and body politic'.[13] At the same time, expressions of emotion are almost exclusively culturally shaped, providing a link between mind and the three bodies, individual, society and body politic. They suggest that the recognition of a 'mindful body' brings us back from the purified ideas that pit the mind versus the body and allow us to understand sickness, both personal and social. A mindful body is one in which emotions and feelings communicate as much as formulated words do.

Given the importance of bodies to our everyday speech, we might well wonder how actual bodies have become so strikingly absent in planning debates. To find out why, we might look at what takes their place. Planning talk tends to focus on abstract qualities such as the 'public good' or competing 'interests'. Financial interests are the easiest for planning to deal with, as they appear to be relatively concrete and apparent. Interestingly, if we call an interest financial, it implies personal gain and is considered slightly suspect. No sin has been more widely renounced in the planning profession than 'nimbyism', where people want to have energy and waste treatment, but they would rather they happened out of sight and 'not in my back yard'. But because the idea of the hypocritical 'nimby' has been so overused, protests against development close to where people live is easily dismissed as personal interest in the value of protesters' own houses, rather than any environmental or political interest that might be in the 'public good'. On the other hand, a broader economic interest is considered to be a shared good and not associated with grubby money-grabbing. The potential for some abstract economic development is likely to be a material consideration. Emotional interest, on the other hand, is considered less material. It will not be news to anyone involved in planning that displays of emotion are seldom welcome in planning debates, least of all in the most formal situations of planning enquiries or examinations. Emotional connection to place is not a material consideration; it is not considered material at all.

This kind of distinction between unreliable emotion and sound reason is constantly reproduced to reinforce an Enlightenment-style adherence to rationality over whim. It is Reason that defines the planning system, not Emotion, and this stricture is repeatedly acted out in planning encounters, in planning statements, debates and decisions. Yet planning is full of contradictions in this area. The planning system places no value on the view from domestic windows – 'you can't buy the view' – yet offers protection to 'areas of outstanding beauty' which are afforded their own acronym, the AOB. Using designations of this type is a way to transform particular interests or preferences into considerations that can

12 I do not wish to belittle either sickness, merely point to how they are often medicalised rather than politicised.

13 Ibid.: 28.

be included in planning debates. They also serve to make things equivalent, part of a national order of things, rather than particular to certain locations. An AOB in Lincolnshire can be understood professionally in a similar way to an AOB in Shropshire, for example. They lend legitimate (nationally recognisable) planning weight to otherwise intangible preferences in order to transform emotional into material considerations. The flimsiness of the device is all too easy to discern if you ask awkward questions about how they actually work. For example, we might wonder from where one should view these outstandingly beautiful areas. The beauty of the hills of the Chilterns AOB are to be enjoyed only from particular perspectives, looking into or within the AOB itself, apparently, since the view from the AOB is not protected at all and provides no material consideration in the approval of very large warehouse hangars[14] in the vicinity. Yet what is the 'outstanding beauty' of the designation but an emotional response to an aesthetic experience?[15] This could be seen merely as a simple illustration of the inconsistency of planning thought that people sometimes dismiss as bureaucratic nonsense.[16]

Yet even in this most disembodied example it is possible to discern a kind of underlying logical flaw that relates to the lack of account for bodies. It is the eyes in the body that see, the bodies that are not considered in the idea of the AOB. If reason is to be thought of as objective and impersonal, then reason must be external to bodies. Since bodies are absolutely personal, so the discourse of planning remains bodiless. It is otherwise difficult to maintain the sanctity of rationality and reason to which planning nails its colours, despite sustained critique over at least half a century. Planners are enjoined not to let their hearts rule their heads but to base their recommendations and analyses on facts and data. That the data might be anything but reliable does not seem to constitute an overwhelming problem, as we showed in 'Rationalities of Planning'. In that case, we showed how the whole of the hierarchy of planning for housing rested on household forecasts that everyone agreed were inaccurate, but since they were there and had the appearance and attributes of technical knowledge, they were used as such and became gradually unassailable.

Rarely are planners asked to question whether it is actually possible to separate heart and head, emotion and reason, mind and body. To do so might threaten the basic logic that maintains an appearance of professionalism which, by definition, requires skills, knowledge, and experience that are exclusive to the profession. But nor can we take for granted that body and mind are separate, since they are

---

14 Which a colleague of mine liked to call the late 20th century disease of 'crinkly sheds'.

15 I will not enter into a treatise on beauty here as it would take us too far from the question in hand.

16 These devices also hint at the lack of rigour of other planning approaches, and the intellectual flaws in the planning project that Reade (1987) outlined in a coruscating attack barely addressed in planning theory – in which he also prophetically outlined all the reasons why planners would ignore his arguments.

always at risk of intermingling again, so the fight must be fought on every front to keep them apart. This is not peculiar to planning but to all stances that rely on a Cartesian approach to culture and nature. Since the 17th century, science has striven to expel superstition, magic and religion into a separate domain,[17] yet still today debates continue over whether this is either right or feasible. The question of whether knowledge can be objective was the core question of the Enlightenment, and although in the West we now take for granted that knowledge has a life outside of bodies, the implications still cause us problems. Enlightenment philosophers promoted the idea that each individual has both a body, which is part of nature, and a separate mind that is not part of nature.[18] Where people decorate their bodies (with tattoos, jewellery, clothes, etc), this is thought of as a cultural practice overlaid onto the natural body. This kind of thinking led to a convention that the body was part of nature, but the mind, instead, was part of culture, and this is a distinction that we now take for granted to an extraordinary degree.

The commitment to a purist Enlightenment rationality is always a struggle. Nature and culture are now categories that we think with and we have to do constant work to sort things into the two realms. Once separate, we have to then find ways to bring them back together, to manage cultural approaches to nature, or to try to examine the links between psychological and physical processes, for example. The boundaries between them are always moving. In the 17th century, according to dominant Western thought only certain human beings were thought fully cultural, and others were more natural, closer to the animal world and hence could be treated differently. Not everybody thought like this, yet anti-slavery campaigners were hugely helped when it became clear to the (limited – yet powerful) reading public that slaves were also thinking people (through the publication of slaves' memoirs). In the 20th century, people have reassessed the place of animals between nature and culture, discovering the culture of apes, for example. Indeed, the rise of animal welfare movements has pushed animals further towards the culture side through the idea that animals have feelings, and thus must have some kind of mind. Wherever the division lies, it seems to persist, and we continue to apply it in all sorts of circumstances, separating nature from culture, and their parallels (or proxies), the body from the mind, heart from head, emotion from reason. And then we try to put them back together to make sense of the world as we meet it in practice.

Bruno Latour calls these two processes purification and translation, twin processes of what we call Modernity.[19] On the one hand, separating mind and body, or reason and emotion, requires the purification of separate entities from the confused mess of lived everyday experience. We imagine truly objective 'rational' discourse as being true whoever says it. Scientific rationality aims to produce knowledge that is external not only to our minds but also our bodies: in Latour's

17 See Tambiah 1990.

18 Morris 1991: 296–8.

19 Latour 1993.

terms, it is abstracted from both nature and society. But the outcome of the work of science has been to apply it to problems, and to do that it has to be brought back into particular times and places, reintroduced through actual people, where nature and culture mix. Latour calls this 'translating' the pure discourse of rationality back into a hybridised nature-culture. For him, being Modern meant keeping these two processes separate, on the one hand, separating nature and culture, while on the other hand, they are applied back together. As soon as we have political decisions about scientific experiments, we are re-hybridising nature and culture. And as soon as we see that the processes of dividing and rehybridising nature and culture, Latour argues that we are no longer really Modern at all. We have never really lived up to the Enlightenment vision of a world governed rationally.

Planning has to be the archetypal rehybridisation. While appealing to statistical arguments over future development, planners are simultaneously suggesting that there are facts about development that are independent of body and mind, but that these can be influenced using various technical and political devices in the planner's toolkit. These include abstract calculations (such as housing forecasts) but also the forms in which they are presented to politicians, for example. All planners know that however robust the knowledge or information they work with, it is always subject to political competition. Planners aim to stand outside the obviously political arena by being impartial or by discarding emotional reason and aiming to remain rational, yet as we know, planners are also involved in negotiations and in trying to persuade residents, investors and politicians too, to choose particular outcomes.[20] So, planning as an occupation is involved in reproducing the idea that mind and body (reason and emotion) can be kept separate, yet aims to effect solutions to social and physical problems by bringing them back down to earth in concrete plans. 'Objective' evidence has to be re-hybridised with actually-existing socio-political conditions on the ground. Politics is always an element in planning, and politics is not disembodied in either process or function. On the contrary, political debate is where we deal with the very cultural issues that cannot be reduced to factual calculation. So, the idea that emotion is not a material consideration is clearly an illusion of outstanding bravura. What it disguises is the work of making certain kinds of knowledge seem more legitimate than others, and this work is achieved through the medium of rationality.

Disciplined bodies

With a concept of the 'mindful body' that can help us to bridge the divide between nature and culture, case studies of the disciplining of bodies in politics start to become both relevant and to look a little different to how we might have seen them before. Not only is the body mindful, but knowledge can be found in our bodies. That is, we both know things with our bodies and body-memory, and we also

20 Forester 1989, 1999.

express certain forms of knowledge with our bodies rather than through words. We all know that our bodies remember certain kinds of skills, like riding a bike, brushing our teeth, playing the piano. Once we have learned to be proficient in this kind of skill, our bodies remember it, even if we could not articulate in words what it is that we have done.[21] We learn these skills through a combination of individual practice, and social learning, so that we gradually socialise our bodies as we grow into adults. Marcel Mauss published an article in 1935 that illustrated the many ways in which our bodies are socialised into moving in particular ways and how we recognise foreign bodies through their different ways of moving. Mauss noticed that soldiers in the First World War could tell each others' nationality from the way they walked, that French soldiers walked differently to British soldiers, for example. They also used different kinds of gesture-language, fashioned their hair differently and ate differently. We know that these differences exist because we laugh when comedians parody them, pretending to be stroppy lanky teenagers or uptight barflies. Physical comedians show us how socially we use our bodies, and they make us laugh either by exaggerating the effects for parody, or portraying people who get it all wrong. In effect, they are showing us how trained we are, or, to use another term, how our bodies are disciplined.

The social sciences can tell us a great deal about discipline, and few more than the French philosopher Michel Foucault.[22] His studies of the invention of prisons and asylums show how inventing a prison also meant inventing a prisoner, and the redesign of prisons in the 18th and 19th centuries also reinvented model prisoners. With attempts to increase the surveillance of prisoners, prisons were trying to give prisoners the feeling they were being watched all the time, so that they would impose discipline on themselves. The invention of an all-seeing prison design was also a means to exert control over prisoners in such a way that they would change their own behaviour, and this is what can be thought of as reinventing the bodies of the prisoners. A prisoner who knows that their actions are being watched will begin to exert surveillance over their own behaviour, rather than waiting for the external surveillance to be acted on. If you know that you will be punished for something, you are likely to avoid doing it if you cannot avoid being caught doing it. Constant surveillance makes us self-conscious of what we are doing, but surveillance doesn't need to be constant to have this effect. If we know that at any point we might be being watched, but we don't know when, then the surveillance encourages us to discipline our bodies.

The idea of discipline doesn't just relate to prisons. Feminist philosophers,[23] have shown how women's bodies have also been disciplined, and how sexuality is squeezed into certain acceptable forms, or punished. It is quite easy to find examples of this nowadays. Mainstream tabloid newspapers and gossip magazines often publish photographs and articles that criticise or ridicule women's appearances.

21 See Polanyi 1966, Schön 1983.

22 Foucault 1979.

23 See Butler 1990, 1993.

Wrinkly thighs or flabby stomachs spotted when celebrities are on the beach are punished through articles that ridicule and insult people whose bodies are anything but ideal (too fat, too thin, too tanned, too pale). It makes it clear that women's bodies are available to be disciplined. But it is not only women's bodies that are disciplined. It is only recently that either men or women have been allowed to exhibit any kind of sexuality other than heterosexuality, on pain of imprisonment, or worse. Indeed, in some countries in the world, homosexuality is still considered to be an offence that merits imprisonment or even execution. Although some brave campaigners resist by flaunting their sexuality, most people are cowed into hiding behaviours that attract such severe punishment. This literal punishment is perhaps the most extreme form, yet public ridicule can also be effective in encouraging people to discipline their own behaviour. Understanding this helps us to see why CCTV, for example, is a way to persuade us that we should behave appropriately, or to understand why some places make us feel uncomfortable. They also show us how some kinds of organisations make our lives feel impossible by making unreasonable demands on us, as well as why we sometimes feel that we can never work hard enough, pushing our bodies to perform more and better, without our problems being resolved. It is not only that we are being disciplined by organisations and institutions from the outside, but that we reproduce the discipline they desire by disciplining ourselves. Self-discipline is a much more powerful tool than imposed discipline, because we barely notice that it is discipline at all.

The concept of bodily or behavioural discipline is very useful for understanding all sorts of situations. If planners feel frustrated when they only ever meet the 'usual suspects' at public consultation events or participative planning groups, then we can use this lens of discipline to show how the way these meetings are organised within a consultative strategy requires participants to be disciplined in particular ways. When public consultation exhibitions are organised to discuss a strategic planning issue, such as the location of new housing, planners can find it very frustrating when people turn up to complain about the dog dirt on the street or the rowdy teenagers 'hanging about'. They are advised who to complain to, or even more likely, who to write to. Refusing verbal communication on the basis that it is irrelevant is a very clear way of trying to discipline people into doing the things you want them to rather than the things they want to. If we say to them, effectively, 'what you are saying is in the wrong context, we do not wish to hear it here', we are attempting to coerce their behaviour to suit our purposes. On the other hand, those people who are willing (perhaps even despite themselves) to discipline themselves and respond in appropriate ways have to put some effort into learning how to do that, and having made that investment they are likely to be alert to new opportunities to participate, and to try to be more effective in their participation. They learn when to put things in writing and in appropriate language, but they also learn when to be present, when to be quiet and when to speak, and generally how to comport their bodies. It is significant, then, that discipline and self-discipline are not just rules or thoughts but they are performed bodily. The way that bodies are held and used reflects a store of knowledge that is rarely made explicit, yet it is crucial to the way we interact and the expectations we have of ourselves and others. Normally, when we talk about people's body language, we are referring to the popularised psychology of non-verbal communication. Magazines sometimes run features explaining to us that when we mirror other people's movements, we are communicating sympathy and empathy, or that when we lean away and fold our arms, we indicate that we are bored or aggressive. But understanding how people use their bodies is not just about personal psychology, but about how we produce and reproduce social and political roles.

The bureaucrat's body

It isn't only the public or citizens or foreigners who have bodies, of course. Planners are also embodied beings, and the way planners use their bodies is also worth thinking about. When do planners speak and when do they sit quietly? How do they listen? Why do they share dress codes or ways of talking? Turning the question round and looking at how planners are in the world can be uncomfortable – just as it can be embarrassing to look at your own face in the mirror when someone else is watching. It can be easier to look at planners elsewhere, both to shift the focus a little and, as with any exploration of things we take for granted, making comparisons often helps us to recognise things that are both familiar and unfamiliar. To do this, in this chapter I will describe some Norwegian public sector planners, because the Norwegian political system has well articulated rules and regulations, and is much more open to public scrutiny – and academic analysis – than the British public sector. Even so, many of the details will be recognisable to those working in other countries and other bureaucratic systems, so the example is not so different that it is irrelevant to other contexts.

During 2000, I spent six months or so doing ethnographic fieldwork in a local authority, or municipality, in southern Norway, a relatively large municipality in the middle of a general bureaucratic reorganisation, and in the early stages of drafting a new general long-term plan. Ethnographic fieldwork includes a wide range of research methods, mostly based on spending a long period of time in the 'field' of investigation, and in this case it included accompanying various municipal officers in their daily activities, attending meetings of various sorts, chatting to people over lunch and other breaks, and interviewing a number of different people within the municipality, including politicians as well as public servants at different levels and sectors of the organisation, as well as accompanying them on residential working parties and consulting various documents. The degree of access offered to me was extraordinary and well beyond what would have been possible in the UK at the time, despite the rhetoric of 'open government' often adopted in the UK public sector. Indeed, I was welcomed into the authority as a visiting anthropologist and offered complete access to any persons or documents, and welcomed into council offices. All public sector documentation except for private personnel information is held in the public domain in Norway, so this openness was not specifically aimed at me as a researcher. All mail in or out of the municipal offices is in the public domain, and journalists from the local newspapers regularly turn up at the municipal offices to read it and report on anything they find interesting. Politics, in that sense, is thus very much a public matter in the Norwegian public sector. During this period of research, I was able to attend public and private meetings, that is, both council and sub-committee meetings, internal administrative meetings and special seminars. As in many public situations, the ritual aspects of meeting procedures are clearer at the top of the committee hierarchy, and lower committees and sub-committees may appear more informal. Even so, among the first things people began to teach me when I arrived in the town hall were the public service ethos and the rules about when council employees can speak in public.

Such basic rules are taught to public servants when they train, they are inculcated in elected members of council through training they receive when they are first elected, but they are also taught in schools through youth-council programmes where young people are invited to form a model council of their own. However, interpreting the significance of such rules for normal council meetings requires a broader perspective. If, as a member of public, you attended a council meeting, you would only see what was in front of your eyes. At a full council meeting in June 2000, the main agenda item was the first quarterly budget report for the year. There were few non-council members of the public, although there was a TV camera recording the meeting for broadcast on the local television channel, as was normal for council meetings.[24] Much of the debate revolved around the use of money raised from the sale of a hydro-electric plant that was previously owned by the municipality. The Chief Executive had put forward a proposal for a revision of the budget that included cuts in certain sectors. An opposition councillor suggested that the council had cried wolf too often on its budget, but seemed to find the money for projects it wanted to support. A member of the ruling coalition commented that the budget report was very well written, and that the budget committee had been fairly unanimous. Several comments were made on the need for prioritisation, and the Mayor criticised an opposition politician for saying she wanted to prioritise health and schools while using half of the budget for other things, such as maintaining the municipal cinema.

The Chair invited the Chief Executive to the podium to explain how five million kroner had appeared in the property budget from a new accounting mechanism and why schools and health budgets could not be cut. The significant point here is that the Chair invited the Chief Executive to speak. In all political meetings, council officers are subservient to the politicians. They have no right to speak but must wait until they are invited. The principle is that the administration has had the opportunity to inform politicians through the support papers they present in advance of meetings, and the point of the meetings is to debate the papers. While

24 A politician confirmed that these broadcasts usually found an audience – she was often told by people that she had been seen on the television, and her children reported friends commenting on having seen her during these broadcasts.

the Mayor and the Chief Executive sit together on the front table, and the Chief Executive may indicate to the Mayor if there is a point of order or information that should be presented, no other council officer may intervene. This is to maintain the clear separation of administrative and political spheres within the council. In Norwegian local authorities, the chief executives and the chairs of the councils hold figurehead positions. That is, the position of 'Rådmann' (pronounced *r-aw-d-man*, literally the advice-man, which I have translated as chief executive) and of 'Ordfører' (*ord-fur-uh*, literally the one who steers the words, or speaker, which I have translated as mayor) stand for the whole of the administration and all the elected representatives respectively. In Acts of parliament, and in council papers, the administration is referred to through the person of the Rådmann, and the political body is referred to through the person of the Ordfører. All papers presented from the administration to political committees are referred to as the Rådmann's proposal, not the administration's proposal, and all political decisions are passed as the decision of the Ordfører.

During full council meetings, the holders of the position of Rådmann and Ordfører adopt the status, and their bodies represent, the administration and political body in this way. This has two implications. One is that when the holder of the office of Ordfører wishes to speak as an elected representative, he symbolically relinquishes his position as Ordfører and becomes a normal councillor by addressing the Ordfører which is now outside his own body and is embodied by a deputy sitting at the front table. When the Mayor made a party political point in the debate I described above, then speaking as a councillor he also began his comments with the address, 'Mayor', to indicate that he had now stepped out of this position. This sounds like the way that British councillors – and indeed people in any relatively formal committee – address their comments through the chairperson by saying 'Chair, I would like to say blah blah blah…', or in the Commons, by beginning any speech with 'Mr Speaker', but there is a rather important, if subtle difference, in that the Ordfører is not merely chairing the meeting and holding it to order, but in his body represents the whole of the council as a political body.

A second consequence is that the Rådmann, who rarely steps outside his role during such meetings – as s/he has no other legitimate reason for being present – carries the responsibility for representing the whole of the administration, and the duty to recommend to the Ordfører when important information needs to be presented. The Rådmann may thus suggest that particular council officers be called forward to indicate the consequences of any new suggestions made by councillors, for example, and must prepare in advance for this possibility, ensuring that the right officers are present and ready to present. On the other hand, if an officer is present and realises that their papers have been misunderstood, or that new information is required that is not in the papers, they have no right to stand up and ask to be heard. They may try to indicate to the Rådmann that they have important information, in which case the Rådmann must decide whether to call them forward, but strictly speaking, they should sit quietly and not interfere.

This requires a certain discipline in council officers, and one that they carry through to less formal meetings. On one particular occasion, members of the municipal cabinet and supporting council officers held an away-day to discuss the future municipal reorganisation. Whereas a meeting of council officers had been a lively event, with lots of debate and argument, at the joint meeting the council officers were remarkably quiet. After a good half hour's discussion of the possible organisation of services for children, where the politicians debated the responsibilities for purchasing and for the admission of children to nurseries, the Rådmann asked the head of nursery services for an explanation of how admissions are operated for nursery places, and how many places were currently available and demanded. Until then, the nursery services director had been sitting quietly observing the discussion until invited to speak, even though what he had to say made most of the previous debate pointless. Afterwards,[25] I asked one of the senior council officers to explain why he would sit in silence through a meeting to which he had something important to say. 'I don't want to appear to be party-political', he said, 'so I think twice before I say anything'. This was the cabinet's seminar, he reminded me, and they had invited the officers to attend, not to lead. In such situations, officers tended to hold back. Yet this was not a generalisable relationship between these people. The away-day was held in a conference hotel in the mountains, with its own swimming pool, and after the day's meetings were over, several of the participants headed for the pool. There, politicians and officers chatted freely, and afterwards, a few met for pre-dinner drinks. A greater contrast is hard to imagine, but it demonstrates how circumscribed our behaviour is, and how clearly those in prominent positions know how to use their bodies in relevant circumstances. It is surely no coincidence that neither the Chief Executive nor the mayor were among those chatting around the pool. For them to retain the authority that is created by the discipline of other bodies, crossing so far into the informal might threaten the security of their legitimacy.

Although in this context council officers are hardly a repressed social group, they exhibit one form of what Ardener has called 'muting'.[26] This particular form of muting is explicit and fairly straightforward – one group is literally unable to speak openly to be heard by another. The rules of propriety forbid their intruding into political debates even in the interests of information. But there are much more subtle forms of muting going on here. Ardener argued that groups were muted when they do not form part of the 'dominant communicative system of the society' expressed through a dominant ideology.[27] Ardener had two situations in mind when making these observations; on the one hand he was describing the situation of female academic anthropologists of the 1960s, and on the other he was thinking about the Bakweri women of Cameroon. The Bakweri women, who Ardener studied in the

25 A discussion that, bizarrely, took place in the hotel swimming pool, as I describe below; ethnographic fieldwork demands total commitment.

26 Ardener 1989.

27 Ibid.:129.

1950s, were generally responsible for the kind of domestic tasks that obliged them to go out into the forests every day, collecting firewood or growing and harvesting yams and collecting other bush produce. Men, on the other hand, spent much of their time within the fenced area of the farm. For Bakweri men, Ardener argued that women are associated with the wild beyond the fence. At the same time, to put it very simply indeed, women take part in complex rituals that associated them with forest spirits and which initiate them into a kind of secret society of women with healing skills. Ardener's point was that Bakweri men tend to articulate models of society that are on a meta-abstract level, and they also define women within their models. In men's models, men's opposites are usually defined as women and the wild, so that women are associated with the wild. Women thus become a problem for men and their models of society, and these models then become a problem for women, who are defined as only partly fitting into that society. When women talk about the forest or forest spirits, men are unable to understand and effectively do not hear the women. Women then learn not to speak about such things to men and effectively become 'muted' to men. Ardener argues that all dominant groups have muting effects. When we hear about teenagers complaining that adults don't hear what they are saying, we should perhaps think about the Bakweri women and wonder what we are unable to hear and why their language doesn't make sense to us.

While in general we are all socialised into knowing that certain things shouldn't be talked about, some groups are more muted than others, and more at some times and places than others. In these council meetings, anyone sitting at the back of the room as part of the audience could have no voice in the debates, and had to hope that their elected representatives were doing an effective job of speaking up for their interests. For this reason, it was extremely important for the politicians to disagree. Although Norwegian politics is renowned for being consensual and not conflictual, all the politicians emphasised the importance of disagreeing. If they all agreed, they clearly were not representing all sides of society, they argued. In fact, this was one of the few things they did agree on. Their role was to voice disagreement and work towards a compromise decision that everyone could settle for. Consensus, in other words, was not the same as agreement. In between politicians and their public, the council officers also saw it as their duty to ensure that all voices were heard, and often went to great lengths to ensure that different views were represented. Yet this was not necessarily apparent during council meetings of the kind discussed above. Stepping outside the meeting into the coffee room – coffee and pastries were always served during a break in council meetings – one of the council directors urged me to see the council meeting not in isolation but as part of a much broader series. Particular cases pass from committee to committee, being edited a little each time they are debated. Over the course of a four-year election period, council officers understand the communication between politicians and the administration, but this does take time and experience. During the apparently polite debate that I had been observing, politicians had been discussing whether to shift sums of money between budget heads. That, he said, was most unusual. Why were they talking about moving millions of Kroner between budget headings when they usually would not move anything? The reason, he proposed, was that the Rådmann had not offered them alternative budgets. Normally, council papers offer two or three alternative decisions that a committee or council could take and spell out the consequences, but this was not the case this evening. There was often talk about financial crisis in the municipality, so the money they were discussing this evening was reserves, but the Rådmann wanted the council to stop over-spending and had tried to hide the reserves by not telling the politicians where the money was, 'and that irritates the politicians a lot', he said. Even though the Rådmann does not want them to use reserves, by talking about shifting millions between budgets, the elected representatives were doing it anyway. Whilst being polite, well behaved, sticking to the rules and using correct language, the politicians were resisting the Rådmann's recommendations in a way that was only understandable through long-term observation and knowledge of the context.

Behind this politeness, we can see that the use of bodies is a subtle discipline that can be resisted. While council meetings order the place of bodies – where they sit, that they sit at all rather than stand or squat on the ground – and the use of voices – when they can speak, to whom and using what language – the rules can still be creatively used wherever they are not totalitarian. They can also be abused and used ineffectively and differently according to styles or regimes of management. This particular Rådmann was enthralled to what is called 'new public management,[28] or NPM. NPM was a wave of organisational change that swept the public sector from the 1980s, encouraged by various consultancy firms looking for new markets beyond the private sector. They introduced commercial management models and ideas to the public sector, encouraging the outsourcing of services to private companies, changing management structures, professional managerialism, and so on. The Rådmann was particularly influenced by a version of NPM promoted by a German organisation called the Bertelmann Institute who pronounced the 100 best local authorities in 1993 based on a list of criteria that included being service-minded, participative, outsourcing services and so on. In this model the council becomes the coordinator rather than the provider of services, paving the way for the privatisation of public services that has been so familiar in the UK in the last couple of decades. The council is re-imagined from being a public office accountable to the citizens to being a corporate body buying and selling services. As services become one-step removed from the council, it is no longer politically accountable for maintaining standards but for policing contracts that may span between or beyond electoral periods. As the electoral feedback loop is broken, Bertelmann suggests that council performance should be assessed through regular surveys of how satisfied constituents are, a procedure this municipality did through what was called a 'well-being' or 'happiness' survey.[29] One of the typical managerial changes

28 Ferlie 1996, McLaughlin 2002.

29 UK readers might recognise this scenario in Prime Minister David Cameron's call for a survey of 'general well being'. See Early Day Motion 149: http://edmi.parliament.

that goes with this transformation is an increased concern with the corporate image. In this Norwegian municipality the Rådmann was particularly concerned with public image, and enforced strict rules about what municipal staff could say in public. While all communication between administration and politicians formally was personified in communication between the Rådmann and Ordfører, this Rådmann tried to enforce this in practice by keeping committee chairs and their secretaries in an extremely formal relationship, limiting the communication of any disagreements within the administration, or the communication of alternative views. At the same time, his relationship with the Ordfører became so close that they were seen by some to be colluding, and he was accused of being political. Eventually he was forced out of office for a number of reasons, but this rather autocratic leadership style was a contributing factor. Perhaps he took the authority lent to him by the disciplined use of bodies rather too much to heart and mistook it for personal authority. Or perhaps he did not clearly distinguish between informal good behaviour and formal silences, restricting the informal communication that is essential for any organisation to function effectively.

Given how difficult it is to manage the communication between administrators and politicians within a municipality, it is not surprising that most municipalities or local authorities struggle greatly with building and sustaining relationships with external groups. Members and employees of councils are taught how to behave and agree to abide by council rules to work within the organisation. Outside parties have no such obligations, but have rights to be heard or make demands to influence policies or services. Such organisations go to great lengths to try to discipline outsiders into behaving in ways that are easiest for them to deal with. When this Norwegian municipality published its general plan, it held a series of public meetings to try to garner responses from the electorate. Planners in one British local authority explained to me that they no longer held public meetings, as they saw no point in having residents come along to complain, or even shout at them, for decisions made by politicians that they often disagreed with themselves. Who can blame them? It is hardly a pleasant work experience to have residents shout at you and condemn you for policies which you, as a public servant, have been obliged to follow in apolitical obedience to your political masters. It is much less painful to deal with written complaints that arrive without bodies attached. This sort of objection can be easily silenced by putting it in the 'inapplicable' pile. It is no coincidence that in many British planning procedures, people are required to make known their objections through written submissions to the authority, often on forms provided for the purpose. In such a situation, the planners – and politicians – need not encounter any bodies at all, and avoid dealing with the messy humanity that planning proposals actually involve. But at the same time, their own bodies are creating and closing spaces for debate, presenting a particular face to the outside world and being disciplined by the council itself.

---

uk/EDMi/EDMDetails.aspx?EDMID=41068 and Channel 4 news 15.11.10: http://www.channel4.com/news/government-to-measure-uk-happiness.

Culture and nature – concluding bodies

So now we have all sorts of bodies in focus what can we say about them? First of all, we can recognise that our bodies are socialised and that each of us organises both where they are and how they are, within various constraints. It also reminds us that planning for places and policies is bound to go wrong if we do not consider the bodies of the people for whom we are planning (i.e. remember that those people are embodied). Bodies that need to get in and out of houses, to move between places, using transport and walking around. We have learned since the 1970s that people need to walk, and that our cities cease to be liveable if we force everyone to get into a motorised vehicle to get from A to B. We are still seeing the results of transport policies that favour motor vehicles, in the bodies of the people becoming increasingly unfit (and obese) not least because we are walking less and less in our daily lives, and relying on transport more. No-one intended this to be the consequence, but it surely follows from a lack of attention to bodies.

A cultural approach to bureaucratic bodies also tells us more about how exclusive bureaucratic practices are. If we can begin to recognise how highly trained our bodies are, we can see how that training makes us react to others. Once we recognise that only disciplined bodies are welcomed into political processes, we can understand more easily how undisciplined bodies are routinely excluded. People whose bodies seem undisciplined are often either inexperienced, do not belong to dominant social groups, or perhaps do not speak majority languages fluently. It is only at that point that we usually start to talk about 'other cultures', often without recognising how cultured our own bodies are, how cultivated our own expectations of 'correct' behaviour, and how easily offended we are by approaches that are not disciplined in the ways we expect. Planning is about ordering bodies, housing them, keeping them warm, safe and dry. But planning is also about keeping bodies tidy, and sedentary if at all possible. It is no coincidence that nomadic groups such as gypsies have always posed a problem for planning on several levels. They are an archetypal muted group for planners in most European (and many other) countries. In England, for example, many gypsies and travellers speak a language that is not English, and may have English as a second language, or may speak English in a way that is difficult for non-gypsies to understand. Gypsies and travellers traditionally express a preference for non-sedentary living, which is well outside the mainstream dominant practice, increasingly so during the latter 20th century when static-home-owning became a mark of civilisation. And gypsies dispose of waste in ways that are quite unlike those of mainstream society, setting the boundaries between clean and polluted much closer to the body, not sharing dominant views that define waste as 'out of sight, out of mind'.[30] Recognising why Gypsies pose such a problem for planning tells us much more about planning than about Gypsies. It tells us that we are constantly producing the idea that Western rationality is superior, and that outsiders threaten it.

30 Okely 1983, Buckler 2007.

Because the way we use our bodies is so closely tied in with how we think about the world, the categories we use to think about it and the way we perceive others, we find problems when we encounter people who do not share these assumptions. When we think that our bodies and minds are separate entities, we produce effects that confirm our assumptions. We continue to reinforce the idea that body and mind, and nature and culture are separable. Often we don't even recognise that we are either socially trained or that we are disciplining ourselves, and when we meet people who do not do that, they can present us with a puzzle, that we often interpret as a kind of moral outrage. It's disgusting that people throw their rubbish into the front garden! It's a bore that the same people always turn up at political meetings to complain or object. And it's threatening to take photographs in the council chamber. Bodies are there, no matter how cleverly we hide them in our plans and policies.

The problem is not that we have never completed the vision of separating nature from culture, or the social from the natural, or mind from body, but that so much energy has been invested, and continues to be spent, in trying to achieve these imaginary pure states, and that the contest between purification and hybridisation still defines much of our contemporary world, either because people continue to pursue separation, or because others work to deal with its consequences. If we are to think about bodies in planning, that is, human bodies in the environment and human bodies in politics, then we have to deal with two parts of the legacy of modern ideas: that the human (culture) is separate from the environment, and that the body is separate from the mind. The former is so entrenched that most Westerners do not even question the idea that humans are bodies situated in an external environment. Yet anthropological research demonstrates that this is just one way to think about the world. Thinking of bodies as separate things bound by skin which presents a border to the outside 'environment' (be that nature, nature-culture, or the built structures of culture) turns out to be another culturally-specific set of concepts, and a set that is well worth challenging, not only to show us how wide the concept of culture can stretch, but also to show us that there are other ways of thinking about nature, environment and what it is to be human. What I hope to have shown in this chapter is that we need not see bodies as separate from minds, but we can think about our bodies as mindful (as expressions of our thoughts and feelings, and embodying memory and experience), and as social (shaped by social experience and learning, and more or less intimately connected to other bodies). This also means that the way we use our bodies tells us something about the context we act in. We can see on the one hand how our bodies are disciplined and cultivated by larger structures such as laws and regulations, but we can also learn by examining how bodies are implicated in the production of such laws and regulations –and local policies such as plans.

Chapter 4
Owning: House Society and Policy

Whereas the last chapter brought bodies back into planning, this chapter looks at where bodies live. It looks at the relations between bodies and houses, to see how we think about people, persons and things. Using examples from recent politics and policy about housing and ownership, it raises questions about what a house is, introducing concepts of personhood. With a focus on the relation of ownership, the chapter brings attention to the parallels between the political pressure for owning a home and owning policies.

When is a house a home?

Planners are used to thinking of housing as a basic function, and of thinking of housing en masse, as dwellings. The term 'dwellings' is an interesting choice. On the one hand, it is a usefully general term to describe places where people live. But, on the other, it covers a multitude of sins. A dwelling can be anything from a single roomed bedsit to a palace, so figures outlining the number of dwellings needed in a region, for example, can only be rather imprecise. Dwellings are also defined in relation to households, which are imagined in standardising terms that do not necessarily reflect who actually lives in dwellings. So even a first glance at where we live shows us that there are some pretty big assumptions involved that might be worth interrogating.

Planning is not only about housing, of course, but housing is both important and interesting in highlighting some of the impacts that planning has and helping to expose the way planning asks us to think about the world. Planning for housing affects people's lives in a very intimate and immediate way. We attribute so many emotional qualities to our home, and we judge people so all-too readily by how and where they live. Clearly the kind of housing we have and its location are fantastically important to our lives and to the way we categorise ourselves and others. And yet, reading forward plans or regeneration plans, you would be hard put to see any of this value in the language of the plans, or in the process by which planning is put into action. Quality of housing has been a concern of planners since the early days of urban design, with Ebenezer Howard's model city designs focused on the quality of life of the inhabitants.[1] Cadbury, Rowntree, Greg[2] and

1 Howard 1898.

2 Greg is perhaps the least well known of these three. Unlike Cadbury and Rowntree, Samuel Greg was not a Quaker, but was closely associated with Manchester non-conformists and Unitarians. Greg founded Quarry Bank Mill near Styal in rural Cheshire

others built their workers' villages out of moral concerns for the conditions of their workers as much as their concern for production quality. Later, in the 1960s, the 'Parker-Morris' standards for the quality of public housing laid down specifications for construction quality and important details such as the size of rooms required,[3] in the interests of the well-being of the inhabitants.

In recent decades, the political emphasis has increasingly been more on the ownership of the home, rather than the condition of housing. Thatcher's government of the 1980s went to great lengths to encourage people to own property rather than renting, by offering advantageous terms for tenants of housing owned by the city council to buy their homes. At the same time, they removed many of the securities that tenants had previously relied on for fair rent and tenancy guarantees. This emphasis on property ownership is not specifically British, but is a general theme in neo-liberal government thinking. Indeed, in the 'New Public Management' that swept through the public sector in the 1980s and 1990s, the idea of owning extended to policies as well as houses. According to this ideology, if owning a house meant that you take responsibility for looking after it, rather than relying on 'the council' to come and maintain it for you, then perhaps owning a policy would make you feel responsible for that too. All sorts of effects are attributed to feeling ownership, and ownership is thought to result from experiences, so this chapter takes a closer look at owning. Taking an approach informed by cultural analysis, we can find out how owning matters for planning.

Owning policy, owning a home

> 'Our success in the longer term depends on more public bodies committing themselves to empowering the communities they work with, so that citizens can take ownership of their shared priorities and play an active part in making their communities better for everyone.' (Blair 2006: 3)

British planning policy for at least a decade has been heavily implicated in a discourse of ownership as much as in participation. When New Labour came into power in 1997, it was with an explicit agenda of reconnecting policy to 'the people', an approach heavily influenced by development theory. Influential politicians such as the first London Deputy Mayor Nicky Gavron pushed hard for a consensual and inclusive approach to policy making, based on the principle that involving people

---

in 1784 to produce cotton cloths using water power from the river Bollin (see Rose 1986). In the 1820s, cottages with kitchen gardens were built for workers in the nearby Styal village, and an apprentice house for child workers was built nearer the mill. The mill has the most powerful water wheel in Britain, that powered five floors of spinning and weaving equipment. It was donated to the National Trust by the Greg family in 1939 and closed in 1959. It was reopened as a museum in 1978. See also Barton 2009.

3 See Ministry of Housing and Local Government 1961.

in the development of policy would lead them to experience feelings of ownership over the final product, and hence smooth its implementation. Among academics and practitioners, great enthusiasm was revived for citizen involvement. It was thought to accommodate superior community knowledge, synergy (the 'mantra of partnership'), a direct impact on social skills and 'social capital', redistribution and participation as a merit good – a good in itself.[4] Commentators also noted the costs of participation, including failings of the participants, such as a lack of professional knowledge among 'ordinary people' who lacked analytical attachment, and the lack of a wider perspective, and, ultimately, prejudice.[5]

In Britain, citizen participation was already creeping into planning policy at the end of the Conservative government of the 1990s, and the link between home ownership and citizenship was quickly cemented. It can be seen in the criticism of tenancies and in the radical move away from state ownership of housing. Government analyses of the trouble with council housing were baldly stated:

> In 1997 the social housing stock was depleted and suffering chronic underinvestment. Social tenants had little choice over where they lived, and local authorities were sidelined and starved of cash. Too many people renting in the private sector were exploited by rogue landlords.[6]

> Despite the intentions of planners and politicians, the drive to build more homes even more quickly led to monolithic estates with too many homes that were cramped, cold and in disrepair. In the 1960s and 1970s, the worst estates had walkways in the sky that became rat runs for robbers.[7]

Although the first explanation is based on underinvestment, the byline for New Labour ideology is in the second cause, a 'lack of choice'.[8] It is hard to disagree that chronic underinvestment in housing maintenance left much of Britain's social housing stock in poor condition, nor that the economic and employment collapse of the 1980s coupled with poor housing policy contributed to a radical decline in social housing conditions. Even so, few housing analysts would press the point that 'choice' of tenancy was the central problem beyond the initial post-war slum clearances. During the period when housing was more abundant, throughout the 1970s, for example, many tenants were able to arrange housing swaps, for example, and to manipulate housing waiting lists and point schemes to move around within

---

4 Ball 2004: 123

5 Ball, as cited above.

6 ODPM 2005: 9

7 ODPM 2005: 10

8 A classic case of a political history being interpreted in line with currently fashionable ideological positions and rhetoric.

the system.[9] For New Labour, though, choice was a central rhetorical and political symbol of the New Labour government, heavily promoted by Tony Blair when Prime Minister and consistently supported by Gordon Brown as both Chancellor of the Exchequer and Prime Minister himself.

One of the diagnoses that they offered for what they believed was the failure of state housing in Britain was that tenants did not feel ownership over their housing, and hence allowed it to fall into decline. Although in policy statements, care was taken to avoid stigmatising council tenants and blame former government policy, the emphasis on 'decent housing'[10] took private owner-occupied housing as a desirable and obvious ideal. For the New Labour government, assisting people with 'low-cost homeownership', and 'supporting individuals and families who need help to meet their housing costs' (through 'Housing Benefit welfare payments') were self-evident goods:

> 'The benefits that this brings are clear: People who are decently housed have a stronger sense of security and place. Decent housing strengthens communities and provides a better setting in which to raise families. It improves health and educational achievement and provides a long-term asset that can be passed on to future generations.[11]

This policy is clearly focused on the quality of housing rather than the legal terms under which it is occupied. But later policy was even more explicit about the value of home-ownership. The 'sustainable communities' policy of 2005 states '*homes are not just places to live, they are assets*'.[12] This, it suggests, is a problem because:

> 'the three in ten households who do not own their own homes gain nothing from rising house prices. They and their children risk being left behind, missing out on the choices and opportunities that owner-occupiers enjoy.'[13]

Perhaps the clearest difference between this and Conservative discourse is that the latter pay less attention to avoiding stigmatisation of council tenants. In a

9 Indeed, council tenants have described to me their strategies for moving to desired locations, and their stories suggest they have little less housing choice than those in the private sector, where no waiting list is available for desirable housing.

10 The term 'decent' is a discursive strategy to avoid making precise specifications of housing policy ambitions. Using a 'commonsense' term has the effect of transforming the goal into a moral imperative.

11 DETR 2000b: 4

12 ODPM 2005: 20.

13 Op. Cit.

2008 report by the 'Centre for Social Justice', a 'think tank' founded by former Conservative Party Leader Ian Duncan Smith,[14] the latter claimed that:

> Over the years, our housing system has ghettoised poverty, creating broken estates where worklessness, dependency, family breakdown and addiction are endemic.[15]

Not afraid to demonise large sections of the population, he goes on to claim that there has been '*a vicious cycle of degeneration, with social housing populated by ever more needy and dispirited individuals*'.[16] While Blair espoused owning policy and New Labour policy emphasised 'decent housing', Duncan Smith argued in a BBC interview that, '*People with assets are more positive, more constructive, more likely to do the right thing*'.[17] While he doesn't specify what 'doing the right thing' might mean, this is actually a rather striking philosophy, that private ownership gives moral superiority.[18] The press release is even more explicit, highlighting the report's assertions that:

> The ownership of an asset encourages a series of behavioural changes. Those who own are more likely to protect their assets, to protect their position of ownership and to engage in constructive behaviours that enable their assets to be protected and enlarged: behaviours that benefit themselves, their families and the community at large.

> ...Having a stake in a home is both a privilege and a responsibility. It would inculcate the values of constructive social behaviour and create, from the vicious cycle, a virtuous cycle that encourages social housing tenants to improve their family's future.[19]

If you stop to think about this, it is an extraordinarily radical idea that an inanimate object, a house, can transform the behaviour of people simply by being owned. It suggests that the house is an agent – it can act as if it were a person – that can transform its occupants from unemployed broken-down families into responsible parents, community members and workers. In other words, the house is an active agent in the behaviour of its owner-occupiers. It has some kind of active

14 Duncan Smith became Secretary of State for Work and Pensions in 2010.

15 Davies 2008: 5.

16 Op Cit.: 54.

17 Ian Duncan Smith interviewed on the BBC Radio 4 Today programme, 2/12/08 (author's transcription).

18 There is little connection made, though, between owner-occupation and private landlordism, where the latter also own houses.

19 CSJ 2008.

personhood in its own right, vested in the relationship with those owner-occupiers, and this relationship is quite different from its relationship with tenant-occupiers. Through ownership, and only through ownership, the occupants develop feelings of obligation towards the house, neighbours, work and, eventually, to the state. This was not adopted Conservative party policy at the time, nor was it commented on by the shadow cabinet, but after the 2010 election Tory ministers continued to cast aspersions on council tenancies, along with the policy of pushing social housing tenants into private ownership, and Duncan-Smith became a minister in the new government. The Government's Spending Review of October 2010 suggested that more social tenants would be offered 'intermediate contracts' nearer to market rents,[20] while cutting funding for social housing by 60 per cent, in what the *Daily Telegraph* described as 'an attempt to end the era of heavily subsidised rents'.[21] More generally, though, the language that links ownership to change in behaviour is also found in the ideology of new citizenship.

Government policy has gone quite a long way in sharing this notion, tempered for a while by the New Labour commitment to social housing through autonomous housing associations, rather than local government-owned or managed housing. In government policy, the emphasis has been stronger on the transformative potential of owning property. Throughout a decade of New Labour government, the language of owning spread, becoming embedded in planning and urban regeneration policy. It was adopted both by state officials and those contracted to work for them, including architectural consultants and planners. While there is some academic research on the impact of owning housing, government policy went well beyond research findings, suggesting that: '*Harnessing the insights, perspectives and talents of local people can improve services, the quality of democracy, and the legitimacy of council leadership*'.[22] By 2006, these claims were becoming increasingly idealised and ideological, with Department of Communities and Local Government documents suggesting a sophisticated philosophy of the connection between action and emotion:

> A clear lesson coming through is that the act of engagement improves services and also improves people's perception of services. If people are involved and engaged in the decisions and choices made, they **naturally feel more ownership of the outcomes**. From their sense of ownership grows increasing confidence and the willingness to tackle further problems and take on more responsibility for the wellbeing of their communities. As this review illustrates, the ethos of community engagement is starting to become part of public bodies' organizational culture, and where citizens are able to participate with the decisions affecting their communities, they reap other benefits such as improved employment opportunities, better health and higher educational attainment.

20 HM Treasury 2010: 48.

21 Porter 2010.

22 Andrews et al 2006: 9.

> Once the approach takes root, it contributes to effective delivery and sustainable results but, most importantly, to the revival of the public realm and a new relationship of trust and shared responsibility between people and government: our shared goal for Together We Can.[23]

This paragraph suggests that ownership can be a transformative relationship not only in relation to physical objects such as houses, but for policies and services too. Ownership becomes both the result of and the content of an almost magical process of transformation where participation in local political debate leads to a utopian shared goal of ever-improving employment, health and education. While it might seem realistic to argue that user-participation in service-design can help to ensure that services meet users' needs, the statement goes well beyond this. It reads as a kind of epidemiological philosophy of the natural flow of emotion from participative processes. It attributes deep and far-reaching qualities to the relationship of owning. It is precisely this relationship between 'harnessing' local knowledge and the production of feelings of 'ownership' that have become a mythical strand of governmental ideology. It claims that transformation can be achieved firstly, through the participation or 'engagement' in policy development that is thought to lead to feelings of ownership of policy, and secondly, through the ownership of housing, sometimes also framed as participation in the housing market, that is thought to create feelings of security and place, that in turn improve health, education and employment.

Such striking assertions deserve further investigation, and one way to investigate them is to look in detail at how people experience ownership in practice. What difference does it make to take ownership of house or policy? At the same time, we can ask why politicians have adopted such utopian ambitions, and what kind of resistance they meet when they confront local conditions. It would be almost too easy to produce a counter-argument by showing that people in Paris or Madrid feel a sense of belonging, responsibility and social obligation even though they live in rented housing, and too susceptible to the politically expedient relativist response that 'they do things differently over there'. Instead, we can go back to Norfolk Park and ask how these different kinds of ownership have intersected there.

Owning policy versus belonging

Looking through the transcripts of formal interviews carried out either by me or by students of planning over the last decade with people involved in the regeneration of Norfolk Park, it is noticeable that none of the residents use the terms ownership or involvement, but that the politicians, developers and council officers use them frequently. The latter asserted, for example, that local residents had been involved in the political process, alongside the sometimes baffling number of different

23 DCLG 2006: 6, emphasis added.

public and private agencies and businesses who have had a role in the regeneration process. On the other hand, there were residents who repeatedly complained of 'not being listened to', of delays in the rebuilding of housing and the lack of new housing that was affordable for younger and lower-income people, especially for former residents of the estate who might have wanted to move back after the regeneration.

This is not surprising given the history of the re-development. From a policy perspective, Norfolk Park was an ideal candidate for regeneration, generally considered in the city to be a 'no-go area', with a reputation as a hang-out for drug users and, as we have seen, with buildings in poor condition and a high crime-rate. Local residents were very keen for improvements. Architectural consultants were hired to develop a masterplan, and held fortnightly meetings on the estate to discuss with tenants how they saw the future of the estate. With a number of tenants heavily involved in redevelopment in order to get government funding, it could be said that at this point tenants did feel that they were central to the process, and certainly that they felt ownership over the estate. The Park was their home and they were fiercely proud of it: they had brought up children there, run social groups (Scouts and Guides, football clubs, social evenings and annual shows), and campaigned for improvements over more than 30 years. Early on in the regeneration their campaigns were partially successful. Early proposals to demolish all the pre-fabricated terraced housing were met with stiff resistance, and the council agreed to retain and improve those in best condition, through the offices of a new housing association. By the end of the consultation, representatives of local residents were relatively satisfied that the plans were satisfactory, if not ideal, but they recognised and mostly respected the compromises that had been made. Even so, there was clearly a battle of wills developing, as one local participant outlined:

> To begin with they used to have design meetings every Tuesday. Used to have them at the [...] church and they used to put lunch on as a little bribe. We were very clever; we knew that if they brought three designs, the one in colour would be the one the developers wanted to be chosen and the others were in black and white. The community would choose the design that they felt was best. So [the developers] weren't very pleased with what the community were asking for.[24]

However, once the Regeneration Plan had been adopted by the City Council as Supplementary Planning Guidance, action on the ground began to deviate from the ideals laid out in the plans and discussed through interminable meetings on the estate. These comments by a woman who worked in the community centre in the neighbouring Victorian park typify the views of many who lived and worked in Norfolk Park:

24 NH-HC 2006. Thanks to Hilary Corcoran for interview data.

> In the beginning the residents were consulted about the Master Plans, but what has happened today does not bear any resemblance to what was asked for or agreed upon.[25]

This statement contains one clue to further issues in planning processes that we rarely take seriously, and that is the time that processes take, an issue that I discuss in the last chapter of this book. As planning processes progress, other things change, new participants appear, other policies change, people shift jobs and so on. The gap between what is agreed early in a planning consultation and what appears on the ground can be rather large, for all these reasons and more, although it is clear that the size of the gap is seen differently by different participants. Despite the residents feeling that the plan was not followed, local councillors, council officials and the commercial developers on the site thought otherwise, with a councillor arguing that:

> The original Master Plan that we had of Norfolk Park I do believe has been more or less followed and I do think it is extremely useful.[26]

One reason this councillor thought the plan had been followed 'more or less' was that she saw the plan as a general scheme, a tool to recruit funding, and a set of goals. Where one or two goals were met (such as demolishing sub-standard property or dividing the whole site into smaller portions to manage separately), then the plan was followed. For residents who were treated to illustrations of what the development would look like, and agreements on the economic development that would be undertaken, the plan looked less true to the consultation discussions. So a verdict on whether the consultation had been effective varied quite substantially between participants. The senior council regeneration officer carefully suggested that:

> The way [the architectural consultants] set about [masterplanning] was to very much involve the community in the development of the Master Plan and to make sure people were as involved as they could be on topics they were interested in.[27]

And the main commercial developer's Regeneration Manager claimed:

> I firmly believe that throughout both the Master Planning process and the re-development process to date that the local community has been fully engaged and consulted within that process.[28]

25 NH-HC 2006 op. cit.
26 JD-SA 2006.
27 SM-SA 2006.
28 DC-SA 2006.

They did also make statements of exception to indicate their awareness that the process might not be perfect, such as the councillor's observation that for the maintenance of local democracy:

> I think it is dependent on the will within the local authority to ensure that local people in the community, which includes all the local voluntary agencies for example and the local forum, are involved and not just involved but they're actually listened to so that you don't just ask them what they want, you actually listen to them, you respond to them and you change accordingly. I actually believe that that's been done, albeit I think it was a very slow process because I do feel that parts of the community believe that they weren't listened to particularly at the beginning.[29]

These interviews were carried out in the context of the filming of a documentary, and clearly the interviewees are doing Public Relations work, stressing the success of the project both for the benefit of government funders, and to maintain confidence in the project among investors. In private conversations, similar claims were tempered with assertions about the difficulty of working with people focused on their immediate problems, as one of the Community Forum officers acknowledged:

> There have been regular regeneration meetings on Norfolk Park, although I think one of the frustrations around that has often been that the meeting which perhaps was called around something quite strategic, with members of the public, sometimes gets bogged down in grass-cutting and blocked drains you know, or water running off a certain site or whatever. These are all genuine concerns in terms of quality of life but I think it has at times frustrated the regeneration team, which have turned up to try and get across maybe something that's quite important around the regeneration from a strategic perspective, but sometimes it has got bogged down in blocked drains.[30]

Getting estate residents to feel that they owned the regeneration as a whole became increasingly difficult. Perhaps the most significant diversion was from the plan's timetable for development. While demolition proceeded according to plan so that it would be completed within the time that public funding was available, the construction company delayed rebuilding significantly. The consequences for the development company were highly beneficial, as the price of housing in the region began to rise dramatically and, over three years, the prices they were able to raise on the new homes built doubled from their original estimates. Consequences for residents and former residents were more serious, though:

---

29 JD-SA 2006.

30 CN-SA 2006.

> Residents were told they would be moved out of their home on a short-term basis, while their new homes were built. In reality half of the estate [population] has disappeared, because half of the new homes have not been built at the same speed as the demolition. Some have moved more than once due to their 'temporary' accommodation needing to be demolished. A lot decided to move off the estate. Obviously if they have been away for 3 years plus, they have made new friends, neighbours, and the children have settled into a new school, so they have made where they have moved to their new homes.

Yet council officers continued to argue that the plan had local ownership:

> I think having that community involvement in that has really added to that Master Plan and added to the ownership of the Master Plan from the local community.[31]

There are strong echoes here of the development practices that David Mosse described in his book, *Cultivating Development*. The public face of the project was maintained through an avoidance of retrospective criticism and a determined focus on seeing the regeneration through to the development of each sub-site of the estate. A rhetorical commitment to 'community involvement' is rarely critically analysed in relationship to the totalising and homogenising concepts of community or involvement it presumes. The difficulties for many residents wanting to participate in this 'involvement' process were pointed out by a member of the senior management of the rebuilt local primary school, who noted that:

> The parents feel that they have been poorly consulted about the new developments. Although there has been a range of consultation evenings, the planners do not understand the fear that these parents have in attending. Many have low literacy levels and are not comfortable entering the school.[32]

He also noted a sense of fear among local parents confronted by unfamiliar faces, suggesting that rebuilding trust would take a long time. His observations underline the former insularity of the estate, an insularity that could also be interpreted as the face-to-face familiarity that constitutes the 'sense of community' sought in ownership policy. On the other hand, a young woman interviewed by students told of the divide between old and new residents who she thought felt themselves better than council tenants. She told the students that because of this, 'there is no longer a sense of community'. An older resident echoed this: 'The spirit, I think, has gone to a large extent because of the depopulation.'

We could sum up these positions as a fundamental difference over the notion of community and ownership. For residents, although the material conditions on the estate had undoubtedly improved, and the removal of open drug dealing

31 SM-SA 2006, Op. Cit.

32 PF-'Annexe A' undated.

was clearly seen as a benefit, regeneration had been a frustrating and dispiriting process of attack on the vibrant community of the estate. It had been threatened by the declining conditions and lack of maintenance prior to regeneration, but it was the process of regeneration itself that had evicted many of the community, friends and relations, and had demolished local amenities such as the shops and community centre, with its ballroom, bar and coffee room. In addition, all four of the pubs on the estate had closed – two being converted into evangelical churches.

While residents told accounts of local differences of opinion and disagreements over the regeneration, the project officers projected complexity, struggle, then triumph. This was recognised in government documents that promoted the Park as an example of successful community-led regeneration (see Fig. 4.1). Only one developer argued differently, and this was the head of a non-profit anti-poverty development trust. He interpreted the process as a policy fashion:

Transformation in Norfolk Park

Norfolk Park in Sheffield is situated within the South Yorkshire Market Renewal Pathfinder. Constructed in the mid 1960s, the area is steadily transforming from a monolithic estate into a high quality urban residential area.

Local people, Sheffield City Council, North British Housing (NBH) and private developers are working together to drive forward this change. 2800 low quality properties and 14 tower blocks have been demolished and 195 new properties built. The replacement housing is a mix of new social and private homes, whilst the remaining older properties have been refurbished. A private £20 million housing development will be completed in early 2005.

The area has a state of the art junior community school and there are plans for a new health centre, shops and community facilities. An *Extra Care Scheme* provides high quality housing and care to elderly people whilst green spaces are being planned and managed by Sheffield Wildlife Trust.

Courtesy of Sheffield City Council

Transforming Norfolk Park

Figure 4.1 Excerpt from *Sustainable Communities: Homes for All*, Chapter 6

Source: ODPM *Sustainable Communities: Homes for All*, Chapter 6

They decide that they'll commission a Master Plan and get some fancy firm of architects to talk to all the locals and then ignore them, and we think it's a real

> waste of money ... everyone seems to commission Master Plans, it's completely bonkers.[33]

The ritual aspects of this approach did not appeal to him. On the contrary, he had a clear view of how to be effective:

> What you should do is sit down a development team with the local community and then devise an implementation plan because [of] the number of regeneration agencies, and I think it applies to [Single Regeneration Budget] programmes, it applies to New Deal for Community programmes,[34] it applies to everybody who is winged in to some local area.

He did not criticise the architects who worked on the project, but the fact that their masterplan bore little resemblance to practice. Indeed, the masterplan included statements on community economic regeneration and the importance of local facilities that were laudable, but were not implemented (and still were not implemented ten years after the process started). What, then, was the point of the process? The local councillor was explicit about the utility of masterplanning:

> I do think it is extremely useful. I think it's mostly useful to obtain funding because if you're going to the government or you're going to any other organisation like European Funding for example, you don't just go along and say we want £40 million to develop [an estate], you have to demonstrate why you need that money and what you're going to do with it. So of course you need it for your funding.

This instrumentality was not the only purpose, and she was careful to refer to the conventional justification for masterplanning policy:

> I think you also need it because you need to be looking at the long term future of an estate and it's not patchwork. So if you've got a Master Plan for the whole estate you're not just doing bits at a time.

What is not evident here is any attention to the experience of living in the estate,[35] or of the memory of homes demolished or to be demolished. Where the categories used in urban regeneration distinguish dwelling types by their ownership (tenancy types, such as rented, shared equity, privately owned, etc), these quickly slip into the categorisation of people in relation to those forms of ownership (ie resident, tenant, home-owner, etc). But for many planners dealing with a wide range of different constituents, these categorisations do not make it any easier to appreciate the reality of the lives lived by

33 JA-SA 2006.

34 Government regeneration policy funding schemes.

35 Or 'on' it, in local parlance.

actual people. If we move the perspective and see things from their point of view, then the categories start to seem less convincing, less suitable and rather arbitrary. Few of the residents talked explicitly about belonging or about ownership. They talked about their families, social clubs they ran or joined, about the steepness of the hills and about the view. But many of them were highly politicised and also talked about their campaigns for tenants' rights, and the frustration of not being listened to.

In our interviews with residents, there were those who stressed the poor conditions of some of the worse towers that were the first to be demolished. These residents were glad to see the end of cold, damp flats with no security and failing lifts. For others, though, the memories were different, especially for those who had lived for longer in towers that had been partially restored with video-phones on the doors and coffee mornings in the lobbies. The elderly residents facing a move into sheltered housing regretted the need to move. They stressed the open balconies in the flats, the majestic views over the moors and the city, and the spacious rooms: 'it's just the view…', and commenting on the new housing, a resident said: 'It's just the balconies really …I miss the view'. Despite the extra amenities offered in the sheltered housing complex, residents remained nostalgic for their tower block flats: 'I liked us to be high up; you could look down on people then and see personal things. If you look out of the window here, it's not part of your world.' The steep hills of Sheffield were spectacular from the flats, as another resident said shortly before moving:

> …we had this fantastic view over the moors and this is the thing I'm going to miss at night, all the lights twinkling. You can see right from the moors all the way down to the Town Hall clock. I shall miss that…

When Peggy Seaton was asked to press the button to demolish the old East Bank tower block at the Norfolk Park housing estate in Sheffield, she says she had mixed feelings seeing her home of 30 years blown to smithereens. Other residents were more emotive. The local newspaper reported local sentiment about the demolition of some terraced housing, with resident June Bell recounting, with tears in her eyes, that this was the second house the council had 'taken off' her through compulsory purchase, the first having been demolished in the 1960s to make way for a ring road. 'This house is where my memories are', she is reported as saying, 'I want to stay here with them'. Another home owner put the argument most succinctly: 'for housing people it's a decision about houses, but for us it's about our homes and lives'.[36] Despite all the talk about partnership in regeneration, there were clearly people on the estate who felt that they were not being respected as full human beings. Certainly it seemed that the various people involved had rather different views of what partnership meant, and even what the point of regeneration was, as well as what the role of residents should or could be. As the interests of residents became progressively marginalised, some have suggested that the intention of regeneration was not to improve the estate, but to remove it; not to improve the conditions on the estate and reduce the poverty through economic investment, but

36 *The Star* 22/10/1998 'We're all losers in council's land grab'.

rather to exchange the population for a wealthier one.[37] Now that the management of the regeneration has been merged with the larger neighbouring estate of older state-owned properties, Joan wryly suggests that Norfolk Park, the estate, the neighbourhood, has 'been abolished'. Perhaps we should ask whether it is surprising that people suspect foul play, when the explanations they are offered seem remote or unconvincing, or when the value of such a fundamental thing as home is not considered a planning issue.

When is a house a person?

Ownership is obviously a relationship. You cannot own something without either an object to own or another person who does not have the possibility of ownership. So ownership is a relationship with the thing owned and with other potential owners. This raises all sorts of questions, but most fundamentally it asks what is a person, who can own, and what is the 'thingness' of a thing that can be owned? While the dictionary definition of a person is first of all a human being, the legal definition is rather more expansive. A legal person might be a firm, partnership, association, corporation, trade union, legal representatives, etc. A government might also be a legal person. A person is not merely a human being, since not all humans are necessarily persons in the eyes of the law at all times. The most obvious example is in the history of slavery in which slaves were not considered persons as free men were, and there is no shortage of histories of men who consider women to be lesser persons than themselves. Persons may also be civilly dead (outlaws) while still humanly alive. Philosophical considerations of such problems consider the extent to which persons have consciousness, and are the locus of moral values. Once discussions recognise that personhood is relational, personhood can be considered on the basis of what John P. Lizza calls 'individual, moral and cultural construction'.[38] Lizza's concern is with the definition of death, but the concept of personhood is used by other philosophers in relation to other living things. Aaltola[39] notes that cognitive ethnologists argue that animals have minds, for example, and that personhood defined by interaction allows for a consideration of animal ethics, for example.

While we tend to think of persons and things as separate entities, various theorists are now arguing that they are increasingly enmeshed. This is evident in areas such as biotechnology, where a thing might become part of your body, such as an artificial joint, or where new transgenic crops are being distributed among networks of farmers

---

37 In other words, of gentrification, although it is not necessarily discussed in these terms.

38 http://ideas.repec.org/a/bla/ajecsc/v66y2007i1p195-216.html
http://www.blackwell-synergy.com/servlet/useragent?func=synergy&synergyAction=showTOC&journalCode=ajes&volume=66&issue=1&year=2007∂=null
American Journal of Economics and Sociology 2007: 195–216.

39 Aaltola 2008: 175–194.

to create human-thing networks.[40] Alain Pottage points out that it is particularly contentious in relation to embryos, which are related to their parents through contract and property, but are also increasingly thought of as persons in their own right.[41] That is, the legal controversy about abortion rests on a question of whether an embryo becomes a person when it becomes a foetus or when it is born. He notes that social and political theories have been slow to recognise these connections, since they, too, have tended to presuppose a basic division between persons and things. Recent debates have begun to remedy this situation, though, and there are many social scientists rethinking the meaning of the term 'person'.

Nor is it only proto-human things that can be thought of as persons, as Kay Milton indicates in her essays on environmentalism. Although persons are generally seen as having a different moral status from other objects, Milton argues that:

> 'some nature protectionists argue that we hold moral responsibilities towards other things…, such as plants, species, ecosystems, life in general and the planet as a whole. In recognizing moral obligations towards these things they are implicitly according them rights, thereby defining them as the kinds of things that can have rights, in other words, as persons.' (2002: 28)

In other words, in Milton's definition, having rights is what defines a person (rather than 'person' automatically implying 'human'). Whereas Pottage was referring to people-technology combinations, or what are sometimes called 'cyborgs',[42] Milton is asking how far things like flowers, whales, forests or ecosystems might also be thought of as persons. If a person is, by definition, that to which we owe moral responsibility, and which has rights to protection then what about inanimate objects? We accord rights not only to landscapes and ecological sites, but to certain buildings too which we consider to have particular historical or aesthetic values. Such buildings play a significant role in our lives, and as well as dwelling in them and with them, we develop emotions and feelings towards them. We think of certain buildings as protective, frightening, secure, threatening, and so on. They appear to be more than inanimate, but take on personalities, embellished by our memories of them and all kinds of associations we have with them, either directly or through others. Even on a domestic scale, homes become significant players in our lives, often defining our family interactions, our relations with friends and foes, as both background and foreground of our everyday lives. In this sense, the house not only demands our attention (we must maintain or repair it, clean it, look after it), but we also require it to do things for us (protect us, provide comfort, enable us to live safely and healthily).

French anthropologist Claude Lévi-Strauss noticed that some societies were actually organised not around the family or tribe, but in relation to a house. While in some cases, this might be an actual building, in others it could be a metaphorical household. Think

40 Pottage 2004.

41 Pottage 2004: 4.

42 See Harraway 1997.

House of Windsor, for example, or other noble European royal houses. Lévi-Strauss noticed that the social organisation of the Kwakiutl of northern Vancouver Island did not match any of the patterns of kinship known elsewhere (such as clan, matriliny, etc). Instead, he recognised houses as moral persons, with an estate of material wealth that is passed down a line that maintains the house, and kinship, class and any other form of social relation can be used.[43] We can think of houses as persons when they become the focal point of social organisation; but outside the realm of 'house societies', houses as buildings may also be conferred personhood that is not necessarily sustained over generations but is repeatedly invested with emotion and care during the course of its inhabitation. Some also have more than others, and we may speculate that the personhood of a house is more secure when a house can be identified as a home, and that the distinction in the language between these two terms indicates a parallel difference in personhood.

For instance, in the process of moving house or inheriting a house, the personhood of the house is first abandoned and its status becomes uncertain.[44] Only when it is re-adopted by its new inhabitees does it start gradually to regain it status as a person. The transformation of a warm, lived-in home to a depersonalised empty shell is something of a literary trope; the forlorn state of a home deserted suggests an object stripped of its humanity, perhaps signified in ghostly form through the traces of former lives. In contexts where homes move with their inhabitants,[45] the personhood of the dwelling is reinstated each time it is reconstructed, and becomes part of the household itself. Carsten and Hugh-Jones indicate how commonly houses are thought of as bodies (1995: 3). The language of the body comes into our thinking about houses: the hearth is the heart of the home, grand houses have wings, the kitchen is the life and soul of the house, a house has to breathe, and so forth. Generally speaking, the house is much, much more than a 'machine for living'.

Of course a house is not a human being, but according to the policies and politicians quoted earlier, houses can be thought of has having agency – being able to do things and have effects on both their environments and their inhabitants, and their owners. Moreover, given the discussion about ownership earlier in the chapter, it is clear that there are ways in which the agency of houses is tied into morality. So it is fruitful to think about houses as part of the socio-technical relations of contemporary urban society; to consider how houses are simultaneously seen as an object but also as something with (moral) agency in policy and in practices related to housing redevelopment.[46]

---

43 Lévi-Strauss 1983. See Carsten and Hugh-Jones 1995.

44 In anthropology, this status is called 'liminal' – the state of transition between two other states, such as before and after a ritual, as suggested by Arnold van Gennep in 1909 (1960).

45 i.e. rather than inhabitants moving from house to house.

46 I have written elsewhere of how buildings act, in the Actor-Network sense (http://www.hrionline.ac.uk/matshef/abram/MSabram.htm).

This way of thinking links usefully to studies of socio-technology that advocate a non-determinate approach to human and non-human actants, or things that act.[47] In other words, we need to observe closely the ways that things we think of as non-human can determine the activities of others. Bruno Latour took such an approach to the development of a hi-tech transport system for Paris,[48] in which he imagined what the machines might be thinking. Giving the machines a voice made it clear that they had effects on others – his aim wasn't really to argue that machines can think like humans, but to show that if we look at the world from their point of view, they do actually intervene in the relations between themselves and other things by the things they can do and the things they can't, the moments when they go wrong or go right. Although Latour does this humorously, he also provokes us into focusing our attention on how technological objects construct human thoughts and activities, and we might add how all non-human or non-animate objects can be constructed as agents or actors rather than bystanders in the performance of daily life. We might ask how the world looks from the point of view of a house or flat, or we might try to find out how the shape of the house, its movements, its changeability and its solidity shape the lives of those who move through it.

We can ask the same of policy, too: How is policy implicated in the ownership and appropriation of knowledge? How do policy-regimes produce subjects that can be managed? And we can go on to ask how both human and non-human actors produce policy regimes and are, in turn, re-made by them. This is not merely to give an account of how a policy comes into being from the perspective of its writers (although they themselves might already be a temporally and spatially extended network), but how concrete objects, landscapes, social and socio-technical formations and assemblages produce a world where policy becomes a meaningful quantity.

This casts into doubt many of the assumptions held in policy related to housing including not only 'housing policy', which usually refers to detailed policies on the allocation and management of public housing, but a wide range of urban and planning policies that regulate the construction, demolition and provision of both private and public housing. Rarely does such policy recognise the moral obligations related to the personhood of housing, yet as we have seen, recent policy has outlined a desire that the occupiers of housing 'take ownership' not only of the housing, but of housing policy itself. In Norfolk Park, the problem was that people were asked to take ownership of policy that proposed to demolish their homes, and that was difficult to swallow.

Owning home, owning policy – conclusions

What I have described in this chapter is a radical and increasingly dominant set of political ideas. The idea that ownership is morally superior to other relations between

47 See Murdoch 1997.

48 Latour 1996.

humans and houses has returned to the political stage, and it is worth interrogating what it implies. I have outlined how it attributes agency to objects such as houses, suggesting that the relationship of owning instils a sense of obligation to property, and that owning thus creates personhood in the house. The house becomes the organising principle of a morally acceptable society. That society is simultaneously conceptualised as a 'community' with local roots, but with a broad commitment to the state through what has been described as good citizenship. In recent years, political movements have urged us to believe that good citizens can also be created through a relationship of owning to policy processes and outcomes. If owning houses and policy changes the behaviour and thoughts of people, then we might argue that both houses and policy have personhood. So this political ideology is based on the relationship of ownership which is thought to bring about a transformation in behaviour and I have suggested that this could be thought of as a kind of political philosophy of personhood. It is expressed through generous phrases such as involvement, engagement, belonging and sharing.

Clearly this is not simple to translate into practice. There is some evidence that desired outcomes may be more achievable in smaller scale architectural projects, and a lot has been learned, at least by architects, since the 1990s when projects like this were getting off the ground. Experienced architects certainly recognise the limitations to their 'visioning' exercises, as participative as they may be, and more radical architects have developed community-owned and community-directed development projects which aim to help empower citizens, as much as to offer improved environments.[49] But there is little evidence that such transformation can be achieved on anything like a general scale in longer or larger policy processes. There are many reasons why this might be the case, some of which I have elaborated elsewhere.[50] These include the problem of the role of time in policy negotiations where open participation is incompatible with progression through deliberation to decisions.[51] They also include the challenge to the authority of elected representatives through unaccountable self-selected participation, and also relate to a critique of planning theories whose notions of coherent communities or actor-equality lack substance.

Similar trends in the promotion of 'owning' policy are found in other European countries. Woltjer summarises planning literature that identifies participation as a means to empower citizens, both as a good in its own right and as a means to

---

49 See the Atelier d'Architecture Autogérée and Petrescu, 2007.

50 Abram 2002, 2000.

51 That is, policy processes usually aim to progress iteratively through time, through deliberation or negotiation, consultation and decision. Open participation inevitably allows new participants to join the process at any point, when they almost inevitably want to object to decisions already made – not having been involved in the process means they are unlikely to have been incorporated into decisions (do not 'own' the decisions), and the ideal smooth flow of the process from decision to decision is interrupted, causing frustration and delay for prior participants.

achieve improved decision outcomes.[52] He identifies in Dutch discourse the desire for 'win-win' outcomes as the goal for participatory planning.[53] Woltjer's conclusion is that Dutch infrastructure planners consider participatory planning '*to be effective mainly in terms of support and acceptance*', primarily '*in its ability to generate public support'*.[54] So, he argues that infrastructure planners use participatory planning as a kind of '*public support machine*', an instrumental tool to smooth the passage of large intrusive projects. Woltjer's conclusions suggest that planners are using participation pragmatically, although it can sound a little cynical, but it also reminds us that we cannot presume what people are doing simply from talk about 'participation'.

What we can conclude is that in Norfolk Park, politicians, council officers and some commercial developers bought into the discourse of ownership through involvement, albeit with the limitations set at different levels. What is striking about the tenants' description of home on Norfolk Park is not that they talked about owning their homes – and indeed many of them were opposed, on political principle, to buying their properties from the council or the housing association to whom their homes were transferred. On the contrary, many of them talked about 'community spirit', and the term 'spirit' is key. As one resident suggested:

> People still wanted to keep community spirit and have more facilities. But they have actually got fewer facilities now. They were also hoping for better housing, which some have got and some haven't.[55]

This is not the magical ownership through involvement that policy envisages, but is a long term experience of shared and personal memory, friendships, family, and time passing, where associations are not the snapshot of contemporary dereliction, but are tied to longer histories of pride and pleasure. Home, in this context, is not only the house or flat that the tenant has rights to, but the spaces between, and the shared spaces among: the coffee lounges, lobbies, community centres, clubs, sports grounds, associations, churches and pubs that tie the estate together. While owner-occupiers might own their flats, they cannot own the public space any more than tenants. And one might argue that they own their flats less, since for usually 25 years such properties are fully or partly owned by the banks, not by mortgagees. Private owners are currently more likely to have their housing repossessed than council tenants, for example. The terrible irony of current regeneration practice is that despite the heavily embedded discourse of community involvement (or perhaps because of its weak form), urban regeneration in many cases has arguably been a process of gentrification,[56] whereby pre-existing long established working-class social groups

52 Woltjer 2002: 441.

53 Ibid.: 446.

54 Ibid.: 446.

55 NH-HC Op Cit.

56 Some have argued that the 'real' purpose of this kind of regeneration has been to move 'problem' tenants out of sight, and to realise the potential capital of the land. The

have been dispersed in favour of privately renting or privately owning residents, often without local history or ties to long-standing residents.

On the estate described above, much of the long-delayed private housing has been bought by landlords and rented to students, the archetypal fleeting temporary resident and not the most likely to make a long-term commitment to the area. With the increased variety of local residents, with different tenancies and very different circumstances, it is more difficult to offer communal activities. As one of the Community Forum observed, 'it's not about poverty any more': there is no core shared experience on which community can automatically be formed, and new kinds of relation must be invented. If this is true, then one could argue that politicians have achieved one of their objectives – to be rid of the 'monolithic' council estates – monolithic not just in architecture, but in class and occupancy. For the former residents, personhood is not merely found in the housing they live in, but in the spirit of community that they have lived. It is over the loss of this spirit that they have felt grief, and over the death of the estate as they knew it in its happier days. The feelings of ownership they describe were much broader than the deeds of their flats and houses, more closely tied to a sense of belonging. In this world, private ownership signified an inward individualism, the opposite of community, and a loss of social interaction that many lament. They do not talk of the new buildings in terms of a rebirth of the estate. But neither did many of them develop the feelings of ownership over the policies that they were supposed to develop, but felt excluded and rejected when they voiced their concerns. Many of the older residents regretted being moved out of high rise flats, even though the move to a care-home has been very timely for some of them. What they expressed in private was anger, but what they expressed in public was more often a resigned acceptance that they would have no control over what would happen anyway.

There are two arguments here. The first is more banal, that policy and practice are severely at odds. This is not surprising, and the more utopian the policy, the further from practice it is likely to be. We can also repeat an easy observation that political rhetoric is inconsistent and note Ball's conclusion that participative policy making represents policy over-optimism.[57] But the second argument concerns the disputed notion that the personhood of housing is instilled in a relationship of being owned by its occupants that is believed to lead to changed behaviours not only within the house but between residents and between them, their employers and the state. The same principle of thought is embedded in the notion that policy becomes owned through some experience of involvement in its development, and that this can generate acceptance of difficult choices. Its participants will feel ownership over it, at least metaphorically, and through their adoption of it will feel obligations towards it, thus somehow engendering feelings of care and sympathy towards it. Despite the lack of evidence for such effects, closer examination of how policies are developed suggests

Centre for Social Justice report makes this explicit: 'While occupied by social tenants social housing has very little value. Turning tenants into owners releases the value of the home and allows the most vulnerable in our society to benefit' (Davies 2008: 70).

57 Ball, 2004: 139.

that the implicit detection of personhood may have worth. Policy may live or die, be cultivated or abandoned, and it may bite back with unintended outcomes. I have also indicated that the notion of community spirit may be less banal than is often assumed, and that it bears a close relationship to the utopian 'good community' that policy aspires to. That policies have been followed that have been accused of killing this spirit shows how these forms of ownership and personhood have been used inconsistently – the ownership that residents felt over their socially rented housing and neighbourhoods was destroyed in the name of creating home ownership to produce community feelings of responsibility. But the consistent reference to a spirit of community should only reinforce our recognition of how highly it is valued. It was simply not the 'kind' of community that policy-promoters desired.

What does this tell us about ownership and personhood? I have outlined a contrast between formal ownership with juridical legitimacy, and sentiments of owning that include proprietorship and shared experience. These are set in the context of the personhood invested in two objects of ownership, housing and policy. In a symmetrical analysis, one could argue that the sentiments of ownership that planners and developers felt for policy might best parallel the sentiments that loyal estate residents had for their estate. Neither correspond to the political ambitions for ownership that are stated in common political statements, including official policy texts and lobbying documents. Rather, the process is inverted; while planners create and use planning policy documents instrumentally to secure partnerships, contracts or funding, the kind of personhood they are attributed from residents is filled with antipathy. Persons are not always benign. Being heavily involved in so-called participative policy-making arouses feelings of despair and rejection from residents at least as much as (and I would argue often more than) feelings of ownership over policy. Although Kay Milton suggests that personhood is intrinsic to objects/beings for which people feel obligations, that obligation may produce antagonism: persons are not always on good terms. Many residents in Norfolk Park fought hard to change policies or parts of policies, which threatened to impinge on their strongly felt attachment to the idea of the estate as a lived community. Ownership of their housing in terms of judicial rights (ie owning the deeds to the property they lived in rather than renting) was less important to residents than the moral ownership of shared lives, and the ownership of the greater estate itself. One long-term tenant, Joan, summed this up effectively in response to an advertising campaign by the developers building housing for private sale. The campaign featured a picture taken from the estate labelled 'My Norfolk Park'. In it, the picture identified 'my pub', 'my gym', 'my work', etc. Joan complained that these included a city centre pub and gym, and the workplace was a bank. 'Is that my Norfolk Park?', she asked, rhetorically. 'It's not *my* Norfolk Park.'

Chapter 5
Citizens and the Public

The previous chapters are bringing us gradually closer to understanding what planning is about by applying different forms of cultural analysis and comparison to elements of planning that are usually taken for granted, or rejected as being in the realm of culture rather than planning. Each chapter has identified a problem or something unsatisfactorily explained in planning and tried to see what new light might be shed by taking a different perspective. The next two chapters look at the idea of the 'public' from two perspectives. In this chapter, the double-bind is the question of the citizen as a kind of constituent part of the public. I focus in this chapter on the question of how we work out which bit of a person is a citizen, or which part of a person's life is citizenship.

Citizen participation as policy (with a life of its own)

In general terms, a citizen can be defined as either the resident of a city, literally, as in the French term '*citadin*', or as a member of the political institution we call a state, as in the French term '*citoyen*'. But beyond these very general categories, governments are often keen to try to redefine what being a citizen means. In 2005 the British government introduced a 'citizenship test' to be passed by any immigrant who wished to get British citizenship or settlement. This suggests that citizenship requires a certain kind of knowledge, but as no British person was ever required to take, never mind pass, this test, it was perhaps not about citizenship at all, but about the control of immigration. Other government policy tried to redefine what it meant to be a citizen for those who already have nationality. Given that the idea of the citizen has to do with the relation between the person and the state, much government discussion of the role of citizens has tried to define what citizens should do in relation to the state. How should citizens participate in state activities, and what is the role of the citizen in making policy? Questions like this imagine an ideal citizen, a model that ordinary people should live up to, so they are actually asking who, how and when is the citizen?

Citizenship talk is found in all sorts of policy at all sorts of levels. There is continuity between, say, UK and EU language of citizenship, not surprisingly, and we can find it in general documents about participation in democracy in general and in policy in particular. The sort of language to be found in governmental or intergovernmental statements about participation gives us some clues to the concept of citizen that is being developed and written, often as the outcome of contentious debates, compromises and diplomacy.

One such statement consolidates the notion of the active citizen as interlocutor of the state. The Council of Europe Committee of Ministers published a recommendation which laid out a position on participative policy making in 2001.[1] In this statement, the ministers recommended that national governments put in place legislation to encourage 'citizens' to 'participate', complete with a set of suggestions on how to monitor, benchmark and evaluate participation. Participation being a complex notion, however, they do not define it directly, but hint at it through a set of related principles, making it the kind of conundrum that anthropologists love to grapple with. In particular, the statements in the excerpt in Figure 5.1 are helpful in relation to the British context, as they reiterate statements made before and after this time in British policy documents, particularly those relating specifically to local government in England.

> Considering that participation of citizens is at the very heart of the idea of democracy and that citizens committed to democratic values, mindful of their civic duties and who become involved in political activity are the lifeblood of any democratic system;
>
> Noting that local democracy has to operate in a new challenging context resulting not only from structural and functional changes in local government organisation, but also from the radical political, economic and social developments that have occurred in Europe and the process of globalisation;
>
> Aware that public expectations have evolved, that local politics are changing form and that this requires more direct, flexible and ad hoc methods of participation;
>
> Considering that, in certain circumstances, the level of trust people have in their elected institutions has declined and that there is a need for state institutions to re-engage with and respond to the public in new ways to maintain the legitimacy of decision-making;
>
> Considering that the right of citizens to have their say in major decisions entailing long-term commitments or choices which are difficult to reverse and concern a majority of citizens is one of the democratic principles common to all member states of the Council of Europe;
>
> Considering that this right can be most directly exercised at local level and that, accordingly, steps should be taken to involve citizens more directly in the management of local affairs, while safeguarding the effectiveness and efficiency of such management;
>
> Reaffirming its belief that representative democracy is part of the common heritage of member states and is the basis of the participation of citizens in public life at national, regional and local level;
>
> Considering that dialogue between citizens and local elected representatives is essential for local democracy, as it strengthens the legitimacy of local democratic institutions and the effectiveness of their action;

Figure 5.1 Extracts from Recommendation Rec(2001)19 of the Committee of Ministers to member states on the participation of citizens in local public life.

1 CECM 2001. Although it is difficult to trace the passage of policy ideas between states, and we should hesitate to draw simple comparisons between states, it is clear that ideas of participative citizenship had reached the European political stage when this document was published.

This play of rhetoric to ideas of common heritage and democratic principles is less a reflection of common practice than a statement of ideals (or 'aspirations' in current policy parlance). There is no attempt to broach the sticky subject of who is included within the category of citizens, or how participatory activities might marry with established formal representative political processes. Nor does it attempt to explain how involving citizens at the local level might be squared with 'safeguarding the effectiveness and efficiency' of the management of local affairs, when one of the key dilemmas within participatory policy making is the time and expense involved in opening up routine and non-routine decision-making processes to wider audiences. These central dilemmas are hinted at within the recommendation but nowhere addressed.

In the context of UK government policy, the theme of participation has resurfaced frequently, and was a central theme in much of the New Labour government's policy from 1997, and continues today. Defining features of contemporary democratic discourse in Britain include the idea that members of the public should be 'involved' in democracy through a number of routes. Throughout the 1990s, it was noticed in political circles that steadily fewer people were politically active. The definition of political activity was based mainly on party membership and election turnout, the standard measures adopted in political science, and both these quantities had been decreasing for some time.[2] Party membership, for example, has more or less collapsed relative to the early post-war period, yet political activity has not disappeared. For many political scientists, the move from joining a political party to joining a campaign is thought of as a weakening of general democratic literacy. From this perspective, activism associated with a principle such as 'environmentalism' or more particular local development issues is interpreted as a 'single issue' which is inferior to generalised political party politics. We now have sufficient knowledge of environmental activists from detailed anthropological studies to demonstrate that environmental activism is no less of a comprehensive ideological standpoint than any established political party,[3] reminding us to be careful of making judgements before considering the evidence.

The extent to which conventional political science ideas penetrate government is apparent in a typically short-lived cross-departmental UK government project, entitled 'Together We Can', whose annual report includes statements from both the then Prime Minister and the Secretary of State for Communities and Local Government implying that there is a problem which needs to be solved. In line with his carefully cultivated rhetorical practices, Blair, as Prime Minister was careful to avoid any negative statements or identification of 'problems', but suggests that the government is working together with citizens, 'to provide more opportunities for people to influence the public policy decisions that affect their lives and communities'.[4] The Secretary of State's statement adopts a common political

2 Not only in the UK: see Jenssen 1999 or Conway 2001.

3 Berglund 1998, Abram and Waldren 1998.

4 Civil Renewal Unit 2006: 3.

avoidance of specifics, claiming to see 'a growing willingness among residents and public bodies to collaborate'. Yet the main document is clear, that there is a 'gulf – real or perceived – between people and public bodies', a 'problem of citizens' disengagement from public issues'. It states that 'the proportion of people in England and Wales who believe they cannot influence decisions affecting their local areas went up from 57 per cent to 62 per cent between 2001 and 2003, and remained at around 61 per cent in 2005'.[5] The consequences it traces from this situation are presented as clear cut:

> When people feel they cannot influence the way problems affecting their communities are tackled, they also come to believe that public authorities have little interest in meeting their needs. They feel their problems will persist regardless of what official announcements are made to the contrary, and that their views on what could be done to turn the problem around are not valued by public authorities. It is not surprising that they withdraw even further and feel increasingly alienated from public bodies. Conversely, when people are able to play an informed and constructive role in shaping the public policies and services which affect them, they not only add vitality to our democracy, they help to ensure public bodies deliver the improvements communities need.[6]

We can recognise the talk of inclusion and involvement from the previous chapter, of course, but here it is interesting to focus on who is to be involved or become an owner of policies. In this document, the citizen has given way to a generalised body of 'people' with ambiguous status. The construction of 'the people' and 'public bodies', or the introduction of 'communities' in relation to 'needed improvements' have been simplified into banality, yet they serve as reminders of the power of rhetorics which divide the world into 'people', 'government' and 'communities'. It is no innovation to use this kind of speech. Since the French and American revolutions, the use of terms such as 'we, the people' has helped to convince us that we do actually constitute a people, that a peoplehood exists whose will can be communicated.[7] Anderson, Gellner and others have argued that we came to imagine that we formed part of a group of people we could think of as 'we, the people' through the spread of certain kinds of printed text: pamphlets, manifestos, newspapers and novels. These texts could not only simultaneously be read by large numbers of people, but used narrative strategies to suggest that we could imagine others who shared our experiences.[8] Whereas before, the world consisted of peasants, aristocrats, bourgeois, etc, the French and American revolutions, and later the Russian revolution were predicated on the existence of equal human beings who constituted 'the people'.

5 Ibid.: 6.

6 Ibid.

7 See Lee 2001 for a detailed account.

8 Anderson 1983, Gellner 1983.

The idea of peoplehood suggested that we could think of ourselves differently, to imagine a new way to be a subject, or a new kind of subjectivity. As we saw in Chapter 2, being a nation may have emerged in the 18th and 19th centuries, but we have now internalised it so far as to find it difficult to extract ourselves from our nationalities. 'The people', like 'the public' is a rhetorical invention that has had profound implications for how we imagine both ourselves and the state. Government initiatives like 'together we can' imply without reflection that 'we' are 'the people'.

The general absence of the term 'citizen' is interesting, but this may be only in order to distinguish these documents from those of other sections of the department, as the term makes frequent appearances in a range of policy and agendas such as the 'Active Citizenship Centre'. This project, also launched within the 'Civil Renewal Unit', emerged in 2005 with its own research commissioning powers, and its remit was defined on its website as including, 'key aspects of civil renewal including greater public involvement in service delivery, social capital and community cohesion'.[9] Reviewing such documents, an image forms of citizenship as a normative symbol which serves to promote what we might call good behaviour, or perhaps co-optation into governmental ambitions. New Labour pursued a line of thought that had been consolidated by their predecessors, that too many people felt that the state owed them something, that a citizen was a person with rights otherwise quite alienated from political life. By urging people to participate in the state itself, they hoped that passive, dependent welfare recipients would emerge as citizens with feelings of responsibility toward the state, as well as demands. This sort of political project had been ongoing throughout the 20th century, with John F. Kennedy famously urging people to ask what they could do for their country, rather than what their country could do for them.

From this perspective, a good citizen not only does what they are told and refrains from doing what they are told not to, but eagerly launches entrepreneurial projects to generate 'communities', to provide welfare in the form of local self-reliant services, and devotes the rest of their time to attending governmental consultancy events, keeping up to date with planning applications in order to send encouraging comments and to assist in the investment strategies of large corporations. They are 'actively involved' in local political debates (although not necessarily through the party system), vote regularly and predictably, and understand that economic growth is the basis on which sustainability might be achieved. On that basis they will, of course, work full time. Insofar as they may have gender or ethnicity, this is to be channelled through organised groups, with clear representatives who can add any extra requirements to normal policy through constructive dialogue. This ideal citizen must be a very busy person indeed.

9 Active Citizenship Centre 2006.

Citizens, stakeholders, participants

In the UK in the 1990s, participation was opened up beyond citizens imagined as individual persons. The term of preference was the 'stakeholder', an expression adopted and popularised by the political commentator and journalist Will Hutton.[10] The stakeholder is not a subset of the citizen (those citizens with a legitimate interest in a particular policy or development), but was designed to include all types of interest, including commercial interests of profit-seeking, ownership and also government agencies. In the field of urban renewal, where large areas of cities have been redeveloped or demolished and rebuilt, government guidance suggested that 'local ownership, capacity development and the active participation of all stakeholders are critical to the long-term success of urban renewal'[11] and in this statement, the key participants are stakeholders, not citizens. Stakeholders were defined as 'all those individuals living and working in the area and organisations interested and involved in the area', although it was acknowledged that 'some stakeholders will not be interested in the Renewal Area', and that 'the team should focus on those that wish to be involved'. The level of confidence in stakeholder participation was high, such that, '[R]enewal Areas should create true participation, with the stakeholders having an equal say in what happens in their area'. This version of democracy, where commercial private interests have an equal say in political decision making as private citizens and public bodies undermines a widely held belief that it is not the state's role to line the pockets of commerce, but that government is by the people and for the people. Yet the simple linguistic shift from citizens to stakeholders changes the very nature of the democratic balance of power.

Stakeholders have since gone out of fashion in government documents, although commercial influence has not. There is clearly a strong belief that government and citizens must work with businesses, rather than act to regulate their excesses. Stakeholder-talk was followed by a discourse of communities, which were rather non-specific quantities. A programme of 'local government reform', referred to as an 'agenda' first established a belief that local government needed to be revived, and that this would be achieved through building trust and engaging local citizens in democratic practice. For example, a white paper on 'community strategies' suggests that 'an espoused objective of community planning is to 'allow local communities… to articulate their aspirations, needs and priorities'.[12] The rather non-specific moralistic emphasis on 'communities' was quite unreflexive early on, yet ministerial statements consistently suggested that 'community' was a morally positive form of sociality which citizens could adopt to mutual benefit. A White Paper on local government in 2001 equated community with the population in a local authority area, seeing councils as 'community leaders' and suggesting that

10 Hutton 1998.

11 DETR 1999.

12 DETR 2000: 6.

'thriving communities and strong democratic leadership go hand in hand'.[13] The White Paper's conception of diversity was that between local authorities, not within them, although it refers back to urban social disorder (i.e. riots) earlier that year as the result of a breakdown in 'community cohesion' related to 'changes in cultural mix'. Such changes in economy, environment and 'social mix'[14] it argued, required, 'positive community relations', 'community cohesion' and 'community leadership'.[15]

At the local level, efforts to improve the participation of citizens in local authority activities had to be organised, and here more prosaic means had to be found. Efforts to broaden the participation of citizens in policy development were often based on drawing up lists of different communities that should be considered and inviting someone as a representative. At a meeting to set up a community-based forum for discussion on planning policy in Sheffield in the early 2000s, for example, council officers had invited a member of the Sheffield and District Afro-Caribbean Community Association, and two men from a Muslim community group. Their presence seemed to stand for all Afro-Caribbean or Muslim residents in the city, whose concerns could be voiced by these representatives. Cross-cutting differences such as gender, age, education, employment, and so on, were thus hidden, as were other, sometimes competing organisations supposedly representing the same sectors of the population. Imagining all black people as belonging to one community homogenises the diverse experiences of citizens who happen to be black, and follows the same logic as nationalism, by imagining a community of fellows who can be represented by an individual. The categories 'black' and 'Muslim' are of quite different orders (one racial, the other religious), yet they were applied to social organisation in a simplistic way.

Conversely, the ideal citizen is a member of, ideally, one community. The individual with an indivisible ethnicity, the unitary citizen, is foreshadowed in much policy literature. It is worth noting also that these communities of citizens were quite ahistorical. If you perhaps have a Caribbean mother and a Scottish father, you would presumably have to choose to which community you belonged for the purposes of being a morally upstanding citizen member of what is often called '*the*' community. Pre-existing alliances, conflicts, or dispersals were barely acknowledged: communities were either already established or – after some hefty campaigning by local activists and community development workers – created as part of 'capacity building'.

The belief that people living and working in renewal areas should have an equal say in what happens to their area has remained important, either as a policy discourse or as a belief among some participants. Many of the community activists I have worked with see this as a central tenet of participative democracy, and still see the inclusion of commercial interests such as a betrayal of public interest. The

13 DTLR 2001: 13.

14 Ibid.

15 Ibid.

principle of some citizen participation has, in fact, been firmly institutionalised through successive policy formulations which have, at least on paper, required the organised representation of local residents in some role in relation to decision-making. Little formal distinction has been made between the categories of local residents and citizens in practice. Although local residents (or whichever grouping is called upon) may present themselves at, say, public meetings, routine managerial meetings and consultations generally require that they be represented through some association, and the most legitimate are those that elect their representatives. This implies immediately a return to representative democratic form, and illustrates one of the significant weaknesses of the participatory democracy principle, that it has no theoretical model for complex populations. It assumes that populations are made up of 'groups', either ethnic, social, residential, interest groups, or other coherent wholes which can be represented through spokespersons. Although this is not always stated explicitly in policy documents, it is an understanding of society which is consistently adopted by local government officers and nowhere more so than in the various planning fields which include urban renewal programmes. Citizens, then, are not undifferentiated, but come in different kinds – different ages, interests, ethnicities, religions, status. They can be talked about, or represented by other citizens so that their relationship to the state can be indirect.

Thinking about the category of citizen in this way seems to have made it more difficult, not less, to detect who the citizen is. If we cannot identify our citizen, how can we discover who the public is, in whose name planning operates? If planning is for the public good, we must at least know who this public is.

Citizen-consumer in the quasi-commercial state?

It might be easier to see things from another perspective, from the ground-up, so to speak, by considering an actual person, and putting the question from the opposite perspective. Which parts of a person is the citizen?

Joan is a volunteer at the Norfolk Park Community Forum. By 2006 she was the only volunteer left, running the Forum's offices, manning the reception, responding to enquiries, replying to consultations, representing the Forum to the local authority, etc. She's been doing this kind of work for a long time, in various forms, more or less ever since she moved to this area in the mid-1960s when the city-council were still building the houses and tower blocks which have now largely been demolished. Joan was featured in a BBC local news film in 1966, talking about her first campaign. She's shown in her 'pinny' hanging out the washing in her garden, explaining how she sent round a petition to ask for an extra row of paving stones in the garden, so she didn't have to get her feet dirty hanging out nappies. That was the start of a lifetime of campaigning, and the inspiration for the tenants' association which she helped found. Nowadays, she always has a story of the dystopian state of the supposed regeneration of the housing estate, which she has long referred to as the *de*generation of the estate.

Today, she's talking about Betty and Norman, long-time residents who are now elderly, and Norman is no longer well. Betty rang Joan to say that the strip-light in her kitchen wasn't working properly. So Joan rang the housing association from whom the couple now rent their house since it was sold by the city council, to ask whose responsibility repairing lighting was. 'It's the tenant's responsibility if it's just the light bulb', they told her, but if there was a problem with the light fitting then they would send an electrical engineer, but if the engineer later found that the problem was just with the bulb, then the couple would be obliged retrospectively to pay back the cost of sending the engineer. Joan leans over her reception desk towards me and says 'I thought, God!, they've got a handyman on the estate! Why can't they just send him round?' The Community Forum's own handyman was away or she would have asked him to call round, but in the end, she called another resident, even though she was recently bereaved, to ask if one of her sons might call in to repair Betty's light, and they were happy to help.

There are various different things going on in this episode. It illustrates the way in which local long-term friendship and family-networks are called on to manage day-to-day problems and, implicitly, the extent of the community bonds which have been created and sustained over 40 years in this large social-housing estate. It also indicates the contrast between the pragmatic within these relationships and the bureaucratic and audit-based forms of organisations involved in the new governmental regimes and structures of housing management. Where Lily's son will call round as a favour, the management organisation will sub-contract an electrician whose each particular deed must be accounted and paid for according to a set of complex rules. Neighbour, in other words, becomes client, and the shift involves a change in the exchange relationship from favour to commercial transaction costed in relation to action. So far, so Modern. That the conversation between Joan and the ALMO representative did not move on to why the handyman could not attend to the light also tells us something about the ways in which knowledge is privileged and sometimes is not used. Joan knew, but she did not say what she knew. She kept this knowledge to share with others (such as myself) based, no doubt, on previous experience and an unwillingness to provoke an argument.

On the other hand, the assumption that an external agent will attend to household repairs also illustrates much about the relationship between tenant and landlord which 'stood for' the relationship between state and citizen when the landlord was the local authority. Like many landlords, it was not a single person, but a bureaucratic organisation whose representatives included the staff at the local housing office, as well as the City Council housing office and local councillors But it was also personified through the chief housing officer and the local elected representatives.

Nowadays, governing roles or roles known as 'service provision' formerly held by the state or its agencies have been taken over by private, semi-private or semi-public organisations. In this complex web of organisations and agencies, individuals may move frequently between different organisations, and roles and relations may become multifaceted rather than cleanly cut and spliced into new formal coordinates. Joan, for instance, can run down the career trajectories of many of the people involved in the regeneration process who she has known for 10 or 20 years or more, yet she is quite clear over who among them is worth working with and who is better avoided, whatever their current position. She also interprets their actions and speech through the lens of these personal relationships, as instances of long-running feuds or career ambitions, and so forth. With little other logical explanation for apparently non-rational decisions and practices, these personal explanations serve to make sense of difficult conditions and the failure of what otherwise looked like promising projects. The citizen, in this account, is the ordinary resident struggling to maintain their home and community in the face of commercial and governmental forces which seem set on achieving the opposite. But this citizen is not an isolated individual in direct relationship to a capable state. On the contrary, a citizen is enmeshed in multifaceted relations, and rather than being an abstract ideal with a singular relationship to the state, a citizen is a person with relationships to persons in organisations which have partly adopted what once were state roles, both political, commercial, and occasionally extending into more emotionally laden realms of 'caring'.

Citizenship as a relation?

So far we have seen that a citizen is someone who holds an array of relationships, and we think of them as a citizen when we are thinking about their relationship with the state and its services. How does the way we think about the citizen colour our dealings with people and organisations? Thinking in terms of citizens covers different sorts of ideas.

Marshall argued that there were three parts to citizenship: civil, political and social, which emerged in that order.[16] Civil citizenship encompassed rights to individual freedom, liberty of the person, freedom of speech, thought, faith, the right to own property, to conclude valid contracts and the right to justice, rights that we would now recognise as civil rights or even human rights. Political citizenship includes the right to participate in the exercise of political power as a member or elector of a body invested with political power, or what is known as suffrage. Social citizenship, on the other hand, includes the right to a degree of economic welfare and security, the right to live the life of a civilized being according to prevailing standards. Such social rights entailed access to education and social services. These rights of citizenship emerged in contrast to the lack of any uniform collection of rights and duties under feudal society, for example, where serfs lived under very different conditions to landowners, and with very different opportunities to change their circumstances. The three strands of citizenship developed gradually and at different rates. Whereas in the Middle Ages participation in politics was felt to

16 Marshall 1950 (based on lectures delivered in 1922).

be part of the duty of the ruling classes, as the institutions of government became increasingly nationalised, access to government began to be claimed as a right. Similarly, in the early nineteenth century, the Poor Law treated the claims of the poor as an alternative to the rights of the citizen, so that the poor had to give up their freedom in return for welfare, by being incarcerated in workhouses. The abolition of the poor law in 1918 effectively secured the social rights of citizens independent of their economic circumstances.

Marshall offers a general definition of citizenship as 'a status bestowed on those who are full members of a community. All who possess the status are equal with respect to the rights and duties with which the status is endowed'.[17] Yet this general definition also has some consequences. In Schnapper's view, the very idea of the citizen is an atomising one, presuming that a population is equally divisible into single persons with equivalent rights. Schnapper argues that societies based on the values and institutions of citizenship can only work if there is a legitimate higher authority that is above the internal divisions among the people. This public sphere, she imagines, 'transcends everyday society, its historical and religious diversities, its divisions and its inequalities'.[18] But such a state reverses the actual social world, which is full of diversity and inequalities. Schnapper suggests that a state that strives to behave in direct contradiction to normal social relations can only ever be fragile, but Iris Marion Young argues straight out that an impersonal, impartial view is, in fact, an impossibility.[19] One could also call it a utopia.[20]

Yet this utopia is grounded through institutions designed to sustain the conditions under which citizenship can be performed. Universal education aims to create the educated electorate that a political democracy requires; universal welfare enables people to share the life of a civilised society. For Marshall, these provisions were not to be understood as singular benefits to individuals, since the social health of a society depends on what he called the 'civilisation' of its members.[21] By the late 1980s, Ruth Lister identified a risk of increasing numbers of people being excluded by poverty from the enjoyment of their rights as citizens.[22] She also recognised a revival of the link between economy and social rights in the spirit of the Poor Law. Right wing politicians from the USA were pushing for a work obligation as a counterpart to social rights to welfare under a rhetoric of active citizenship. The active citizen began to emerge in the model we saw above, not only earning their own keep, but giving to charity and doing voluntary work. Talk of citizen's rights was becoming restricted to those of the consumer

17 Ibid.: 18.

18 Schnapper 2002: 3.

19 Young 1990: 103.

20 Schnapper, 2002: 4, argues that this is why political institutions are so important, since, by being predominantly national, they provide an abstract principle of legitimacy which allows individuals to live together.

21 Op. Cit.: 16.

22 Lister 1990.

in a marketplace. The problem for Lister was that this idea of the active citizen obscures and reinforces inequalities of power, resources and status, since it denies that citizen participation is limited by other social determinants such as health, gender, race, or disability. Only with social and economic rights can citizens exert their political rights. Or, in other words, simply put, you cannot access justice if you cannot afford to pay a lawyer, and you cannot get to a polling station if you are not mobile. In this sense, a distinction is commonly made between being a citizen and acting as a citizen, between status and practice.

But citizenship is also commonly used to refer to a broader range of concepts, such as to legitimate belonging in a nation-state, or to membership of a corporate body governed by a particular state organisation. Such definitions rely on sets of abstracted categorical definitions of cohorts of persons into theoretical groups, such as all those with rights to make claims on a particular state, who otherwise may share little in terms of interest, identities or intentions. The great contradiction in the standardisation of citizenship is the suggestion that all citizens have equal status in relation to the state, society and the law, yet citizens are subject to social class, a system of inequality that was not diminished by the growth of capitalism. Economic inequality affects the quality of citizenship for different citizens. Access to education and justice, for example, are crucial factors for who can most fully enact their citizenship. So, the principles of citizenship urge us to imagine all people as separate, self-willed, and un-entangled in their relations to the state. Such a model does not recognise either the difference between people or the relationships between them. It is used to imagine a world where all citizens are autonomous whole individuals, and rather ignores the way that people are already actually associated. The notion of citizenship has the effect of setting up an opposition between citizen and state (or sometimes a three-way one including non-state organisations), as the UK governmental version does. So the term 'citizen' has different registers of meaning that it is important to recognise. We should not unquestioningly adopt the version given out by government, for example, which would restrict our analytical horizons and our abilities to understand the everyday encounters through which citizenship is played out. Even if we understand the citizen as having this direct relationship with the state, parts of the state are simultaneously trying to suggest how citizens might also have relationships to each other. 'Together we can' imagines citizens as those socially-inclined persons who also work together for the public good, who care about people other than their immediate family. These citizens join community groups, attend neighbourhood meetings, participate in government consultations and 'area panel' meetings to discuss local policy. Still, they should do this in a certain way, through co-operation with the state, putting the public interest above their own interest (as politicians are supposed to do), and in groups that are not political, single-issue or exclusive, although ethnic groups are encouraged to find spokespersons to speak for them as though they were corporate bodies.

Categories into which people are ordered form a central axis of language and social organisation, as they illuminate the subtleties of social relations, and they also demonstrate the very different ways in which people think about the world. Anthropologists have long recognised the importance of categories, and one of the ways they have investigated them is through the study of kinship – the ways that people are thought to be related. We might take for granted that a family has parents, children and grandparents, but we also know that a lot of families have step-parents, step-children, uncles, aunts, great uncles and aunts, and so on. What struck British anthropologists early in the 20th century was how the relatives people have in other parts of the world did not fit into this model. Looking at the language of being related in other places showed that not all languages have terms that correspond in the same way to different relations. Even within Europe there are different terms. In Scandinavian languages, for example, there are different terms for maternal and paternal grandparents, and rather than one term for cousins differentiated as first, second or third, there are separate terms for different kinds of cousins. In fact, the way we categorise our relatives varies quite dramatically. Even terms that we think of as quite basic, such as 'mother' and 'father' are not universal. In some societies the word used for a mother is the same word used for all a mother's sisters, for example, so mother and mother's sisters are all one category of relations. And when I was growing up, I was taught to refer to all my mother's friends as 'auntie' and 'uncle'. Such different terminologies force us to rethink the 'naturalness' of the categories we use ourselves.

One controversy in kinship-studies has been the accusation that too many anthropologists used Western family biology theory as the basic model to define other forms of kinship, when they have described family models that include non-biological relations as 'fictive' kin.[23] To define systems that include what we think of as non-blood relatives as less real than our own is to misunderstand the point of comparing kinship systems, which is that kinship is actually a way of defining social relations, not a natural system of identifying genetics. Having terms for our relatives actually defines those relations, it does not simply reflect them. Although we might think that we define our family based on biological relations (or genetic connections), all our genealogies miss some relatives off. The way we draw our family trees actually makes this inevitable, since at each generation we have to choose which side of the family to trace. It is not unusual for people to discover 'long lost' relatives, who they hadn't known existed before. Even drawing a family tree demonstrates that we categorise the relations that we consider the most natural of all. These categorisations are not limited just to family, though. We are constantly categorising people – family, friends, colleagues, team-mates, acquaintances, celebrities, politicians, public servants, and so on – and these categories actually reveal the principles by which we organise and imagine social life. If we want to understand these, we have to try not to take for granted categories that are presented to us, but interrogate them to see what they tell us about the relations they describe.

23 Schneider 1984.

Categories used by governing organisations like states or local authorities (or health services, or housing associations, etc.) also offer insight into the concepts of social organisation that form the basis for governing – in the broadest sense of trying to organise the bodies, practices and places of others. Some categories disappear into the background through everyday familiarity and others disappear through non-usage, while new ones are always being invented. Some may be unuttered yet profoundly significant. Citizenship is a term which occupies all of these positions, being central to policy discourse on immigration and in education, where 'citizenship' has itself become a subject of study. In the encounter between officials and elected representatives in local government and their constituents, the roles which people living in the city take on and which are allocated to them may not be discussed under the rubric of citizenship, but they are implicitly defined by and define the nature of contemporary democracy.

So far we have recognised citizenship as a kind of status – 'do you have citizenship' – which tends to push us into considering only the juridical kind of citizenship (or nationality), or as specific practices – such as casting a vote or making public speeches – which envisages political rights as individual. But we need to add the idea of citizenship founded in relations between people and categories. If citizenship is merely the relationship of an individual to the state, then how can we understand the practice of citizens who are always and already in relationships with each other? In order to enact any of our rights or duties as citizens, we have to act together with other people, whether that is through political parties, working with lawyers through the courts, dealing with administrators to get access to welfare, or navigating the complex arrangements of political and administrative processes that is the planning system. In other words, our citizenship relies on relations that are performed in the encounters between persons in different relations to authority. Thinking of citizenship as a series of relationships, it is possible to relate the abstract concept to mundane and often inchoate or incomplete practices of states. After all, Sharma and Gupta[24] remind us that the state itself is a cultural construction whose meanings are produced through cultural struggles in the sphere of both representation and everyday practices of state agencies, and, we might add, citizens. As Philip Abrams argued in 1977, 'the state' isn't something that is there, it is a model of the world to which we lend a kind of concreteness by talking about it and identifying people with it. The state is actually a rather abstract concept that we conjecture from a set of effects that we infer, or imaginatively trace back to some apparently concrete whole. Of course, it is a very effective model, and since we share some ideas of what the model is, and because we identify it with certain concrete things and people – parliament, Whitehall, the benefits agency, the education authority, or the planning office – we think of it as a real thing. In the same way, because we can point to people and call them citizens, we think that a citizen is a person. But what I have argued above is that citizens and states only exist in relation to each other, and that we can think

24 Sharma and Gupta 2006: 11.

of them as sets of relations themselves. We can also think of these relations being performed, as well as citizenship status being performed, since we know someone is a citizen only when they do something involving their relationship to the state (paying taxes, voting, or applying for and receiving, or not receiving, a passport). That is to say, that these relationships are not just there, but have to be done,[25] so we can think of citizenship as something we do by enacting selected relationships on relevant occasions. Citizens are not simply people out there, but being a citizen is something we do through relationships with others, relationships that can also be materialised through things (such as money paid in taxes to be distributed to other people and back to us), through actions (such as voting as members of the electorate, turning up to political meetings to debate issues with other people), and through social interaction, as well as through our family relationships. Because each of these areas is complex, the way we do our citizenship relationships is also very many and varied, and changes according to time and occasion, and throughout our lives as our experiences change.

Nowadays models of citizenship are complicated by the fragmentation of both state and market. This is most clear in public housing, where not only do British local authorities no longer act as actual landlords to tenants, but public housing is managed through a range of semi-public or private quasi-market organisations. The relationship between state and citizen is mediated by more and more intervening relationships. Yet government policy addressing the construction of good citizens flows fast and free, both in individual European states and in the European Union.

Back to the particular: Rebuilding Norfolk Park

Citizenship is only one of many different kinds of relations that are called on in planning activities. One can think of Urban Regeneration as a long performance of complex relations both institutional and personal. Regeneration managers need to try to ensure that investors build confidence in the project and make, or continue to make, investments in the regeneration. Developers need to work with construction companies to build when the market is right, while making regeneration managers believe that they really do want regeneration for its own sake, even though they are dependent on market conditions. And tenants try to keep their home lives or their businesses going in uncertain times, trying to create trust between themselves and their landlords, or to get information out of official actors such as elected representatives or local authority officers. Urban regeneration can equally be considered an instance of more generalised governmental principles and actions, such as ideas that the state will act in the public interest, that politicians take some responsibility for the housing conditions of the population and try to improve the living and working conditions of those worst off. At the same time, as representatives of the state, politicians can be shamed by the dereliction and

25 The political philosophy of performativity is outlined by Barad 2003.

breakdown of areas of major cities, and can see the benefit of creating wealth and gathering greater taxes. Either way, the delegation of public housing to 'arms length management organisations', of housing maintenance and construction to private development companies, and the redefinition of public stakeholders to include commercial organisations illustrates the increasingly muddied water between what appear to be simple categories of public and private, state and market, or state and civil society, dichotomies which are now very difficult to map onto the messy world of material change and fragmented institutionalisation. Whereas ownership of the housing rented by residents in Norfolk Park, for example, was held by the corporate legal body of the City Council (and its predecessors with changing institutional structures), and delegated to the authority of officers employed by that City Council, it is now organised through externalised contracts through the offices of several other organisations, including the ALMO, housing associations, and the other commercial organisations to whom they sub-contract.

Transferring state operations such as housing management actually transforms the nature of citizenship. Tenants are now treated as clients of the ALMO and they stand in a customer-provider relationship, and although this does imply a potentially less paternalistic relationship, tenants have no choice to change to another provider. They cannot purchase these services elsewhere, so the customer-provider relationship is one of monopoly, yet without the routes of democratic accountability in place that once offered them some – at least potential – access to senior management. Joan recollects the early days of the Tenants' Association, when they were able to call the City's Director of Housing and arrange a meeting, where they could put their questions and demands face to face, and get an immediate reply, with assurances, from the Director. Nowadays, it is no longer the Director of Housing who is responsible, local regeneration managers say that housing allocation is organised by the housing associations or the ALMO, and site management of particular development areas is sub-contracted via private developers. In comparison with the development practices of the 1960s, current chains of command and accountability can only be described as opaque. Whereas they previously held a contract with the City Council, tenants are now pseudo-customers in a quasi-commercial state.

Similarly, the associations that tenants and residents have of their own have also diversified. The TARA still exists to represent them in relation to now various landlords. The Community Forum was created and officially recognised as the agency of community representation in the regeneration programme. The Forum was supposed to set up community companies and provide employment training and information. It was to be funded through the ground rents from the new housing that would be built on the estate, and through a one-off grant of £50,000. Since the construction of housing on the estate was delayed by around four years, clearly the ground rents did not appear. The Forum, having been a lively organisation providing a range of courses and services, dwindled to encompass a volunteer and a financial officer. Over the years, two community companies were set up, a catering company and a maintenance company, but only £17,000 of the promised grant money was handed over to the Forum. Joan explains that 'they' (ie the regeneration team of the City Council) say the Forum hasn't put forward a business plan, yet business plans have been produced in order to set up the community company. The Forum have struggled to put together a business plan without knowing what the Council's spending plan for the estate was, so they were left in a stalemate. Joan explained that the companies were set up with business plans, but the Forum can't write a business plan without knowing when the ground rents will start to come through. It became less clear what the different remits of the TARA and the Forum might be, and, in some instances, they seem to be played off against each other.

It is Joan's clear perception that she is not seen as an active citizen devoting her time to community service, but as a trouble-maker. 'That's the trouble', she says 'it's never what you say, it's "oh it's them"'. A senior member of the Council's regeneration division has said more or less this to Joan, saying 'you're always objecting', and Joan replies that it's her job to respond on behalf of residents, and 'I'll carry on doing so until you do something about it'. Colleagues of Joan have also told me that important meetings have been held where only the amenable members of the TARA have been invited, to avoid any difficult questions being asked. By 2006 the future of the Forum was looking very doubtful, and despite transforming itself into a Development Trust, the Forum finally closed down shortly after.[26]

Citizens and people

Even before the Skeffington report of 1969, planners and politicians worried about how to involve members of the public in plan-making and planning decisions. As we have seen already, one of the justifying pillars of a planning system is that it should be in the public interest, but the questions of who this public is, and what is good for it, are not so easily answerable as we might first imagine. In searching for who might be a member of the public and who might reasonably be involved in planning, we often find ourselves thinking about citizens, those ideal members of the political community who attract the protection of the state and owe to it their loyalty. Rather than looking for culture in the inclusion or exclusion of foreigners from citizenship where it has been most commonly sought, we can actually find out more about planning ideas and our cultural assumptions if we look directly at who we think is a member of the public.

If the citizens are the public, the embodiment of the public good, then we ought to know a little more about who we think they are. By looking at things from the point of view of people we expect to be citizens, we see reflections that tell us more about our own ideas about the relationship between states and people. What kind of an image of the citizen do we use, and how does this affect how we act towards

26 Due also to management problems – but this is another story.

them and between ourselves? If the citizen is a body that represents some kind of ideal person, then it is a category of person, and like any other category into which we put people, it needs to be explored if we are to understand it properly. What do we expect of citizens and who do we think they might be?

We have seen that the ambition to involve people in policy and plans is organised so that it constructs the idealised citizen, yet that this ideal citizen corresponds poorly to actual living people. They are not isolated individuals who stand in equal relationship to the state, but are actual people steeped in other kinds of relationship that affect their interactions with state agencies or agents very profoundly. In practice, citizenship describes a set of relationships rather than defining a set of people. If the idea of a citizen corresponds so poorly to the lives of actual people, then we are left with the problem of why it is so popular in policy. While local policy-makers might be pragmatic or cynical about their encounters with actual 'participants', the policy remains ever blue-eyed about the potential for citizen engagement, or what we might call the creation of engaged citizens. It might be seen as a kind of internal colonisation, one that aims to transform an unruly population into a cohort of ordered citizens.[27] Even if that colonisation happens within the state, and not as the product of imperial expansion, it is no less colonial as a process, through the creation of a new category of person, that well-behaved citizen.[28] From this perspective, the idea of the participating citizen could be seen as an attempt to domesticate resistance. Rather than have angry mobs hammering on the doors of the town hall, we prefer to have citizens who voice their concerns through a structured participation process. The process is double-edged, since theoretically it both offers people a recognised route to influencing policy, and uses that process to delegitimise other forms of protest. We should bear in mind here that resistance to participative policy can also take the form of apathy. People do choose to be apathetic, to not participate, so apathy can be understood as a kind of political strategy, rather than ignorance, and it might reflect a deep-seated mistrust of the value of action.

There is an irony here, in that participative practices have been brought into the mainstream from their origins in resistance to the imposition of overseas development dependency. As it has been incorporated into Western government practice, it has been seen as a way of increasing accountability for policy, and as a way of undermining welfare-dependency by pushing people to take responsibility for difficult political decisions. In the process, the idea of participation has created a new kind of relationship that defines a good citizen. Despite the flaws in the practice of participatory policy-making and despite the lack of a proper theoretical model of how it fits into representative democracy, the political rhetoric of participation has been extremely resilient. It has replaced the notion of 'public good' as a virtue in its own right. Even though citizen-relations are increasingly

27 Selznick 1949, Robertson 1984.

28 In a parallel to the production of what Foucault called 'docile bodies' (cf Chapter 6): Foucault 1979.

complex and harder for (former) council tenants to manage, these very people are constantly being implored to be part of their own development, to engage with development plans and companies, to be glad to do it, and to be happy with its results, even where those might include the demolition of their own homes.[29]

Seeing citizenship as a set of relations, rather than a self-evident role, means that we can recognise it as a specific cultural practice of politics and policy. Looking at the idea of the citizen from different sides shows how the concept is used in quite different ways. From the perspective of the state looking at the people, the citizen is a category that is good to think with. From the citizen's point of view, citizenship includes a set of relations which make the category of citizen seem rather ill-fitting, since we are only citizens in relationship to something particular, rather than thinking of ourselves as citizens the whole time. Seeing the category itself from different sides shows that it contains a number of contradictions. It might enable us to see that talk about citizen engagement lives a life of its own, often separate from the way that our fellow citizens live their own lives. The citizen can only ever be part of a person's life, in other words, because none of us live unconnected, independent and unencumbered, with the time to engage in myriad local government procedures like the ideal citizen. We have duties and obligations to others, we have relationships of care, sympathy, obligation and duty that over-ride our role as consumers, service-users, or participants. Thinking about citizen-relations from the point of view of the subjects, rather than the governors who desire well-behaved citizens, can reveal cultures of citizenship and give us much food for thought.

And as I pointed out above, rather than thinking of the citizen as a person with rights and habits, we might usefully think about citizenship as something we do. The citizen is also something that people conjure up when trying to evoke the state as though it were a concrete thing, even though we know that it is an idea that seems real because we act as though it were. Of course, in extreme situations the state seems very real – when the police or army use violence to control people in the name of the state, it suddenly seems very real indeed. When council workers are digging in the street outside our door, or when we see the council's emblems on information about schools or social services, again it feels like a solid something. But the state is only concrete through its effects – the school buildings (although these can be privatised), policemen on the beat, the building inspector visiting a building site, the park ranger teaching people how to plant hedges. And in the same way, we can perform the citizen by enacting our citizenship with the help of others, through casting our vote, using our passport, or demanding services or benefits. And increasingly, through joining local action groups or attending planning consultation events, whether or not our participation changes the decisions that are made.

Remembering that the citizen and the person – the ideal political subject and the related, divided and multiple person – are not identical helps to explain why

29 A point that Damer and Hague made already in 1971: 226.

policies on citizenship rarely achieve what we hope from them. Because the ideal citizen is not a real person, our calls for participation fail to attract the anonymous cipher we imagine but brings us people with histories, existing relationships, entrenched views and partialities who rarely fulfil the roles laid out for them in planning policies. The myriad personal ways that people are related are usually categorised separately from their citizenship, so that people's family or faith relationships are classified in planning as 'culture' and deemed of secondary importance, or even outside the reach of planning altogether. If we see them, instead, as the effects of the way we categorise, then all relations can be opened up to examination, including those implicit in the idea of a 'public', an idea that emerged historically and developed differently in particular contexts.[30] Citizenship can be seen as one dimension of these relationships, one that can sometimes be difficult to reconcile with others. This is partly because people who exercise their citizenship also have bodies, a factor often missed in literature about citizens, but which we have considered in Chapter 4. In the next chapter, the citizen emerges in a different light, as part of the public, another concept that deserves to be considered in detail.

30 Warner 2003, 1990.

Chapter 6
The Public and Time

> What the majority of people consider to be 'reasonable' is that about which there is agreement, if not among all, at least among a substantial number of people; 'reasonable' for most people, has nothing to do with reason, but with consensus. [Erich Fromm: *The Heart of Man*]

Imagining the public

This chapter looks at how the public is imagined in planning. It shows how 'the public' is less a term to denote a set of people than an idea used to organise planning processes. Using the familiar concept of the public, we operate in ways that have consequences for the people we want to plan for. Questioning our concepts of the public also raises questions about time, and this chapter goes on to raise questions about the kinds of time that are used in planning.

I started to consider, in Chapter 5, why interactions between planners and citizens often fail to work out in the way we imagine, by showing how the citizen is an ideal category that maps only awkwardly onto actual people. We lead complicated, often messy, lives and usually fail to fit into the normal categories that are used to organise people. This chapter looks again at why public consultations and participative politics often fall short of our hopes, but this time the focus is on the public and I ask who the public is and why it seems to cause so many problems.

Anyone who has worked in planning practice can recognise these questions: Why do so few people turn up to routine public consultations? Why is it always the same people who come to public meetings? Why do so many people act like NIMBYs (Not In My Back Yard) rather than being public-spirited or open-minded? Why do people find it so difficult to think strategically about life in 20 years time? If we are to do something about these questions, we need to do more than berate members of the public for being apathetic. Instead, we can interrogate our expectations.

A disappointing public

We've all been there – one of those dreary or infuriating public meetings where the planners want to talk about the future of housing or transport, and local residents want to complain about dog mess in the street or broken street lights. If you haven't been there, then you have either been to very few public meetings or you have been extremely lucky. I've certainly been to all kinds of public meetings over the years. There was a public consultation 'surgery' about the district forward plan one snowy January morning in Aylesbury Vale in 1997, where three planners chatted to me over a very leisurely cup of tea while waiting for a total of about a dozen people who wandered in over the space of three hours. Or the public consultation over the new retail site for Norfolk Park in Sheffield in the mid 2000s, where a list of 20 visitors to the community centre over the course of an evening included 6 students from my own research methods course at the university doing a coursework 'task'.

On the other hand, there are those meetings that planners dread, where a furious community hall overflows with residents angry about a planned new housing estate, waste site, factory, supermarket, wall, or whatever new development has roused people's ire. A series of public meetings were held in Haddenham, in Buckinghamshire in 1995 about proposals to build a spice factory, where hundreds of residents turned up to hear arguments for and against, in increasingly angry exchanges between householders, planners, politicians and company representatives.[1] Generally speaking, planners in Aylesbury Vale, reasonably enough, preferred not to hold public meetings where there was a risk of things turning hostile or where they might get shouted at. On the one hand, they were very keen to engage members of the public with their visions for future new housing areas, and they wanted people to be sympathetic to their ambitions and to understand that they wanted what was best for everyone: to provide housing for people who needed it. On the other hand, they suffered the frustration of being attacked for decisions made by politicians who seemed less inclined to turn up and defend their priorities. In their conversations with me, they described feeling themselves caught in the middle, between their professional aim of facilitating development in the interests of housing and employment for future generations, while being blamed for intruding on the comfortable lives of the better off residents, who liked things just the way they were, thank you very much. Why should the planners have to be attacked by angry residents for implementing planning decisions made by others?

There have been various diagnoses made for these dilemmas. Perhaps the plans don't represent people's interests, or maybe they have been decided by the wrong people, or presented badly. Complaints are made that plans have sometimes been imposed on people who don't want them, and the remedy offered is for a more collaborative approach to be taken in preparing those plans. On the other hand, some politicians – and some planners – have told me that in the 'real world' you can't please all of the people all of the time, and you can always expect that some people won't like plans, so you must weather the attacks in the interests of the good of a broader general public, especially the public of the future rather than just

1 See Abram 2004b.

the people who shout now. Or sometimes politicians argue that most people only have their own interests in mind, and only politicians have the broad overview of the whole range of competing interests to enable them to take decisions for the good of the whole public rather than just one sector. After all, in a democracy you have to accept things that don't suit you in the interests of tolerance for other people. There are also commentators who argue that planners need to learn to communicate with the public better so that people understand why they propose particular compromises over others.

But perhaps the problem is not that the public don't appreciate what planners do, but that the public is a figment of the planners' imagination. A radical thought, perhaps, but it is often the most common concepts that channel us into narrow ways of thinking, and that we most need to think through again. Unless we challenge common terms, we risk failing again and again to locate the source of problems and always attack on the wrong front.

Lauderdale cautioned in 1819 against received understandings, chiding his readers against unreflected use of common terms:

> ...when we find a phrase in general use, we are apt to regard it as conveying the common testimony of mankind in favour of that species of reasoning which at first sight appears to have suggested it; and adopt, from a supposed idea of authority, opinions, which a little examination would make us reject. By such carelessness, men often become habituated to the common use of phrases and expressions, without having even called in question their propriety; and these, forming the basis of further reasoning, give birth to ideas founded on a series of misconceptions, and consequently to new phrases and turns of expression that tend to perpetuate fallacies. It is by these means that language has, in all sciences, been often found a most powerful supporter of prejudice, and a most active promoter of error.[2]

Lauderdale was elegantly expressing the tendency to take for granted received ideas rather than asking what they actually mean. Is 'the public' just such a linguistic expression that we have used too carelessly? It is certainly not a concept that has escaped the attention of planners, and the question of 'public good' is closely considered. Less attention is perhaps paid to the rhetorical use of 'the public', not only as a political tool, but as a bureaucratic motif. In tracing what we know about the public, through familiar and less familiar routes, this chapter sheds light on some of the most persistent problems in planning practice.

2 Lauderdale1819: 2–3.

Talking about the public

If the public is a concept rather than a living thing, then it is a concept that we know because we talk about it a lot, and we act on the basis that it exists. But talk is neither simple nor transparent, and there is always more going on in any discussion than just the content of the words might suggest. In political and academic debates, just as in business-talk or newspaper headlines, talking is also a jostling for position, the basis for creating and maintaining relationships and discovering what we think. Over time, some terms become established and then are generally accepted as 'true', as common sense – that is, a sense that is common to most people.[3]

Sometimes statements that very closely represent the world are accepted as obvious truths, ideas that people think are true whoever states them, but this condition can just as easily be the outcome of prior labour than a particularly close tie to reality, as Susan Gal and Kathryn Woolard[4] argue. Popular opinions are not necessarily supported by evidence, but can be used rhetorically to persuade people to support particular arguments. Politicians know that if you state something often enough, it will begin to gain traction, and people will start to talk about it. US Tea Party activists know that if they keep telling people that they will go back to the real America, they will gain popularity. That there is and never has been such a 'real America', and that we can never go back into the past are facts that need trouble them little. The phrases and slogans conjure up something that their followers desire and it motivates them into action. The rise of extreme right wing politics across Europe relies on large numbers of people accepting the idea that foreigners are dangerous and take 'our' money, yet all research shows that immigrants generally boost local economies and generate more tax income all round. Yet many people choose to believe the former, and the idea gains the status of a truth among them.

Erich Fromm seems to have meant something similar when he remarked that ideas thought of as reasonable are usually judged more by how many people agree with them rather than by having been arrived at through the application of reason.[5] In just this way, if someone can appear to talk on behalf of the public, they may seem to have the majority with them, and this lends credibility to their speech. How we claim that we speak for the public is very much at the heart of politics, and one of the most persuasive strategies of the last century has been to use statistics as a proxy for speaking for the majority. If the majority of the population are known to live in houses, then speaking on behalf of those who live in houses sounds like a credible interest. If we can talk about living in houses as though our truths emerge from the house-living itself, rather than our opinions about houses, then we have

3 See Geertz 1983 for a discussion of what is common to whom about common sense.

4 Gal and Woolard 2001.

5 Fromm 1965.

dominated any future discussion about houses by privileging one set of views as more 'objective' than others. In the past, we would hear politicians speaking on behalf of the working classes, for example, who could be assumed to share an interest in maximising their wages or needing better housing, whereas now we are told about 'hard working families' (which, although it infers that there are families who aren't hard working, is rarely used to attack the upper classes). Who would argue against the right of 'hard working families' to live a decent life? Similarly Conservative politicians urge people to 'do the right thing', without explaining what constitutes 'right', yet it would hardly be sensible to argue for people to do the wrong thing. A moral rhetoric of rightness and goodness remains sufficiently open for all sorts of things to be thrown in when they are convenient. When a political party – or anyone else – has succeeded in getting their view accepted as the obvious one, then they are in a position of strength.

Clearly, 'the public' is politicians' favourite rhetorical flourish, but it is so widely used – by theorists, commentators, advertisers and journalists – that we utterly take it for granted and fall straight into Lauderdale's trap. 'The public' is more than a rhetorical device, though, since the idea of the public is a key political tool of statecraft, and without it we would struggle to imagine the nation at all. As noted in Chapter 1, it is our belief in a nation of people with shared concerns that lends legitimacy to the state in the first place. The central model of legitimate countries since at least the 20th century is the nation-state, where it is the people of a nation who elect a state to govern them. The centrality of the link between people and state can explain why so many people struggle with the concept of the multicultural society. If a state is the legitimate organisation that governs all of us who belong to the nation, then legitimising a state that governs over multiple nations is a slightly more complex task. Hence the extraordinary lengths that the United States government goes to to inculcate citizens with a sense of an American nation – saluting the flag and singing the national anthem in schools, flying US flags on public buildings and elsewhere, so that people demonstrate their Americanness on a daily basis, no matter where in the world they might have been born.[6] The point is that everything to do with the contemporary state is based on the idea that there is a body of people out there with something in common, as I have explained. The concepts of the nation, 'the people' and the public are closely related. We know already that the nation is a fairly ambitious imaginative concept, and its history is well documented, so we need now to ask where the idea of a public comes from.

How has the idea that there is a body of people who we can call 'the public' established itself as the obvious truth? The very word, 'public', might be antique, but its usage has changed. Derived from the Latin *publicus,* it is related to people, and to publication (making public). It appears to have replaced the term 'folk' to

6 Hence the USA can have a president whose father was not a US citizen, although conspiracy theories that circulated in 2009 that President Obama was born outside the US show that becoming American might not be so straightforward after all.

refer to *the* people, or the community as a whole, in the 15th century[7] to distinguish said common people from the nobility. An early English usage referring to the public house was recorded in the 1650s.[8] But the idea of the public as the popular citizenry served by the state seems to have emerged later. Terms to describe general populations only make sense once a general population is there to be imagined, of course. In medieval Britain, the largest number of people were peasants or serfs, not members of a public. The idea of all classes of people forming one society emerged only as a post-revolutionary term.[9] So, although the idea of a difference between public and private, and between the people and the nobility has a longer history, the idea that all the people living in the country constitute the public seems to be somewhat more recent.

According to the German philosopher, Jürgen Habermas,[10] the public (or more precisely the 'public sphere') is a product of bourgeois society that emerged in Western Europe in the 17th and 18th centuries. With the rise of printed news circulation, urban society, growing long-distance travel and a sector of society with leisure to pass in discussions in coffee shops, a public sphere emerged as a challenge to the established royal courts. Such institutions and everyday practices created a legitimate space for opinions to be shared in larger social groups, so that city dwellers could believe that there was a recognisable shared public opinion that could be identified. Various critics have pointed out that Habermas's view of the early public sphere is somewhat romanticised in order to criticise what he saw as the debasement of the public sphere in the 20th century. Feminist critics,[11] for example, have pointed out that the public spheres of 18th century Europe actually excluded large sections of the population – such as women and working people. Bourgeois men were able to participate in public society because of the segregation of men's and women's responsibilities, for example, and even since the 17th century, one could argue that there have been multiple publics: proletarian, regional, religious, and so forth.

Having identified the public as an idea with a history, and not simply a universal human concept, we can look again at how the term is used in planning. The idea of ordinary people was opened up in Chapter 5 in relation to citizenship; if our ideal public is a host of citizens, and we have recast the ideal of the citizen, then we need to do some more work on the public to make a new kind of sense out of this. One way to make this new sense is to look at how our belief in a public is acted out in our everyday lives. Why do we think there is a public, and how do we act on this knowledge? We can ask this both of ourselves in our everyday lives and

7 See "public" in Hoad 1996: <http://www.oxfordreference.com/views/ENTRY.html?subview=Main&entry=t27.e12085>

8 See "public" in Cressell 2010: <http://www.oxfordreference.com/views/ENTRY.html?subview=Main&entry=t292.e3964>

9 See Wittrock 2000 for a discussion of Manent 1994 and Heilbron 1995.

10 Habermas 1989.

11 Particularly Young 1990.

of planners in their professional lives. How does the idea – or ideal – of a public survive?

Whether or not Habermas has his historical facts in order, students of his work have noted that the idea of a public has worked to legitimate political action, but furthermore that this public gets its authority from being anonymous. It is because the public is no-one-in-particular that it can represent everyone, and Gal and Woolard argue that this is in direct contrast to the personified interests of absolute monarchs. The argument also works in relation to any private or particular interest. We make grand claims about a class of people that we would be hard pressed to attach to any one individual. For example, recent scandals about city bonuses show how categories can work in this way. City brokers, bankers and analysts who receive large cash bonuses out of all proportion to their labour are accused of being 'fat cats'. Individual brokers[12] and business executives are identified by the media as being in receipt of absurd remunerations (preferably, from the journalists' point of view, while simultaneously demanding wage restraint from state employees). Individual businessmen who are known to have taken very large bonuses are talked about as though they exemplify the whole group. They are then seen in opposition to people on an average wage, who exemplify the 'ordinary public'. How many people in the banking sector receive million-pound bonuses, or whether other people see bonuses as a normal and routine means of incentivising workers becomes irrelevant once an archetype has been established of the 'greedy banker'. If, the next day, we meet a banker who seems to be a perfectly considerate person with concerns about the environment and the welfare of workers, we are confused. We are in danger of saying 'I hate bankers – not you, of course, you're different'. We are caught in perspective games, like the images of Giuseppe Arcimboldo of arrangements of fruit and vegetables that can be seen as a face or a body depending on your depth of focus. What in one perspective looks like a single image (a face, a person), on closer inspection is made up of a whole range of disparate objects thrown together that are quite varied and dissimilar. We are once again in the territory of the stereotype setting up a character whose features are assumed to define a particular class of people. Keeping with the art theme, we could say it is a figure-ground game where we can see either one image or another depending on which way we look at things.[13] We can only see the profile of the greedy banker in the reflection of the 'ordinary people on normal wages' that we imagine as his opposite, and vice versa: the 'public' emerges as the figure against the background of the particular.

Often it is during election campaigns that political parties identify a person who they adopt as an icon of the public, a little girl denied an ear operation, or a working person unable to afford their mortgage payments. This can be a red rag to investigative journalists, who can usually come up with unsavoury details about

12 I use the term 'broker' quite unfairly to denote anyone who works in the City and routinely receives large bonuses.

13 See Gell, 1998: 137–8 or Peterson 1991.

the person's family or habits that undermine their status as 'ordinary member of the public'. That this is done so routinely ought to warn us not necessarily that political parties aren't to be trusted, but that no-one truly embodies ordinariness. The public must remain anonymous, because as soon as we identify actual people, they differ from the norm. The norm, as Ian Hacking points out,[14] is a statistical construct. If we look at statistical spreads of the number of people in a household, then the norm might be 4.2 people. But the graph that shows us the norm will also show us the less normal households with 1, 3, 6 or 20 people in them. In defining the norm, we have also defined out the non-normal. To put it another way, averages never correspond to actual people? What Hacking shows is that the norm was invented, not simply discovered. The norm is a product of the science of the state – statistics. Once the state identifies norms and legislates according to them, Hacking argues that people start to try to conform to those norms, in order either to get the benefits that accrue from being normal, or to avoid the disadvantages or even punishments of being abnormal.

If we go back a little further, we can see that society as a whole also had to be invented. It is well know that Margaret Thatcher, radical British Prime Minister from 1979 to 1992, famously stated that there is no such thing as society, only the individual and family. She was actually arguing that people should not be dependent on the state, and claimed to have been acknowledging that 'society' is an abstract category. What she did not say is that there is no such thing as the public, which is rather interesting, since one must assume that she did acknowledge that she had an electorate, even if she sincerely believed that they were merely an anarchic crowd of individuals. Her statement was rhetorically confused, though, not merely for the obvious reasons (e.g., does that mean that political parties are not legitimate forms of collective action?). On the one hand, she acknowledged the concept of society, while on the other hand refusing to believe in it as a means to organise welfare. Given the discussion of magic and belief earlier in the book, we might be tempted to agree with her that society is a concept that one may or may not choose to believe in. From a historian's perspective, the notion of society was discovered (or perhaps invented) as part of the historical development of Modernity. In denying society, Thatcher denied the discoveries of the 18th century philosopher Jean-Jaques Rousseau and more or less all subsequent political theorists, although it seems unlikely that she had thought it through quite as carefully as such a statement suggests. According to Pierre Manent,[15] Rousseau's discovery was the ultimate expression of modern political thought. Until then, liberal thought was focused on distinguishing civil society and the state, and most liberal arguments were justified in relation to different explanations of nature. The Western liberal obsession with 'primitive people' (that itself gave rise to the discipline of Anthropology) was a search for political organisation that could be thought to be more 'natural' than that found in European states that were, by definition, civilised, and hence less natural

14 Hacking 1986.

15 Manent 1994.

(one might in religious terms say 'corrupt'). Rousseau saw that civil society and the state could only be seen in opposition as part of a greater whole, which he termed society, and within this society, men were either more or less equal. Instead of politics being discussed in terms of nature, it could now be thought of in relation to liberty and history, but we must remember that this only became possible in the context of bloody revolution.[16]

In this light it is rather interesting that the population should be described as one body of the public, for whose good the state is supposed to act. To recognise this public, we have to look in the mirror for its alternatives. What interests are not those of the public? Are they those of the aristocracy? Of business? Or is the opposite of the public a set of clans, or what are often called 'tribes'? If society is the product of revolution that tore us away from a system of peasants, nobles and tradesmen, then what is the 'public' producing instead?

We reach a point where we can see that the public may not really be the collective of all people in reality, but a concept that helps us manage the complexity of political organisation. The difficulty for us is to make the connection between an idea of the public as a body politic, and people we actually meet. Habermas's concept of an authentic public sphere is based on the idea that face-to-face contact is the truest form of communication in a collective, but Anderson has shown us that the nation (as I mentioned above) is not based on face-to-face contact, but is an extrapolation from it. It is supported by a range of communicative sleights that are often easier to see in other contexts. Take, for instance, the emergence of documentation of folk tales and folk tunes in the 19th century. Folklore collections included tales where the authors were deliberately not acknowledged, and replaced by 'the authentic folk who are everyone because no one'.[17]

The idea of there being a 'public' out there waiting to be consulted is built up through all of these activities, the election that demands an electorate, the peculiar that demands a general normality, the rhetoric of politics. So, if we are expecting the public to turn up to planning consultations, who exactly are we expecting? What happens when the anonymous public of our imagination materialises in the form of actual people? The first thing we are confronted with is the re-emergence of categories into which we fit different people. While we can imagine a general public, a nation or a multicultural population, what we meet is a retired school secretary who's been a council tenant for 40 years, a Bengali businessman whose sons now run the family grocery shop threatened with demolition, a care assistant from the old people's home, or a semi-retired wealthy property owner who knows more about planning than the planners. None of them represent everybody, because they are all somebody, situated in particular circumstances, and each have their own private interests that they are concerned to protect, and some kind of commitment to the general interest, be they concrete (my family, my community) or abstract (the economy, the environment, etc).

16 See Wittrock 2000.

17 Gal and Woolard 2001: 9.

This conundrum has consequences, beyond the effectiveness of certain aspects of 'common' (public) sense. Firstly, for example, while the participation of 'the public' is theoretically welcome in some state activities such as planning, the participation of private interests is more problematic and more work must be done for them to appear legitimate. While professional lobbying organisations are well equipped to do this extra work, it can be rather more difficult for others. People whose views can be categorised as not being those of the 'general public', but a particular interest, can be sidelined quite effectively. It is easy, from this perspective, to see why the idea of the 'NIMBY' came about in the 1990s. Local authorities attempting to make strategic plans tried to see problems that concerned the whole district – such as where to accommodate new housing and business development sites as required under regional plans. In Aylesbury Vale, for example, the district needed to identify sites for tens of thousands of new dwellings, with much of the district identified as protected landscape. At the same time, policy on sustainability argued quite sensibly that if houses were dotted around all over the countryside, then it would be uneconomic to run public transport, so it would be better to concentrate housing in existing settlements. In principle, these are worthy aims, but, in practice, they implied packing development into villages and small towns where residents felt they were already reeling from dramatic expansion in previous decades. So, on the one hand, they agreed that generally speaking, there was a shortage of housing, but they didn't want to see more fields allocated for housing in their village – a classic 'not in my back yard' (NIMBY) response.

At the same time, though, much of the housing that was being built was 'executive' or 'luxury' housing that was most profitable for developers, leaving low-income and homeless families still without access to housing. So, many village protection societies were formed, to argue that what was actually needed was small, cheap housing for young families in village centres, and that allocating more and more fields for estates of detached commuter housing was not welcome. In fact, these are quite acceptable planning arguments. The term 'NIMBY' was used by developers to try to rubbish the resistance to expansion plans, for which their organisations had lobbied long and hard at government level, and from which they stood to make a profit (or 'maintain our business and keep people employed' in the language of the House Builders' Association). In this way, they had attempted to engineer the view of increasing housing development as that central, 'objective', and 'natural' fact around which everything else should revolve. By labelling resisters 'NIMBY', almost whatever their objection, they were fairly effective in reducing the legitimacy of any objection to their proposals. Yet people living in the district did resist. Rather than be able to have Habermasian rational conversations in which their reasoned point of view was heard, they had to work extremely hard to make their quite logical arguments cut through the overwhelmingly negative interpretation that was put on them once they were labelled NIMBY. The point here is not only that calling them names was an efficient short-hand for dismissing their arguments, but that calling them something other than 'the general public' left the 'public interest' available to be claimed by planners and developers. At the same time, having established that being a NIMBY is something undesirable, anyone concerned about what was happening in their local area could be labelled a NIMBY and excluded from important discussions about future development.

Secondly, if the public are, by definition, not particular trained professionals, then they lack sufficient knowledge of planning procedures to participate effectively in them. Participating in planning actually requires quite a lot of specialist knowledge, and public participation in planning in the UK was established on the basis that the public needed to be educated about planning, rather than vice versa.[18] After learning what plans are, and which kind of plan has which kind of outcome, and at which point in the planning process one can intervene, one must know how to frame arguments in writing addressed to particular policies, proposals or clauses, what kind of arguments are acceptable (such as what constitutes a material consideration), potentially how to present a case at a public inquiry, how to appoint a QC if the money is available, and so on. Once a person knows these things, though, they can no longer be considered to be an 'ordinary member of the public' (who, by definition, does not have specialist knowledge). In other words, effectiveness in planning participation is in inverse proportion to ordinary 'public-ness', making a kind of self-perpetuating exclusive system.

Some of these mechanisms were at work in Norfolk Park in the consultation I mentioned in the last chapter, that seemed like an endless series of meetings held between the Community Forum and the Council's regeneration team. These meetings were open to anyone, and when the regeneration was at its most active, they were held every two weeks, but were later wound down to once a month, and then once every few months. Their aim was for the regeneration team to keep the local residents informed about the progress of the development scheme, and to hear local concerns. But not so very long into the regeneration, the developers stopped coming to public meetings, leaving the Council's regeneration team to answer questions and become go-betweens, being put in the position of having to answer for problems and delays that were caused by the developers. When members of the Forum came to meetings to complain, they ceased to be ordinary residents or members of the public, but were gradually identified as 'the usual suspects', as difficult complainers, and they started to feel that their representation was being undermined. As mentioned previously, Joan told me that she knows that the Community Forum have been seen as a nuisance.[19]Joan was insistent that it was her role as a member of the Forum to speak up on behalf of residents, and when residents came to her with complaints or difficulties, she raised these issues at meetings. She tried hard to persuade residents to go to the regeneration meetings

18 See Damer and Hague 1971.

19 'It' included a lack of rental housing available, long delays in reconstruction, unfinished paths and handrails, lack of economic regeneration activity, delays in grants being delivered to the forum, and so on.

themselves, so that the planners would see it wasn't just the Forum who were complaining, but they rarely did and, as Joan added, 'who can blame them?'. Joan and other forum members were immediately caught in the trap – having learned enough to respond knowledgably to planning issues, they could no longer be seen as ordinary members of the public, but as particular people with special interests.

Public participation as a conundrum

These problems go right to the heart of current ideas about democracy. The idea of participative democracy, in which governmental bodies invite people to have some role in the processes that lead to decisions (if not those that lead to actions) is a promising ideal, but it suffers under several mismatches. Firstly, the set of categories used to define who is to be included is constructed from the perspective of an idealistic state with little reference to the profuse historical social relations which are already in place before policies are embarked upon. That is, planners and politicians identify the kinds of people they want to be included in participation, either as residents, citizens, local representatives, or representatives of ethnic minorities, and so forth. Most consultation processes, too, start sensibly with a list of relevant people to be consulted. But if you want to get involved in either a consultation or a participative process, you first of all need to find a role that suits you as a participant: Should I join in as a local resident, as a member of a local organisation, as a qualified employee, or as someone with a belief in environmental ideals? If I simply join in as myself, then my contribution will sooner or later be challenged by the question of who I am to make comments. And to find out who I am, that is, on what basis what I say should be listened to, I have to work out the different roles that are on offer.

For an ordinary person to engage with organisations and institutions whose actions are based on such abstract categories requires enormous commitment in time and energy (as well as other resources) to become familiar with the rhetoric and practices of these organisations. That is, to be a good participant, you need to study the expectations of the relevant public and private organisations to whom you are required to communicate and to do that on their terms, rather than your own. And on top of that, if you want to be taken seriously, you have to know your way around planning law and guidance, and to keep your comments 'relevant' to what can be done by those running the participative process. This takes a considerable amount of work, reading policies, learning how governmental systems work, and so on, so it is a fairly hefty investment.

Secondly, in the light of the enormous persistence required to participate in policy organisations by those not directly employed by them, only a few people are in a position to be able to respond to the invitations to participate. They must have both the necessary resources and the interest, or will, to devote significant amounts of their lives to the process: If they are to be critical of policy processes, rather than simply amenable, that is, if they are to be politically astute, the demands are greater. It is perhaps not surprising that they then will keep re-engaging with the processes, and get involved in further activities. This presents a problem for planners who aim to involve as many people as possible, when on a daily basis they end up feeling that they always meet 'the usual suspects'. When the usual suspects keep pushing a line that perhaps doesn't work with the plans, or doesn't move forward, the only option seems to be to try to work round them. The problem for planners and politicians, or those seeking 'wide participation', is that the public they seek is made up of unknown people. Once people who make the effort to learn how to participate are known to them, they are no longer unknown and cease to be representatives of the greater anonymous 'public'. Since, as we have seen already in this chapter, the public derives its authority from being anonymous,[20] so those people we know are no longer the public we seek.

So, the effort to include a broad 'public' is always either extremely fleeting or it is done in vain. If the definition of the public is the opposite of people who have trained to participate effectively, and in this process have become known to councillors and council officers, then the process will always be self-defeating. Once members of the public actually become good citizens by learning how to participate in public life, they cease to be general members of the public because the categories don't overlap. What we are faced with is a kind of category mistake,[21] where the category of public cannot correspond with the category of person, since the public is an ideal political construct for the purposes of thinking about how the state works, and a person is bound in layers of social relations, with complex personal history, and a multifaceted life to lead. The concepts 'ordinary person' and 'the public' are conceptual ideas that tempt us to believe that abstract people exist, with the outcome that our ambitions to be participative are bound to be frustrated. What we effectively have is two models of democracy that we have yet to reconcile. On the one hand, we have an abstract model of democracy whose public elect representatives but may also participate directly in certain activities, and whose workings we know through statistical or theoretical materials (sometimes called 'macro' studies). On the other, we have quite a lot of examples of inspiring participative actions that are often based on particular examples (sometimes called 'micro' studies) where certain people with specific experiences, qualities and personalities managed particular circumstances to reach unique outcomes. What we do not have is any understanding of how incompatible these two models are, yet if we analyse our assumptions about basic categories and language, such as 'the public' and 'ordinary people', we might be able to see where the incompatibility lies and think more realistically about whether they can work.

20 Gal and Woolard 2001: 6.

21 Ryle 1949.

When is the public?

One further issue is lurking in this discussion about the public. In a brief reference to Aylesbury Vale planners, I reported planners talking about their visions for the future population of the new housing they hoped to put in place. When I asked municipal planners in Norway who their plans were for, they responded – with a certain air of surprise at the question – that the plans were for the residents of the district, the constituents, the people who had elected the council, and their families, the people who paid their wages through local taxes. But the British planners were far more equivocal about this. For them, the people they had to consider were those people who would come to live in the area in the future. How, the Norwegian planners asked, could you possibly represent these people given that you couldn't yet know who they were? I admit that this was a difficult question, but it is clear that there are planners who feel that the forecasts and predictions about future populations are sufficient knowledge on which to imagine the society of the future and to make plans to accommodate them. This is a different sense in which we imagine the public – we don't only imagine a public out there now, but we frequently and commonly use forecasts and trends to imagine how our public might be at some time in the future.

There is something of a time paradox at work here. Planning is always about the future. We don't make plans for the past; when we plan in the present, we call it management. Yet the future is something we can never be sure of. We are always adjusting and remaking our plans depending on how the present matches up to how we thought it might be when we imagined the future, and the one thing that is always true is that the two never match exactly. So, we know that time is an issue in planning, and that if it is difficult to know much about the public now, it is even harder to know about the public in the future.

Ottar Brox likens planning to a sailing trip, with the planner as navigator.[22] We might set out with a destination in mind, and we set our sights accordingly and aim for a point we imagine, based on memory, hope or evidence like a map. The navigator has to keep finding new sights on the horizon to aim for, and adjust the course constantly from one point to the next. But along the way, the wind might change, one of the people on board might feel sick and want to get off, or we might decide we would prefer to go somewhere else. The navigator has to keep changing the point to which the boat steers, and in the end, the destination might change completely if the people on board all decide on a new harbour. Although we might have agreed on a long-term goal, we still have to attend to intermediate goals and adjust the longer-term aim accordingly.

But there are other ways of thinking about these kinds of time rather than simply as the near, middle or distant future. The headline time horizon in plans tends to contrast an immediate future that we are dealing with now, and a rather hazier distant future that we should aim for in 10, 12 or perhaps 20 years.

22 Brox 1995.

Norwegian anthropologist Halvard Vike sees a change in the significance of these time horizons.[23] The early welfare state was based on a kind of utopian future, good enough to enthuse people to work towards it, yet far enough away to inspire a degree of patience. That future was on what Vike calls 'the horizon of the possible'. People recognised that their efforts today were but a partial contribution towards a better world in the future, and they were relatively satisfied to make an effort in the hope that the future would be a better place than the present. As the welfare state matured, and new political movements emerged, and indeed as the quality of services and of people's daily lives improved, a different future emerged, which Vike calls the 'contemporary future'. The contemporary future is one that we expect to achieve now, or very soon. It is a future based on market-transaction time, putting extreme pressure on welfare services for perfection now, rather than having the patience to trust that measures carefully planned now will lead to better services in the future. The change that he outlines is a radical shift from the kind of democratic enlightened planning that planning theorists such as Friedman have called for. Our models of democratic planning imagine it as a broad deliberative process for formulating goals for the future and the means to achieve them, but the reality of government has moved significantly. Now, planning is increasingly used as a kind of organisational or managerial tool, not the mobilising force that sustains real democracy, and the kinds of future imagined are changed at the same time.

Planning the past

Planning is not only a practice of making policies about the future and then trying to enforce the future to cohere to our plans. Sometimes plans are almost entirely post-hoc and serve to regularise the past. At the same time, plans often pay scant attention to the historical development of sites, so that the historical depth of plans can be remarkably thin (as we will see below). This combination can serve to produce anomalies that have a kind of logic in the present, but make little sense in relation to things that have happened before, memories or experiences that can be extremely significant for inhabitants. In this timeless future-present, plans can be used to resolve irregularities as well as to define future action. This is particularly clear in contexts were large parts of the population are not afforded full citizenship, for example. Urban planning is not only used in Western states, but has been developed in countries where sometimes quite large sectors of the population are not considered full citizens and where housing and services are not provided for many of the lowest paid workers or those without jobs. In Brazil or Peru, for example, large parts of the cities are occupied by people of Indian descent '*Indianos*' and others who are not accounted full rights as citizens, who

23 Vike forthcoming.

have collectively invaded tracts of land to make places to live. In these contexts, plans and similar regulatory structures struggle to catch up with practice.

The city authorities in Lima take years to agree land tenure contracts with people living in the city to try to regulate development long after it has happened, as people need to live in the city but the city states have not kept up with the demand.[24] In a context of civil upheaval, where appropriation of land has been used strategically by all parties, land reform and land invasions have been used by homeless migrants and urban organisers to prevent usurpation of land rights as well as to create settlements for workers and homes for migrants who fled areas of unrest during the civil war. Urban invasions are not random spontaneous acts, but carefully organised and planned strategic actions, organised by federations and supported by NGOs, often foreign aid organisations. Because land titles are often disputed, years can pass in legal process, appeals and counter-appeals, before the status of land is secured. In the meantime, settlements can gain recognition as housing lots appear, infrastructure is built, community associations are formed and gardens are tilled. Eventually, if things go right, titles and plans may emerge to confirm the existence of what is already on the ground, and the settlements can be regularised and incorporated into city strategy. As Lund explains:

> In dealings between invaders and officials, there is a sense that individual bureaucrats are only people with shared cultural experiences and that necessarily many rules will be bent simply through attrition because people without housing must make homes for themselves as best they can. Their simple presence, vulnerability, and unmet needs cannot be denied. Over the course of years, room is made for the incorporation of the invaded state lands into recognized urban spaces and eventually even private property.'[25]

Planning time seems to scoop round on itself and meet itself coming back. This doesn't only happen in Peruvian cities, of course. Retrospective planning decisions are made in Britain too, and some businesses use it as a strategic tactic. There are large chain stores well known for altering buildings and opening coffee-shops in urban high streets without applying for planning permission, and then applying for retrospective planning permission once the enforcement officers catch up with them. Of course, big commercial chains have much larger budgets to spend on legal activities than local authorities, so this kind of tactic can work extremely well for them. What it means is that planning is not only about the future, but that we plan the past as well.

---

24 See Lund forthcoming a.

25 Lund forthcoming b.

Planning takes time!

It also seems easy to forget how planning takes time. We know that planning is a process and that implies that it proceeds through time, but we often fail to properly take account of this. One way in which we have acknowledged this time is to talk about risks in planning. Risks in the changing of a market are one issue, and one that can be fully manipulated by developers. In Norfolk Park it was not clear to an outsider why the rebuilding took so long to get going. The Deputy Chief-Executive of the forum thought that the problem was that the developer was over-extended, prioritising another more prestigious and profitable housing development in the city centre. It was well known that there was a shortage of labour, and development companies have to manage their investments and their labour force, so it was a credible argument that the company were spacing out their work. On the other hand, it may have been coincidence that housing markets started to take off as the publicly-funded Norfolk Park demolitions came to an end, and as land values rose it made sense for the developer to put off selling property until the market neared a peak. Certainly the developers' project manager was not prepared to offer any explanation for the delay, and the regeneration planning officer could only try his hardest to get the developer to start building. With few tools at his disposal to get them into action, it must have been a very frustrating time for him (indeed, 'frustrating' was the word he chose to describe the whole regeneration process).

Even without added delays in construction, there are huge implications of the time planning takes for public participation or consultation. Throughout the late 90s and early 2000s, planners' and politicians' ambitions for public participation seemed to grow unheeded. Claims were made for all-inclusive participatory democracy, where everyone would be involved in making policies and plans, as we've seen above. What might this mean in practice, though? I have mentioned already the time it takes to learn how to be a good citizen. But if our aim is to have a fully open and transparent process, where the public can be involved at every stage, then we soon encounter another perennial problem. Policy processes generally move in a hierarchical and linear way through time. They aim to set ground rules, decide general aims, and gradually to specify these more closely until a detailed set of plans can be produced. So, the process through time is mirrored by a hierarchical approach to planning, from general to specific. Now, imagine we are into the second round of our planning process. After six months of negotiation, we have agreed that all the maisonettes on Norfolk Park will be demolished, all but one of the tower blocks and half of the terraced houses. Now we are ready to discuss the layout of the new housing areas, and how to renovate the housing that remains. But at this point, 14 residents of Park View turn up to a meeting and say that they have only just realised that they were being consulted, and they do not want their terraces to be demolished, indeed it is an absolute scandal to demolish such high quality housing, when all they need is a new roof to make them into valuable homes for another 50 years. What do we do now? Do we go back a stage in the process and renegotiate which housing will be demolished and which retained? Do we say that this will set the whole process back by six months and cost many more thousands of pounds which we cannot afford? Do we therefore say that our consultation is now closed to new participants, and thereby disenfranchise a significant group of residents?

A truly open consultation will always confront this kind of temporal problem. The process presumes that time proceeds in an orderly manner, but open participation with an unspecified public will always produce new participants all through the process, and for them the time that has already passed is meaningless. Participatory time does not proceed in a linear way, but meanders in and out of people's other activities, to the frustration of all those people who get involved at the beginning and want to see things through to the end. Once again, the premise that planners start with – their perspective as full-time employees with a task in hand – is a rather poor match for the people who are not professionally engaged with planning. Of course, I am not arguing that we should cease to hold broad participative planning activities, nor that we should cease to allow people to be consulted, because it takes time, which costs money. On the contrary, I cannot see how planning would be anything but totalitarian if it could not be properly challenged at any stage of the process. Part of the problem here is related to our category of the public being too solid and too whole. Our imagined singular public works on one timescale, whereas, in practice, we are dealing with a whole range of different times and temporal scales.

Qualities of time

So, time is rather important, and it has difference qualities. What other kinds of time should we take account of if we are going to explore both what time is and how we imagine the public? There is cyclical or repetitive time that we use to think about our daily lives. What time do you usually get up in the morning? When do you break for lunch? This kind of daily time is the one we deal with most immediately and most of the time. There are broader cyclical periods, of course, the annual cycle of seasons is significant for any society outside the equatorial region, but even there, annual cycles are created by states and other bureaucracies. There are annual calendars with significant ritual moments – religious holidays, bank holidays, state memorial holidays (saints days, constitution days, war memorial days) and passages of time such as school holidays that remind us of the cyclical nature of life. And Robertson reminds us that there are longer cycles, too, that should be considered more important for planners in particular.[26] We may recognise in theory that we have a life-cycle, birth, childhood, adolescence, adulthood, maturity, old age, for example. But studies of households also show that they have lifecycles of their own that have great significance for how we plan.

26 Robertson forthcoming.

In many Western societies adulthood is ideally marked by a move to a new home, and the setting up of a new household. Over time, households grow with the birth of children, grandparents may or may not live in the same house for some time, and later as children grow up and leave and older generations die, the household gets smaller again. In some societies these changes correspond to the building that the household lives in. Robertson reminds us that the income of households is also cyclical, with younger people earning less while bearing the cost of having children, and older people earning more but needing less space.

In contrast, Maurice Bloch writes of the Zafimaniry people of Madagascar that a man entering into a marriage will start by building a simple house with a hearth made of three stones in a wooden frame and three posts.[27] The walls at this stage are usually made of woven bamboo and are easily seen through, and it is possible to hold a conversation through the walls with people looking in. Gradually, as the family grows, work is done on the house to replace the walls with old hard wood into which decoration is gradually carved. By the time the house is quite solid and fully decorated, or 'hardened up', the children may already be embarking on their own marriages, but will still keep returning to the parental house at various times. The history of the house-building is a kind of chronicle of the history of the family. As the parents get older, the youngest son might divide the house instead of moving out, keeping the original marriage alive in the body of the house.

In contrast to this house that grows with the family, Robertson argues that in Western planning we tend to think of houses as solid and unchanging. To the extent that we plan for different household types, we imagine them as discrete and provide small houses for young singles or couples or elderly people, and larger houses with more bedrooms for people with children. We tend to think of them as separate units, not as stages that families move through cyclically. Rather than making flexible housing, we expect people to be flexible, and to move from house to house as the shape of their household or their housing needs change. Robertson's point is that the housing we can afford and the housing we need rarely run in parallel throughout our life-course, with young families unable to afford space, while older people whose families have left home might have higher incomes that they no longer need. In fact, it is financial flexibility that is used to compensate for these effects, when wealthy parents subsidise their children's housing. Whether in the private market or through municipal housing, we generally expect people to move to a house that suits them, rather than providing housing that adapts to the changing household. Recently attempts have been made to change this, with various imaginative architects proposing more flexible housing, but this remains very much the exception and barely registers in either volume housebuilders' developments or planning practices. The timescale of a family's development, or lifecycle, is treated quite differently in these two contexts, but it is clear from both that that scale is significant.

27 Bloch 1995.

There are yet other qualities of time,[28] too, such as pace or duration, time that goes quickly or drags, and different kinds of time past as well as time future and present. Thomas Hylland Eriksen regrets the crowding in of pressing demands, in what he calls the 'tyranny of the moment', the need to answer phones, emails and texts now, the way we are bombarded with news and advertising almost constantly.[29] Time past is also very often carved up and thought of in different ways. We distinguish daily life from our life-cycle and then again from history as a time of longer duration and greater scope. Even without our own life-times we often register the before and after of significant events, and we often think of social time as before and after, too. Françoise Zonabend writes of the way people in a southern French village think about the period before the Second World War as a kind of general before-time, the long process of developing time that was cruelly confronted with total war,[30] and time since then as being much more detailed and immediate. As generations shift, too, time and experience begin to shift from lived memory into a general domain of history beyond our immediate personal memory and into a general more social sense of time passed.

It is a different kind of time past that is very often eclipsed in planning practice, though. Plans being very future oriented, they rarely include any real analysis of what conditions have led us to where we are today. Instead, they look to how we can get to where we want to be tomorrow and build on the basis that some things will remain the same while others will change, in what Vike characterises as 'the social organisation of hope'.[31] But often we meet resistance or difficulties precisely because plans treat now as a start and not as a stage in the progression through time. This is especially important in our understanding of the public, because not only is the public anonymous but it is also timeless. When Aylesbury Vale planners set out proposals for new housing sites in the district plan for public consultation, they expected an ahistorical public to respond to the proposals from the perspective of the demand for development land now and in the future. What they actually met was residents who had lived through previous expansions and felt that they were at the end of a period of growth, not merely in the middle or even at the beginning. People with memory, experience and history brought a quite different response to the plans than was expected.

A similar problem emerged in Sheffield in trying to deal with the regeneration of public housing. Talking to older residents about the need to move house, they were articulate and lyrical in describing why they did not want to move. They told us about the years of living in their homes, reminisced about the social groups they had founded and enjoyed, the scouts and guides groups they had led, the football team/church choir founded by Mrs Seaton, the community centre fought for by the residents' association set up in the 1960s. As well as a fondness for the views

28 See James and Mills 2005.

29 Eriksen 2001.

30 Zonabend 1984.

31 Ibid.

over the hills they had from high-rise flats, there was a wealth of memory soaked into the walls. While there clearly were physical problems with the buildings, some residents held public demonstrations and petitioned to retain the block that had been dedicated to older residents, to have it renovated and modernised so they could carry on living in their homes. The problem here was not so much for the regeneration team or the politicians to find a way to pursue the regeneration. The real problems arose for those residents who wanted to stay. Once a decision was made that they must move, very many of them suffered health problems related to the stress of moving – high blood pressure, heart problems, depression – a stress exacerbated by having to move a lifetime's possessions into smaller flats. In such situations we ought to pay attention to the fact that it is not planners who suffer, but residents whose lives are changed whether or not they wish to move themselves.

The senior planner's approach was to emphasise the road forward. Things had been difficult, he agreed, with financial pressure, difficulties in getting developers to contribute to social or economic projects, or even to develop at all for some time, but whatever had happened before, the job to be done now was to move forward together and achieve a good outcome. This takes us back to the discussion in Chapter 2 about the problem of 'negativity' in contemporary government-mentalities, where discussing, analysing and documenting past failure is seen as a kind of bad omen, a way to risk 'loss of confidence', and a risk to the future. Yet we cannot pretend that the past has not happened, nor that people have memories of it. What we need, instead, are broader ways to think about the significance of time in its multiple layers and qualities, so that we might just anticipate where it will intrude not only in the present but in the future as well. This would demand a more historically informed approach to planning rather than a ground-zero approach. A strong historical awareness would then imply that we acknowledge local specificity, that particular things happen in particular places, and that a planning idea that works in one place might not work in another. It would require planners and politicians to pay much more attention to particular conditions, and to tailor plans to existing populations and their anticipated and desired futures. It might require them to pay closer attention to local arguments and the social relations they emerge from, and to exert more sophisticated judgement. There are a few planners who do this already, of course, but it would help them to consider the difficulties openly and start to search for ways and means to support them.

Time, as we have seen, is neither straightforward nor purely a physical phenomenon. In this chapter, I have barely ventured out of the familiar planning system, and I have not mentioned any of the brain-befuddling 'other' concepts of time that can be found in the records of anthropological research. But having used exotic examples here and there in the book, and having opened up the use of 'culture' as a concept to think with, it has been possible to challenge our concepts of public and time in their own right without recourse to radically different cases. Those examples are available, though, in relation to time[32] or the future,[33] and even in the context of planning and urban development,[34] where various authors are now writing about alternative concepts of time and development. What matters for the argument here is to recognise that there are many kinds of time and that time has many different qualities that affect the way that we think about, talk about and do planning, development and policy-making. If we really want to improve the way we do planning, we will need to step outside the familiar ways that we know, the familiar arguments we trace backwards and forwards (*for* consultation and time, *against* extra costs and *for* efficiency) and think in a completely new way about plans.

32 See James and Mills 2005.

33 See Abram and Weszkalnys forthcoming.

34 See Bear and Feuchtwang 2009.

Chapter 7
Bringing it Together – Renewing Planning

The journey this book takes through planning ideas and practices is rather unusual. If you were expecting a book that told you how to 'do' culture, or how to manage cultural conflicts, then this book may have been a little surprising. There are many books that attempt to do this, but they often struggle with the fact that culture is a complex concept, and what we think of as 'cultures' vary and change. Certainly, if you were hoping to find an easy answer to questions about cultures of planning, then the book will probably have been quite challenging. Instead of telling you what people in 'other' cultures do, this book has used contemporary critical scholarship about culture to rethink our approaches to plans and planning. Or to mash metaphors, this work on culture can be used to reflect on planning, but it is more like Alice's looking-glass than a perfect mirror.

Of course, I am not suggesting that it is not important to try to understand other ways of doing things and how other people think. It is essential to avoid judging other people on our own terms, before understanding things from their perspective. This might be on a national scale, such as Mbiba's explanations about the meaning of time in Zimbabwe,[1] or Watson's indications of how deep difference can be,[2] or it might be a comparison between administrators and politicians.[3] Increasing efforts have been made to acknowledge cultural differences and the ways that planners might understand them,[4] and these are very valuable. Comparisons between different planning systems are an important element of planning studies too, and even though such comparisons are fraught with potential misunderstanding,[5] when they are done well they are immensely valuable in telling us how to understand the contexts that mean that some policies work better in one setting than another.

A great deal of scholarship exists that enables us to understand context and make sense of how 'other' people do things or to explain about them, but to make it accessible, it sometimes needs to be translated, not only into the kind of language that we are otherwise familiar with, but also into the contexts that we work in. Generally speaking, planners and planning theorists translate from the disciplines they are most familiar with, and these are largely economics, geography and political science. Occasionally things go a bit more sociological, although Eric Reade was pretty clear that planners responded badly to sociological critique. Perhaps 25

1 Mbiba 2003.

2 Watson 2003.

3 Abram 2004a.

4 See also Umemoto 2001.

5 Such as those explained in Abram and Cowell 2004.

years after his book was published, planners may feel less defensive and might be ready to go along with the kind of thought-experiments I have proposed. It is still rare to see ideas from anthropology making much of an impact in planning, even though they are occasionally referred to,[6] and despite excellent, accessible work being available.[7] There are good reasons for this. Anthropologists have their own language and their own references, and scholarly articles can be pretty difficult to understand for the uninitiated. Popular anthropology books tend to focus on key ideas such as kinship, ethnicity, ritual, religion, exchange, and so on, but it is rare that these are re-interpreted in ways that seem relevant for planning. What this book does is not to demand that planners become experts in religion or ritual, and it certainly doesn't ask all planners to become experts in anthropology. On the contrary, we can all be like anthropologists in a different way, by stepping outside our insecurities, and subjecting our everyday assumptions to some exceptional examination. Happily for planners, there are more anthropologists researching and writing about planning in increasingly accessible ways, and these publications should help to open up a new frame of reference for planning studies.[8]

Given that the concept of everyday culture was invented in anthropology over a century ago, and that anthropologists have been discussing it ever since, it would seem to be an obvious source to help us understand culture now. But culture has long since escaped the discipline itself, and is widely used in all sorts of ways, as I indicated in the introduction. The Norwegian anthropologist Fredrik Barth realised that culture was a potentially dangerous term some time ago.[9] He was worried that people use culture as shorthand for everything that is different about *other* people, and that made them seem exotic rather than understandable. Using the term in that way represents people only partially, and often fails to fully account for their reasoning. If we think of people as part of an exotic other culture, we are less likely to see that they have everyday interactions as human beings, and are more likely to rely on stereotypes.[10] Barth was most concerned that 'culture' and 'identity' used in these ways were ripe for political entrepreneurship, allowing people to claim to be speaking on behalf of others in a way that disempowers those people. A very crass example of this is the way that many councils in setting up participative or consultative activities tend to look for 'groups' to include. In Sheffield, as I have mentioned above, there have been examples of elderly imams of particular mosques being invited to consultations as though they represent all Muslims in the city, with no effort being made to consult with Muslim women, for example, and no acknowledgement that elderly imams may not share life-experience or political views with younger people from Muslim families, nor indeed that there are very

6 See, for example, Healey 1997.

7 See, for example, Peattie 1968a, b, 1981, 1987.

8 See, for example, Alexander 2001, Alexander and Buchli 2007, Abram and Weszkalnys forthcoming, Weszkalnys 2010.

9 Barth 1995.

10 See Alexander 2000.

widely different Muslim traditions and mosques even within the same cities in Britain. As Ulf Hannerz has put it, the term culture has gone from being associated with education and cultivation, to suggesting problems and conflicts. There is a danger of being fatalistic about cultures, seeing cultural problems as unresolvable and conflicts as irreconcilable.[11] This kind of 'cultural fundamentalism'[12] is neither helpful nor particularly useful.

Barth proposed instead that it might be more useful now to think in terms of knowledge rather than culture. Whereas culture has a kind of blanketing effect, washing over large numbers of people and treating them as more or less homogenous groups, knowledge is more closely related to personal experience that is embedded in a cultural context. What is it that people know, and how do they know it? We can ask how that knowledge is transmitted. We can acknowledge that knowledge can be embodied as well as externalised, that there are things that our bodies remember or skills that take time to learn. Knowledge is usually partial and generally situated in some way. Most knowledge is shared, but much of that sharing is not comprehensive. What knowledge potentially does is reflect experience, and it has the potential to make people equal in their potential for knowledge. Now, this is an interesting approach, but it does have dangers for planning. The clearest danger, as I see it, is that one might argue that if people could just be given the right knowledge, then they would be equally able to fully participate in policy-making. This is the very attitude that prompted the introduction of ideas about culture into planning in the first place, and we must be very wary indeed of going backwards as a way out of what are sometimes called 'wicked' problems – those that have many complex dimensions and are resistant to straightforward solutions. Assuming that 'our' knowledge is superior to 'their' knowledge is an aspect of imperialism that we constantly need to unlearn.

Instead, it is time to go into those sometimes baffling but also enlightening discussions about knowing and being (epistemology and ontology) rather than pretending they do not exist. The link that is missing between the focus on knowledge and the assumption that we can just educate people into thinking like us, is the question of how knowledge is learned. New research on how knowledge is created, transmitted and owned among different people can show us how it is not straightforward.[13] As I suggested earlier, knowledge is not the same as information, which is thought to be independent of the knower. Even information is not quite independent, though; it circulates, and the paths of its circulation are neither unlimited nor separate from other social conditions. Knowledge, though, is explicitly held by particular people and is always under transformation. We gain knowledge through experience, and shape our knowledge through our interaction with both the world and with other people. So, our knowledge is usually a shared creation, in the context of our lives, our epoch, and our society. In fact,

11 Hannerz 1999.

12 See Stolcke 1995.

13 See Marchand 2010a.

the variety of factors that shape knowledge can be overwhelmingly large.[14] So, gaining knowledge, or learning, is not only about getting information. Much of what we know is gained through informal learning. Whereas a conventional view of learning might be that it is something we do at school or university, say, under explicit instruction, there are many other models of learning. Apprenticeship, for example, is a much older model, that presumes a master and a learner, and the learning happens through what has been called 'proximal' experience.[15] This means that there is much that we learn by being on the edge of other people's activities, watching, listening, perhaps participating in a minor role, helping with a larger task, for example. Gradually, as we become more confident, we might take on a larger role, and eventually become a central knowledgeable person in that context. The value of this other kind of learning is recognised by our professional institutions, which require us to have work experience before we can become full members of the profession. While we need to have information about planning, its laws, regulations and practices, learning how to use that information can be a long and difficult process, and relies on formal or informal tutoring from experienced people, as well as direct personal experience that we reflect on and learn from.

Thinking about knowledge offers a rather different perspective than thinking about culture. Asking how participants in planning contexts might learn about planning, and how planners might gain knowledge about them immediately puts us in a different frame that offers some equality of status and opportunity for creating new knowledge through shared experience. Rather than seeing cultural difference as a barrier to be surmounted, we might look to shared knowledge as a domain to be created; it shifts the focus from difference (barriers) to learning (opportunities). And rather than using the label 'culture' to rule out anything that fits badly with our notions of rationality, we might ask what is the knowledge or experience that is being articulated in an unfamiliar way.

Focusing on knowledge rather than culture is just one way that planning might move into a new domain and interrogate its own practices. While planning theorists have developed reflective analysis, sometimes students find theorising a rather alienating practice. If theory is presented as a separate study, then it will be hard to reintegrate it into practice. Reflecting on knowledge can help us to reintegrate theoretical nuance into practical planning. This is not a substitute for addressing processes or practices, or for self-aware politically nuanced action. But action without well-considered theoretical analysis is a kind of floundering around in a dimly lit space where we cannot apprehend the walls, nor see beyond them. If we believe that planning is a useful activity, that there are ways it could be improved or that we could understand it better, then we need to keep looking for different ways of understanding it, using comparative analysis, philosophical interrogation, and seeking perspectives from our colleagues in other disciplines.

---

14 See Marchand 2010b.

15 See Lave and Wenger 1991, Vygotsky 1978.

Such new frames of reference are anticipated here, where I have turned round the usual discussion of culture to raise some pressing issues. I started by showing how many of our ideas about culture are actually ideas about nationalism. If we see culture not as a set of things we do or stuff we have, but instead think about culture as a concept with its own history, then its roots become more apparent. Tracing some of that history, even briefly, reveals what our talk of culture does without us realising. How often do we use stereotypes instead of finding out how things actually are, or thinking things through? How easily can culture-talk disguise a kind of banal nationalism, even racism? Culture is both a tremendously useful concept, and an immensely powerful term that we use for all sorts of purposes. If you were to make a note of every time you used the term culture in the course of a week and thought about the context in which you used it, could you divine the range of meanings that you attributed to it? And when we use the term, we do not only move words around, we perform an utterance that has consequences for ourselves and for others. Once we start to ask ourselves what it is we *do* when we talk about culture, we clearly get some unexpected discoveries.

It is not an easy task to challenge concepts that we are utterly familiar with, and it is not easy to think outside our normal language, so sometimes we need to be shocked into thinking differently. If we allow ourselves to think challenging things, then we sometimes gain a better understanding of why certain things are unthinkable, and whether they should or should not remain so. Thinking about planning as a kind of magic and allowing ourselves to admit all the things that cannot be rationally explained is just such a move. If we take away the usual explanations – that things that are not rational in planning are political (either the result of politicians machinations or power plays between officials) or cultural (down to people's bizarre customs and beliefs), what are we left with? Without our usual rhetorical crutches we actually have to think through whether the usual explanations actually explain anything. Perhaps the delusion that planning is more rational than emotional is blinding us to what planning really means? Or perhaps it preserves our feeling of legitimacy, our professional status, or our complacency about our role? But however we use it, it is irresponsible – if not immoral – to keep ignoring its consequences. What we need is a new set of tools to understand what it is we are doing.

Rather than berating planners for ignoring culture, or pretending that changing the management culture of planning offices will solve planning dilemmas,[16] I have shown that planners are constantly in the process of actually producing culture. Most of the time, 'culture' is a separate category that contains everything planners either cannot explain or feel they cannot influence. Most obviously, as I argued in the introduction, culture has been used as a repository for things considered to not be rational, and, in particular, not to be part of the rationality we call economic. Somers says as much about the idea of political culture – that it was adopted as a way of accounting for the outcomes that economics and political science could not

16 See Shaw and Lord 2007.

explain.[17] Life is complicated and planners cannot do everything, so, particularly in Britain, planners have focused on instrumental issues, such as land-use, economic development, material urban design, etc., and paid attention to regulations and policies on use-classes, boundaries, zones, building shapes and so on. All the issues that make life meaningful, such as our knowledge, our bodies, our emotional lives, our desires, our families, friendships and fun, and even aesthetics, have become 'culture' that is not the concern of people we usually refer to as planners.[18] In sidelining so many issues and in ruling out so many areas of activity, or passing them on to other people, planners produce a category of culture that is then a problem. Having produced this problematic area, it becomes increasingly difficult to deal with it, and yet it keeps coming back and threatening to cause disruption and difficulties. Whenever we propose public participation of any sort in planning activities, people turn up with all their 'culture' problems, their messy personal relationships and their awkward bodies, and disrupt the smooth flow of planning. We try our best to discipline them into thinking like planners (and getting them to write things down rather than talking to us is one typical manoeuvre), but we don't actually like it when they do act like planners, partly because they are able to challenge us on our own terms, and partly because they risk becoming constant foes, instead of being anonymous members of the public. We will never escape this dilemma by trying to do 'better' public participation, or by excluding the public from planning. The only way out is to recognise that we have created the problem ourselves through the way that we have made our categories, of people, of policy, of politics and so on.

Rehearsing old arguments about culture will not help us much here. There is a great risk, as planners start to enjoy debates about planning cultures, or pay more attention to changing cultures of planning, that we will merely remain stuck in a rather outdated discussion that leads us round in well-meaning but ultimately futile circles. In particular, there is a risk that planners remain ignorant of debates that are highly relevant. What I hope to have achieved here is to reinterpret just a few of those debates in ways that relate to planning. With these new perspectives in place, perhaps there really can be a future for planning.

17 Somers 1995.

18 It should be clear by now that I am not addressing people who work in cultural-policy, for example.

References

Aaltola, E. (2008). 'Personhood and Animals' *Environmental Ethics* 30, 2, 175–194.

Abram, S. (2004a). 'Personality and professionalism in a Norwegian district council'. *Planning Theory* 3, 21—40.

——— (2004b). 'The smell of money: Minor risks and olfactory sensibilities (the anatomy of a protest)'. In Å. Boholm and R. E. V. Löfstedt *Facility Siting: Risk, Power and Identity in Land-use Planning*. London, Earthscan: 72—88.

——— (2003). 'Anthropologies in policies, anthropologies in places.' In T. Hylland Eriksen *Globalisation — Studies in Anthropology: Methodological Issues*. London, Pluto Press: 138—157.

——— (2002). 'Planning and public-making in municipal government.' *Focaal* 40: 21—34.

——— (2000). 'Planning the public: Some comments on empirical problems for planning theory.' *Journal of Planning Education and Research* 19(4): 351—357.

Abram, S. and C. Allam (2005). *Living Through Regeneration*. UK, University of Sheffield: 27—30, http://web.me.com/s.abram/Site_5/LTR.html.

Abram, S and H. Vike (2001). 'People Out of Place?' In S. Connelly, S. Abram and T. Richardson (Eds.) *Perspectives on Participation*. Working Paper in Town and Regional Planning TRP143, Sheffield University.

Abram, S. and R. Cowell (2004). 'Learning Policy: The Contextual Curtain and Conceptual Barriers.' *European Planning Studies* 12(2): 209—228.

Abram, S. A. and J. Waldren (1998). *Anthropological Perspectives on Local Development : Knowledge and Sentiments in Conflict*. London, Routledge.

Abram, S. and G. Weszkalnys (Eds.) forthcoming. *Elusive Promises: Planning in the Contemporary World* Oxford: Berghahn.

Abrams, P. (1988 (1977)). 'Notes on the Difficulty of Studying the State.' *Journal of Historical Sociology* 1(1): 58—89.

Active Citizenship Centre (2006) 'Active Citizenship Centre', http://www.togetherwecan.info/acc/ Visited August 2006.

Adam, B. (2005) *Futures Told, Tamed and Traded*. ESRC PF Futures TTT http://www.cf.ac.uk/socsi/futures/wp_ba_futurestamed200306.pdf

Anderson, B. R. O. G. (1983). *Imagined Communities: Reflections on the Origin and Spread of Nationalism*. London, Verso.

Andrews, R., R. Cowell, et al. (2006). *Promoting Effective Citizenship and Community Empowerment: A Guide for Local Authorities on Enhancing Capacity for Public Participation*. C. U. Centre for Local & Regional Government Research. London, Office of the Deputy Prime Minister.

Alexander, C. (2001). 'Legal and binding: Time, change and long-term transactions' *Journal of the Royal Anthropological Institute* 7: 467—485.

——— (2002). *Personal States: Making Connections between People and Bureaucracy in Turkey*. Oxford, Oxford University Press.

Alexander, C. E., V. Buchli, et al. (2007). *Urban Life in post-Soviet Asia*. London, UCL Press.

Alexander, C. E. (2000). *The Asian Gang: Ethnicity, Identity, Masculinity*. Oxford; New York, Berg.

Aterlier d'Architecture Autogérée. http://www.urbantactics.org/ (accessed 1.12.08).

Ardener, E. (1989). 'The problem revisited'. In M. Chapman *The Voice of Prophecy and Other Essays*. Oxford, Basil Blackwell: 127—133.

Austin, J. L. (1978). *How to Do Things with Words: The William James' Lectures Delivered at Harvard University in 1955*. Oxford, Oxford University Press.

Ball, M. (2004). 'Co-operation with the community in property-led urban regeneration.'*Journal of Property Research* 21(2): 119—142.

Barad, K. (2003). 'Posthumanist performativity: Toward an understanding of how matter comes to matter.' *Signs: Journal of Women in Culture and Society* 28(3): 801—831.

Barclay, C. (2009). *Housing Density and Gardens*, House of Commons Library. Science and Environment Section.

Barker, K. (2006). *Barker Review of Land Use Planning. Final Report — Recommendations*. HM Treasury, Her Majesty's Stationery Office, UK.

Barth, F. (1969). *Ethnic Groups and Boundaries: The Social Organization of Culture Difference*. Oslo, Universitetsforlaget.

Barth, F. (1995). 'Other Knowledge and Other Ways of Knowing.' *Journal of Anthropological Research* 51(1): 65—68.

Barton, L. (2009). 'Barton's Britain: Quarry Bank Mill, Styal'. *The Guardian*. London.

Bateson, G. (1973). *Steps to an Ecology of M: Collected Essays in Anthropology, Psychiatry, Evolution, and Epistemology*. St Albans, Australia, Paladin.

Bear, L. and S. Feuchtwang (2009). 'Planning and the Mediation of the Risk and Chaos of the Future'. *Conflicts in Time: Rethinking 'Contemporary' Globalisation*. Edinburgh University March 2009, ESRC Seminar Series.

Berglund, E. K. (1998). *Knowing Nature, Knowing Science: An Ethnography of Environmental Activism*. Cambridge, White Horse Press.

Binde, P and Å Boholm (2004).. 'Schismogenesis in a Swedish Case of Rail Track Planning'. In Å. Boholm and R. E. V. Löfstedt *Facility Siting: Risk, Power and Identity in Land Use Planning*. London, Earthscan: 160—176.

Bloch, M. (1995). 'The Resurrection of the House Among the Zafimaniry of Madagascar'. In J. Carsten and S. Hugh-Jones *About the House: Lévi-Strauss and Beyond*. Cambridge, Cambridge University Press: 69—83.

Booth, P. (1993). 'The Cultural Dimension in Comparative Research: Making Sense of Development Control in France.' *European Planning Studies* 2(1): 217—229.

——— (2009). 'Planning and the Culture of Governance: Local Institutions and Reform in France.' *European Planning Studies* 17(5): 677—695.

Bowen, E. S. (1954). *Return to Laughter*. London, Gollancz.

Brox, O. (1995). *Dit vi ikke vil : ikke-utopisk planlegging for neste århundre*, Oslo: Exil.

Buckler, S. (2007). *Fire in the Dark: Telling Gypsiness in North East England*. New York; Oxford, Berghahn Books.

Butler, J. (1990). *Gender Trouble: Feminism and the Subversion of Identity*. New York; London, Routledge.

——— (1993). *Bodies that Matter: On the Discursive Limits of "Sex"*. New York; London, Routledge.

C.E.C.M. (Council of Europe Committee of Ministers) (2001). *Recommendation Rec(2001)19 of the Committee of Ministers to Member States on the Participation of Citizens in Local Public Life* (Adopted by the Committee of Ministers on 6 December 2001 at the 776th meeting of the Ministers' Deputies)

C.N.R.S. (ed.) (1970—79). *l'Aubrac* (Recherche Coopérative sur Programme du C.N.R.S. Paris: Editions du C.N.R.S.

——— (1974). *l'Aubrac: dix ans d'evolution, 1964—73* (Recherche Coopérative sur Programme du C.N.R.S. Paris: Editions du C.N.R.S.

CRU, Civil Renewal Unit (2006). *Together We Can Annual Review 2005/06*. Civil Renewal Unit, Department for Communities and Local Government, HM Government (UK).

Cambridge Centre for Housing and Planning Research (2009). *Continuous Recording of Lettings (CORE): Weighting and Imputation Methodology*. UK Dept of Communities and Local Government. www.communities.gov.uk/publications/housing/weightingimputationmethod

Carley, M. (2002). *Norfolk Park, Sheffield: Moving to the Leading Edge of Sustainability and Regeneration*. Glasgow, Heriot-Watt University: 13.

Carston, J. and S. Hugh-Jones, Eds. (1995). *About the House: Levi-Strauss and Beyond*. Cambridge, Cambridge University Press.

Clavel, P. (1983). *Opposition Planning in Wales and Appalachia*. Cardiff, University of Wales Press.

Clifford, J., G. E. Marcus, et al. (1986). *Writing Culture: The Poetics and Politics of Ethnography*. Berkeley; London, University of California Press.

Cohen, A. P. (1989). *The Symbolic Construction of Community*. London, Routledge.

——— (1986). *Symbolising Boundaries: Identity and Diversity in British Cultures*. Manchester, Manchester University Press.

Conway, M. M. (2001). 'Women and Political Participation.' *American Political Science Association* 34(2): 231—233.

Corsín Jiménez, A. (2005). 'After Trust.' *Cambridge Anthropology* 25(2): 64—78.

CSJ (Centre for Social Justice). 2008. *Council Tenants Who Look For Work Should Be Given Stake In Their Homes — New Report*. London: Centre for Social Justice.

Cullen, S. (1994). 'Culture, Gender and Organizational Change in British Welfare Benefits Services'. In S. Wright *Anthropology of Organizations*. London, Routledge: 141—157.

Cullingworth, J. B. (1993). *The Political Culture of Planning: American Land Use Planning in Comparative Perspective*. New York, Routledge.

Damer, S. and C. Hague (1971). 'Public Participation in Planning: A Review.' *Town Planning Review* 42(3): 217—232.

Davis, J. (1992). *Exchange*. Buckingham, Open University Press.

de Boeck, F. and R. Devisch (1994). 'Ndembu, Luunda and Yaka Divination Compared: From Representation and Social Engineering to Embodiment and Worldmaking' *Journal of Religion in Africa* 24(2): 98—133.

Dept for Communities and Local Government (DCLG) (2006). *Annual Review 2005/06 Together We Can*. London: HM Government.

DETR (Department of the Environment, Transport and the Regions) (2000a). *Community Strategies White Paper*. London: HMSO.

——— (2000b) *Quality and Choice: A Decent Home for All: The Housing Green Paper* (*Summary*) Department of the Environment: HM Government.

——— 1999 *Running and Sustaining Renewal Areas: Good Practice Guide* London: HMSO.

Douglas, M. (1987). *Constructive Drinking: Perspectives on Drink from Anthropology*. Cambridge, Cambridge University Press.

——— (2003). *Natural Symbols: Explorations in Cosmology*. London, Routledge.

DTLR (Department for Transport, Local Government and the Regions) (2001). *Local Government White Paper*. London: HMSO

Eriksen, T. H. (2001). *Tyranny of the Moment: Fast and Slow Time in the Information Age*. London, Pluto Press.

Evans-Pritchard, E. E. (1937). *Witchcraft, Oracles and Magic Among the Azande*. Oxford, Clarendon Press.

——— (1940). *The Nuer: A Description of the Modes of Livelihood and Political Institutions of a Nilotic People*. Oxford, Clarendon Press.

Fabian, J. (1983). *Time and the Other: How Anthropology Makes Its Object*. New York, Columbia University Press.

Faludi, A. (2005). 'The Netherlands: A Culture with a Soft Spot for Planning'. In B. Sanyal *Comparative Planning Cultures*. NY and London, Routledge: 442—454.

Favret-Saada, J. (1980). *Deadly Words: Witchcraft in the Bocage*. Cambridge: Cambridge University Press.

——— (1985). *Les mots, la mort, les sorts*. Paris, Gallimard.

Ferguson, J. (1990). *The Anti-politics Machine 'development', Depoliticization, and Bureaucratic Power in Lesotho*. Cambridge, Cambridge University Press.

Ferlie, E. (1996). *The New Public Management in Action*. Oxford, Oxford University Press.

Fischler, R. (2006). 'Teaching History to Planners.' *Journal of Planning History* 5(4): 280—288.

Forester, J. (1989). *Planning in the Face of Power*. Berkeley, Calif.; London, University of California Press.

——— (1996). 'The Rationality of Listening, Emotional Sensitivity, and Moral Vision'. In S. L. Mandelbaum, L. Mazza and R. W. Burchell *Explorations in Planning Theory*. New Brunswick, Center for Urban Policy Research: 204—224.

——— (1999). *The Deliberative Practitioner: Encouraging Participatory Planning Processes*. Cambridge, Mass.; London, MIT Press.

Foucault, M. (1978/1991). 'Governmentality'. In G. Burchell, C. Gordon and P. Miller *The Foucault Effect: Studies in Governmentality*. London, Harvester Wheatsheaf: 87—104.

——— (1979). *Discipline and Punish: The Birth of the Prison*. Harmondsworth, Penguin Books.

Fox, K. (2004). *Watching the English: The Hidden Rules of English Behaviour*. London, Hodder & Stoughton.

Frankenburg, R. (1957). *Village on the Border*. Prospect Heights, Illinois, Waveland Press.

Friedmann, J. (2005). 'Globalization and the emerging culture of planning.' *Progress in Planning* 64: 183—234.

Fromm, E. (1965). *The Heart of Man: Its Genius for Good and Evil*. London, Routledge & Kegan Paul.

Gal, S. and K. A. Woolard (2001). 'Constructing languages and publics: Authority and representation.' In S. Gal and K. A. Woolard *Languages and Publics: The Making of Authority*. Manchester and Northampton, Massachusetts, St. Jerome Publishing: 1—12.

Geertz, C. (1975). *The Interpretation of Cultures: Selected Essays*. London, Hutchinson.

——— (1983). 'Common sense as a cultural system'. In C. Geertz *Local Knowledge*. London, Fontana Press: 73—93.

Gell, A. (1999). *The Art of Anthropology: Essays and Diagrams*. London, Athlone Press.

Gellner, E. (1983). *Nations and Nationalism*. Oxford, Basil Blackwell.

Gennep, A. V. (1960). *The Rites of Passage*. London, Routledge & Kegan Paul.

Geschiere, P. (2003). 'Witch doctors and spin doctors'. In B. Meyer and P. Pels *Magic and Modernity: Interfaces of Revelation and Concealment*. Stanford, Stanford University Press: 159—182.

Giddens, A. (2006). 'Misunderstanding multiculturalism'. *Guardian*. http://commentisfree.guardian.co.uk/anthony_giddens/2006/10/tony_giddens.html October 14, 2006 4:50 PM

Gullestad, M. (2006). *Plausible Prejudice Everyday Experiences and Social Images of Nation, Culture and Race*. Oslo, Universitetsforlaget.

Gupta, A. and J. Ferguson (1992). “””culture”: space, identity, and the politics of difference.” *Cultural Anthropology* 7: 6—23.

——— (1997). *Anthropological Locations: Boundaries and Grounds of a Field Science*. Berkeley; London, University of California Press.

Guy, S., J. Henneberry, et al. (2002). ‘Development Cultures and Urban Regeneration.’ *Urban Studies* 39(7): 1181—1196.

Gruber, B. (2007). ‘Iceland: Searching for Elves and Hidden People.’ Retrieved 5.1.2010, from http://www.dw-world.de/dw/article/0,2786922,00.html.

HM Treasury (2010) *Spending Review 2010*. TSO (The Stationery Office Limited).

Habermas, J. (1989). *The Structural Transformation of the Public Sphere*. Cambridge, MIT Press.

Hacking, I. (1986). ‘Making up People’. In T. C. Heller, M. Sosna and D. E. Wellberry *Reconstructing Individualism: Autonomy, Individuality and the Self in Western Thought*. Stanford, California, Stanford University Press: 222—36.

——— (1990). *The Taming of Chance*. Cambridge, Cambridge University Press.

Hannerz, U. (1999). ‘Världsbild, kultursyn, medborgarskap’. In *Globaliseringen: Demokratiutredningens forskarvolym IX*, Statens Offentliga Utredningar. SOU 1999:83: 365—383.

Haraway, D. J. (1997). *Modest-Witness@Second-Millennium.FemaleMan-Meets-OncoMouse: Feminism and Technoscience*. New York; London, Routledge.

Healey, P. (1997). *Collaborative Planning: Shaping Places in Fragmented Societies*. Basingstoke, Macmillan.

Herzfeld, M. (1992). *The Social Production of Indifference: Exploring the Symbolic Roots of Western Bureaucracy*. New York; Oxford, Berg.

Heilbron, J. (1995). *The Rise of Social Theory*. Cambridge, Polity Press.

Hillier, J. (1999). ‘Culture, community and communication in the planning process’. In C. Greed (Ed.) *Social Town Planning*. London, Routledge: 221—239.

Hillier, J. and E. Rooksby (2002). *Habitus: A Sense of Place*. Aldershot, Ashgate.

Hobsbawm, E. J. (1990). *Nations and Nationalism Since 1780: Programme, Myth, Reality*. Cambridge, Cambridge University Press.

Hobsbawm, E. J. and T. O. Ranger (1983). *The Invention of Tradition*. Cambridge, Cambridge University Press.

Howard, E. (1898). *Tomorrow: A Peaceful Path to Real Reform*. London, S. Sonnenschein.

Howe, J. and C. Langdon (2002). ‘Towards a Reflexive Planning Theory.’ *Planning Theory* 1(3): 209—225.

Hutton, W. (1998). *The Stakeholding Society: Writings on Politics and Economics*. Cambridge, Polity Press.

Innes, J. E. (1996). ‘Group processes and the social construction of growth management’. In S. L. Mandelbaum, L. Mazza and R. W. Burchell (Eds)

Explorations in Planning Theory. New Brunswick, N.J., Center for Urban Policy Research: 164—187.
Ipsos MORI (2009). *Attitudes to Housing: Findings from Ipsos MORI Public Affairs Monitor Omnibus Survey (England)* UK Dept of Communities and Local Government: communities.gsi.gov.uk.
James, W. and D. Mills (2005). *The Qualities of Time: Anthropological Approaches*. Oxford, Berg.
Jenks, C. (1993). *Culture*. London, Routledge.
Jenssen, A. T. (1999). 'All that is Solid Melts into Air: Party Identification in Norway.' *Scandinavian Political Studies* 22(1): 1—27.
Kalland, A. (1996). 'Geomancy and Town Planning in a Japanese Community.' *Ethnology* 35(1): 17—32.
Kaneff, D. and A. D. King (2004). 'Introduction: Owning Culture.' *Focaal, European Journal of Anthropology* 44: 3—19.
Kerfoot, D. and D. Knights (1994). 'The Gendered Terrains of Paternalism'. In S. Wright *Anthropology of Organizations*. London, Routledge: 124—139.
Latour, B. (1996). *Aramis, or The Love of Technology*. Cambridge, Mass., Harvard University Press.
——— (1986). 'The powers of association'. In J. Law *Power, Action and Belief*. London, Routledge & Kegan Paul.
——— (1993). *We Have Never Been Modern*. New York, Harvester Wheatsheaf.
Lave, J. and E. Wenger (1991). *Situated Learning: Legitimate Peripheral Participation*. Cambridge, Cambridge University Press.
Lee, B. (2001). 'Circulating the People'. In S. Gal and K. Woolard *Languages and Publics: The Making of Authority*. Manchester, St. Jerome Publishing: 164—181.
Lévi-Strauss, C. (1983). *The Way of the Masks*. London, Cape.
Lindblom, C. (1959). 'The Science of Muddling Through.' *Public Administration Review* 19(2): 79—88.
Lister, R. (1990). *The Exclusive Society: Citizenship and the Poor*. London, CPAG.
Lizza, J. P. (2007) 'Lizza on Personhood'. *American Journal of Economics and Sociology* 66(1): 195—216.
Lovering, J. (2009). 'The Recession and the End of Planning as We have Known It.' *International Planning Studies* 14(1): 1—6.
Lund, S. (forthcoming a). 'Invaded city: structuring urban landscapes on the margins of the possible (Peru's southern highlands)'. *Focaal*.
——— (forthcoming b). 'The Invaded City: Structuring an urban landscape on the margins of the possible'. In S. Abram and G. Weszkalnys *Elusive Promises: Planning in the Contemporary World*. Oxford, Berghahn.
Lyall, S. (2005). 'Building in Iceland? Better clear it with the elves first.' *The New York Times* Retrieved 4.1.2010, 2010, from http://www.nytimes.com/2005/07/13/international/europe/13elves.html.
Manent, P. (1994). *An Intellectual History of Liberalism*. Princeton, Princeton University Press.

Marchand, T. (2010a). *Making Knowledge*. London, Wiley.
——— (2010b). 'Making knowledge: Explorations of the indissoluble relation between minds, bodies and environment.' *Journal of the Royal Anthropological Institute* Special Issue 2010: S1—S21.
Marshall, T. H. (1950). *Citizenship and Social Class And Other Essays*. Cambridge, University Press.
Martin, K. (2010). 'Robert McNamara and the Limits of "Bean Counting".' *Anthropology Today* 26(3): 16—19.
Mauss, M. (1925). *Essai sur le don. Forme et raison de l'échange dans les sociétés archaïques*.
——— (1973). 'Techniques of the body.' *Economy and Society* 2(1): 70—88.
——— (2002). *The Gift: The Form and Reason for Exchange in Archaic Societies*. London, Routledge.
Mbiba, B. (2003). 'A Clash of Time Cultures and Planning: Reflections from Zimbabwe.' *Planning Theory and Practice* 4(4): 477—480.
Mcdonald, M. (1993). 'An Anthropological Approach to Stereotypes'. In S. Macdonald *Inside European Identities*. Oxford, Berg: 219—236.
McLaughlin, K., S. P. Osborne, et al. (2002). *New Public Management: Current Trends and Future Prospects*. London, Routledge.
McNulty, T. (2003). *Putting Planning First: Culture in the Planning Profession*, London: DCLG.
Mills, D. (2006). '"Popular" Anthropology'. *Anthropology Today* 22(2): 1—2.
Milton, K. (2002). *Loving Nature: Towards an Ecology of Emotion*. London, Routledge.
Ministry of Housing and Local Government (1961). *Homes for Today & Tomorrow*. London, H.M. Stationery Office.
Mosse, D. (2005). *Cultivating Development: An Ethnography of Aid Policy and Practice*. London, Pluto Press.
——— (2006). 'Anti-social anthropology? Objectivity, objection, and the ethnography of public policy and professional communities.' *JRAI* (N.S.) 12(3): 935—956.
Murdoch, J. (1997). 'Inhuman/nonhuman/human: Actor-network theory and the prospects for a nondualistic and symmetrical perspective on nature and society.' *Environment and Planning D* 15(6): 731—756.
Murdoch, J. and S. Abram (2002). *Rationalities of Planning*. London, Ashgate.
National Statistics (2004) 'Households: Muslims have largest households'. National statistics online http://www.statistics.gov.uk/cci/nugget.asp?id=961 accessed 12.8.09
——— (2003) 'Households: One-person households up to 30%'. National Statistics online. http://www.statistics.gov.uk/cci/nugget.asp?id=350 accessed 12.8.09
Nazir-Ali, M. (2006). 'Multiculturalism is to blame for perverting young Muslims'. *Telegraph*.http://www.telegraph.co.uk/opinion/main.jhtml?xml=/opinion/2006/08/15/do1501.xml Last Updated: 12:01am BST 15/08/2006

Needham, R. (1983). *Against the Tranquility of Axioms*. Berkeley; London, University of California Press.
North, P. (1998). '"Save our Solsbury!": The anatomy of an anti-roads protest.' *Environmental Politics* 7(3): 1—25.
ODPM (2005). *The Planning System: General Principles*. London: Office of the Deputy Prime Minister.
ODPM (2005b). *Sustainable Communities: Homes for All*. London: HMSO.
Okely, J. (1983). *The Traveller-gypsies*. Cambridge, Cambridge University Press.
Olwig, K. F. and K. Hastrup, Eds. (1997). *Siting Culture: The Shifting Anthropological Object*. London, Routledge.
Parry, J. P. and M. Bloch (1989). *Money and the Morality of Exchange*. Cambridge, Cambridge University Press.
Paul, R. (1976). 'The Sherpa Temple as a Model of the Psyche'. *American Ethnologist* 3: 131—146.
Peattie, L. R. (1968). *The Ethnography of Economic Development*. Dissertation, University of Chicago.
——— (1968). *The View from the Barrio*. Ann Arbor, University of Michigan Press.
——— (1981). *Thinking About Development*. New York, Plenum Press.
——— (1987). *Planning, Rethinking Ciudad Guayana*. Ann Arbor, University of Michigan Press.
Pels, P. (2003). 'Introduction'. In B. Meyer and P. Pels *Magic and Modernity: Interfaces of Revelation and Concealment*. Stanford, Stanford University Press: 1—38.
Petrescu, Doina (2007) *How to Make a Community as Well as the Space for It*. Re-public: Reimagining Democracy. http://www.re-public.gr/en/?p=60 (accessed 1.12.08).
Polanyi, M. (1966). *The Tacit Dimension*. Garden City, N.Y, Doubleday.
Pottage, A. (2004). 'Introduction: The fabrication of persons and things'. In A. Pottage and M. Mundy *Law, Anthropology, and the Constitution of the Social: Making Persons and Things*. Cambridge, Cambridge University Press: 1—39.
Read, K. E. (1955). 'Morality and the Concept of the Person Among the Gahuku-Gama'. *Oceania* 25: 233—282.
Reade, E. (1987). *British Town and Country Planning*. Milton Keynes, Open University Press.
Renn, O., T. Webler, et al. (1995). 'A Need for Discourse on Citizen Participation'. In *Fairness and Competence in Citizen Participation: Evaluating Models for Environmental Discourse*. Dordrecht, Kluwer Academic Publishers: 1—15.
Robertson, A. J. (forthcoming) 'Planning for life: Regeneration, sustainable communities and flexible housing. In S. Abram and G. Weszkalnys (Eds) *Elusive Promises: Planning in the Contemporary World.* Oxford: Berghahn.
Robertson, A. F. (2006). 'Misunderstanding Corruption.' *Anthropology Today* 22(2): 8—11.

Rose, M. B. (1986). *The Gregs of Quarry Bank Mill: The Rise and Decline of a Family Firm, 1750—1914*. Cambridge, Cambridge University Press.

Rose, N. (1991). 'Governing by Numbers: Figuring Out Democracy'. *Accounting, Organisation and Society* 10.

Ryle, G. (1949). *The Concept of Mind*. London, Hutchinson.

Salamon, K. L. (2000a). 'No Borders in Business: The Management Discourse of Organisational Holism'. In *Cultural Capitalism: Politics after New Labour*. T. Bewes and J. Gilbert. London, Lawrence & Wishart: 134—157.

——— (2000b). 'Faith brought to work. A spiritual movement in business management.' *Anthropology in Action: Journal for Applied Anthropology in Policy and Practice* 7(3): 24—29.

——— (2005). 'Possessed by Enterprise: Values and Value-creation in Mandrake Management.' In *Magic, Culture and the New Economy*. O. Löfgren and R. Willim. Oxford, Berg.

Sandercock, L. (2000). 'When Strangers Become Neighbours: Managing Cities of Difference.' *Planning Theory & Practice* 1(1): 13—30.

——— (2006). 'Cosmopolitan Urbanism: A love song to our mongrel cities'. In J. Binnie, J. Holloway, S. Millington and C. Young *Cosmopolitan Urbanism*. London, Routledge: 37—52.

Sanyal, B., Ed. (2005). *Comparative Planning Cultures*. New York and London, Routledge.

Scheper-Hughes, N. and M. M. Lock (1987). 'The Mindful Body: A Prolegomenon to Future Work in Medical Anthropology' *Medical Anthropology Quarterly* New Series, Vol. 1(1): 6—41.

Schnapper, D. (2002). 'Citizenship and National Identity in Europe.' *Nations and Nationalism* 8(1): 1—14.

Schneider, D. M. (1984). *A Critique of the Study of Kinship*. Ann Arbor, University of Michigan Press.

Schön, D. A. (1983). *The Reflective Practitioner: How Professionals Think in Action*. New York, Basic Books.

Scott, J. C. (1998). *Seeing Like a State: How Certain Schemes to Improve the Human Condition have Failed*. New Haven, Yale University Press.

Selznick, P. (1949). *TVA and the Grass Roots: A Study in the Sociology of Formal Organization*. Berkeley, University of California Press.

Sharma, A. and A. Gupta (2006). *The Anthropology of the State: A Reader*. Malden, Mass.; Oxford, Blackwell.

Shaw, D. and A. Lord (2007). 'The Cultural Turn? Culture change and what it means for spatial planning in England.' *Planning Practice and Research* 22(1): 63—78.

Sheffield City Architect (1962). *Ten years of Housing in Sheffield, 1953—1963*. Sheffield, Eng., Housing Development Committee of the Corporation of Sheffield.

Smith, A. D. (2001). *Nationalism: Theory, Ideology, History*. Cambridge: Polity Press.

——— (1998). *Nationalism and Modernism: A Critical Survey of Recent Theories of Nations and Nationalism*. London: Routledge.

Smith, J. H. (2008). *Bewitching Development: Witchcraft and the Reinvention of Development in Neoliberal Kenya*. Chicago; London, University of Chicago Press.

Somers, M. R. (1995). 'What's Political or Cultural about Political Culture and the Public Sphere? Toward an Historical Sociology of Concept Formation.' *Sociological Theory*, Vol. 13 (2): 113—144.

Stapley, L. (1996). *The Personality of the Organisation: A Psycho-dynamic Explanation of Culture and Change*. London, Free Association Books.

Stolcke, V. (1995). 'Talking Culture: New Boundaries, New Rhetorics of Exclusion in Europe.' *Current Anthropology* 36: 1—13.

Swift, J. (1726). *Travels into Several Remote Nations of the World. In Four Parts. By Lemuel Gulliver*. London, printed for Benj. Motte.

Sykes, K. M. (2005). *Arguing with Anthropology: An Introduction to Critical Theories of the Gift*. London, Routledge.

Tambiah, S. J. (1990). *Magic, Science, Religion, and the Scope of Rationality*. Cambridge, Cambridge University Press.

Taussig, M. (1997). *The Magic of the State*. London and NY, Routledge.

Thomas, H. (2000). *Race and Planning: The UK Experience*. London, UCL Press.

Tylor, E. B. (1873). *Primitive Culture: Researches into the Development of Mythology, Philosophy, Religion, Art, and Custom*. London.

Tönnies, F. (1955). *Community and Association* (Gemeinschaft und Gesellschaft). London: Routledge & Kegan Paul.

Umemoto, K. (2001). 'Walking in Another's Shoes: Epistemological Challenges in Participatory Planning.' *Journal of Planning Education and Research* 21: 17—31.

Vike, H. (forthcoming) 'Utopian time and contemporary time: Temporal dimensions of planning and reform in the Norwegian Welfare State'. in S. Abram and G. Weszkalnys (Eds) *Elusive Promises: Planning in the Contemporary World*. Oxford: Berghahn.

Vries, P. D. (2005). 'Critiquing Governmentality: The social construction of participation and accountability in the Atlantic zone of Costa Rica.' *Focaal* 45: 94—111.

Vygotsky, L. S. (1978). *Mind and Society*. Cambridge, Mass, Harvard University Press.

Warner, M. (2003). 'The Mass Public and the Mass Subject'. *In American Literary Studies: A Methodological Reader.* M. A. Elliott and C. Stokes. New York, New York University Press: 243—263.

——— (1990). *The Letters of the Republic: Publication and the Public Sphere in Eighteenth-Century America* Cambridge: Harvard University Press.

Watson, V. (2003). 'Conflicting rationalities: Implications for planning theory and ethics.' *Planning Theory and Practice* 4(4): 395—407.

Weiner, M. J. (2003). 'Hidden Forces: Colonialism and the politics of magic in the Netherlands Indies'. In B. Meyer and P. Pels. *Magic and Modernity: Interfaces of revelation and Concealment.* Stanford, Stanford University Press: 129—158.

Weszkalnys, G. (2010). *Berlin, Alexanderplatz: Transforming Place in a Unified Germany*. Oxford, Berghahn.

Williams, R. (1976). *Keywords: A vocabulary of Culture and Society*, Fontana/ Croom Helm.

Wittrock, B. (2000). 'Modernity: One, none, or many? European origins and modernity as a global condition.' *Daedalus* 129(1): 31—60.

Wolf, E. R. (1982). *Europe and the People Without History*. London; Berkeley, University of California Press.

Woltjer, J. (2002). 'The "Public Support Machine": Notions of the Function of Participatory Planning by Dutch Infrastructure Planners.' *Planning Practice and Research* 17(4): 437—454.

Wright, S. (1994). '"Culture" in Anthropology and Organizational Studies'. In S. Wright *Anthropology of Organizations*. London, Routledge: 1—31.

Young, G. (2008a). 'The Culturization of Planning.' *Planning Theory* 7(1): 71—91.

——— (2008b). *Reshaping Planning with Culture*. Aldershot, Ashgate.

Young, I. M. (1990) *Justice and the Politics of Difference*. Princeton: Princeton University Press

Zonabend, F. (1984). *The Enduring Memory: Time and History in a French Village.* Manchester, Manchester University Press.

Index

'abnormals' 31–2, 41
Abrams, P. 104
Active Citizenship Centre 95
Africa, witchcraft in 35–6, 37, 40
Anderson, B.R.O.G. 7, 94, 119
anthropological perspective 8–13, 134
  Bakweri people, Cameroon 64–5
  bodies 52–3
  categories of social relations and organisations 102–4
  Europeans' magical beliefs 37–8
  Hagener people, Papua New Guinea 52, 53
  Kayapo people, Brazil 52–3
  kinship studies 103
  time issues 125–6, 129, 131–2
  witchcraft 35–6, 37, 40, 44
  Zafimaniry people, Madagascar 129
Ardener, E. 63–4
'areas of outstanding beauty' (AOBs) 54–5
Aylesbury Vale 112, 120, 130

Bakweri people, Cameroon 63–4
Barth, F. 9, 16, 134, 135
belief-system, planning as 21–2, 33–4
Bertelmann Institute 65
Blair, T. 70, 72, 73, 93
Bloch, M. 129
body 49–57
  bureaucrat 60–6
  communication 59–60
  culture and nature 67–8
  disciplined 57–60
  and houses 85
  metaphors 53
  mindful 54, 57–8
  skills 57–8
  social 52–3, 58
  women's 58–9
body politic 53–4
body-self 52
Bohannan, L. 35
Brazil, Kayapo people 52–3
Brox, O. 124
bureaucrats
  body 60–6
  rational 22
  rituals 37
  vs family/friend-networks 99–100
  see also organizations

Cameroon, Bakweri people of 63–4
Carley, M. 42–3
Carsten, J. and Hugh-Jones, S. 85
categories of social relations and organisations 102–4
citizens/citizenship
  definitions and models of 100–5
  participation and home ownership 71, 74–5, 87–8, 89–90
  participation as policy 91–5
  and people 107–10
  stakeholders and participants 96–8
  state–citizen relationship 98–100, 104–5, 107–10, 118–19
civil citizenship 100–1
Civil Renewal Unit 95
civil society 118–19
Clifford, J.G.E. et al. 10
communication
  body 59–60
  muting 51, 63–4
  political and administrative spheres 61–2, 64–6
  see also knowledge; language
Community Forum *see under* Norfolk Park, Sheffield (NPCF)
community spirit 88, 89, 90
Conservative and New Labour government policies 70–5

consumers, citizens as 98–100
controversies/criticisms 21–2, 34, 42–4, 45, 46–7, 111–13
Corsin-Jiminez, A. 32
council housing *vs* home ownership 70–5
culture
  definitions and conceptions of 1–4, 8, 15, 137–8
  see also ethnicity; nationalism

de Boeck, F. and Devisch, R. 40, 46
demolition 24, 25, 42, 45, 78–9, 80, 82, 127–8
Department of Communities and Local Government 74–5
development planning 36–7
disappointing public 111–13
disciplined bodies 57–60
divination 30–1, 40–1, 46
Douglas, M. 3, 52, 53
Duncan Smith, I. 72–3, 74
'dwellings' 69

emotion
  home ownership and participation 74–5
  and rationality 54–7
enforcement of planning 20
Eriksen, T.H. 130
ethnicity
  and culture 7–13, 16–17, 134–5
  multiculturalism/multinationalism 6–7, 13–16, 17
  Sheffield 97, 134–5
EU and UK policy 91–2
  CECM Recommendation on citizenship participation 92–3
Europeans 12
  housing policies 87–8
  magical beliefs 37–8
evaluation/effectiveness of planning 20, 34
Evans-Prichard, E.E. 9, 35, 39
expert practitioners, perceptions of 33–4

Faludi, A. 2
family
  kinship studies 103
  vs bureaucratic organisations 99–100
Favret-Saada, J. 44
feminist perspective 58–9, 116
flexible housing 129
Foucault, M. 41, 58
fragile networks 31, 45
Friedman, J. 1, 2–3
Fromm, E. 111, 114
funding 41
  Norfolk Park, Sheffield 23, 25, 106–7

Gal, S. and Woolard, K.A. 114, 117
Gavron, N. 70–1
Geertz, C. 10, 17
Giddens, A. 6–7
green-homes 32
Gullestad, M. 6, 14–15
Gypsies 12, 67

Habermas, J. 42, 116, 117, 119
Hacking, I. 118
Hagener people, Papua New Guinea 52, 53
home ownership
  citizenship participation 71, 74–5, 87–8, 89–90
  European policies 87–8
  house/home distinction 69–70
  and personhood 83–6, 89–90
  political ideology of 86–7
  UK government policy 70–5
  vs belonging 75–83
housing associations 25, 26, 74, 76, 88, 99, 106
Housing Defects Survey (1985) *25*
housing estates *see* Norfolk Park, Sheffield
human and non-human actants 86
human-non-human planning 31–3

ideal citizen 95, 97, 108, 109, 110
ideal speech situation 42

Java, European colonials in 37–8

Kayapo people, Brazil 52–3
knowledge 39–42, 135–6
  body skills 57–8
  and information 32–3
  local 41

language 41–2, 113, 115–16

categories of social relations 102–3
of witchcraft 44
see also communication
Latour, B. 31, 56–7, 86
Lévi-Strauss, C. 84–5
Lister, R. 101–2
Lizza, J.P. 83
local democracy 78
local knowledge 41
local participation *see* citizens/citizenship; public
Lund, S. 126

Madagascar, Zafimaniry people 129
magic/ritual
belief-system 21–2, 33–4
how planning works 19–23
human–non-human planning 31–3
as metaphor 45–7
non-rationality and intangibility 35–9
and rational approach 39–45
Marshall, T.H. 100, 101
Martin, K. 1–2
masterplans 22–3
Norfolk Park, Sheffield 26–7, *28–9*, 30–1, 77, 80–1
Mauss, M. 58
meetings, council and public 62–3, 64–6, 111–12, 121–2
Milton, K. 84, 90
'mindful body' 54, 57–8
Modernity: purification and translation 56–7
moral person/moral responsibility 84, 85
Mosse, D. 43, 79
multiculturalism/multinationalism 6–7, 13–16, 17
muting of communication 51, 63–4

nationalism
and culture 4–7, 137
multiculturalism/multinationalism 6–7, 13–16, 17
'negativity' 43–4, 131
New Labour policies 93–5, 96–8
and Conservative policies 70–5
new public management (NPM) 65–6, 70
NIMBYism 34, 54, 111, 120–1
nomads 12
non-human elements 31–3, 86
non-rationality and intangibility 35–9
Norfolk Park, Sheffield 23–31
citizenship 105–7
Community Forum 25, 26, 27, 41, 42–3, 78, 89, 98–100, 106–7, 121–2
criticism 42–4, 45
funding 23, 25, 106–7
human–non-human planning 31–2
knowledge/information 32, 33
owning *vs* belonging 75–83, 88–9, 90
planning meeting 112, 121–2
Regeneration Team 25, 27, 121–2
residents 33, 41, 45, 49–50, 82–3
tenants and residents' association (TARA) 27–9, 106–7
time issues 127–8, 130–1
winds 49, 51
Norway 14–16
council study 60–3, 64–6, 124

objections/criticisms 21–2, 34, 42–4, 45, 46–7, 111–13
Office of the Deputy Prime Minister (ODPM) 50, 71, 72, 80
organisations
categories of 104
'personality' of 44–5
see also bureaucrats

Papua New Guinea, Hagener people 52, 53
participation *see* citizens/citizenship; public
participatory time 128
'personality' of organisations 44–5
personhood
citizens 107–10
home ownership 83–6, 89–90
Peru 125–6
place–culture nexus 12
political citizenship 100–1
political ideology of home ownership 86–7
political leaders 38–9
political rhetoric 114, 115, 119
political unrest 53–4
politicians

and administrators 61–2, 64–6
and public 115, 117–19
Pottage, A. 84
power 35–6, 41–2
public 114–22
disappointing 111–13
historical idea of 115–16
participation as conundrum 122–3
and politicians 115, 117–19
public sphere 116, 119
purification and translation in Modernity 56–7

rationality
bureaucratic 22
and emotion 54–7
non-rationality and intangibility 35–9
Reade, E. 20, 36, 133–4
Regeneration Team *see under* Norfolk Park, Sheffield
rehybridisation 57
Renewal Areas 96
residents *see under* Norfolk Park, Sheffield
ritual *see* magic/ritual
Robertson, S. 36, 53, 128, 129
Rousseau, J.-J. 118–19

Salamon, K.L. 44
Sandercock, L. 7
Scheper-Hughes, N. and Lock, M. 52, 53–4
Schnapper, D. 101
Scott, J.C. 32
Secretary of State for Communities and Local Government 93–4
'service provision' 99–100
Sharma, A. and Gupta, A. 104
Sheffield
ethnicity 97, 134–5
see also Norfolk Park, Sheffield
social body 52–3, 58
social citizenship 100–1
social and economic rights 101–2
social housing *vs* home ownership 70–5
social problems 25–6, 31, 79–80
social relations, categories of 102–3
society, concept of 118–19
speech acts 42–3
spirit possession 38–9
stakeholders, citizens and participants 96–8
state–citizen relationship 98–100, 104–5, 107–10, 118–19
Strathern, M. 52, 53
surveillance 58

Taussig, M. 38–9
Ten Years of Housing (Sheffield City Architects) 24
tenants and residents' association (TARA) 27–9, 106–7
Thatcher, M. 70, 118
time issues 21, 124–5, 127–8
planning the past 125–6
qualities 128–32
'Together We Can' project 75, 93–5, 102
Tönnies, F. 11
Tylor, E.B. 8

urban regeneration *see* Norfolk Park, Sheffield

Vike, H. 125, 130

Weber, M. 10, 22
Weiner, M. 37–8
Wikan, U. 14–15
winds 49, 51
witchcraft
in Africa 35–6, 37, 40
in France 44
Woltjer, J. 87–8
women's bodies 58–9

Young, I.M. 13, 101

Zonabend, F. 130